WADDESDON MANOR

WADDESDON

MANOR

THE HERITAGE OF A ROTHSCHILD HOUSE

Foreword by
Lord Rothschild

Text by
Michael Hall

Photography by
John Bigelow Taylor

SCALA

This edition © 2009 Waddesdon Manor
Text and photography © Waddesdon Manor

Revised edition published 2009 by
Scala Publishers Ltd
Northburgh House
10 Northburgh St
London EC1V 0AT
www.scalapublishers.com

In association with Waddesdon Manor

First published 2002 by Harry N. Abrams, Incorporated, New York.

ISBN: 978 1 85759 623 6

PROJECT DIRECTOR FOR WADDESDON MANOR: Philippa Glanville
EDITOR: Adele Westbrook
DESIGNERS: Joel Avirom and Jason Snyder
EDITORIAL DIRECTION FOR 2ND EDITION: Pippa Shirley and Kim Hallett

Printed in China

10 9 8 7 6 5 4 3 2 1

CONTENTS

PRELUDE: SUMMER 1891

A DAY IN THE LIFE
OF WADDESDON

It is six o'clock in the morning on Saturday, June 12, 1891. High on a hill in the centre of Buckinghamshire, the turrets and windows of Waddesdon Manor catch the early morning light. The birds in the Aviary stir and begin to chatter, and the llamas and the mountain deer in their pen await their early-morning feed. Ten gardeners, led by their foremen, Henry Walters, George Rogers, and George Knowles, are leaving their bothy at the bottom of the hill to begin their walk up to the glasshouses. A group of men gathers in the estate yard to collect brooms and rakes and sets off in inspection of the gravel paths; another has already left to trim the verges. As they descend the hill, they pass the Dairy, where the maids, Catherine and Ellen Kingdom, are taking in the milk brought up from the home farm. In the stables, the grooms are feeding the horses, and George Lawson, one of the coachmen, is polishing the carriages that will be needed today.

Inside the house, the footmen are already busy: George Doubleday is cleaning the lamps and Charles Lovett is polishing boots. By eight, the housemaids have swept the carpets and dusted the downstairs rooms. At seven-thirty the bustle increases. Breakfast is being prepared by the cook, Susan Smith. The housekeeper, Sarah Dodd, emerges from her room, and sorts out the table linen and china for breakfast, which the footmen take to the small Dining Room, where they lay the table. Two gardeners arrive with a horse and float from the glasshouses, bringing flowers, fruit and vegetables, and then head back down the hill, for their breakfast at eight. The lawns and paths have been swept and tidied and the flowers in the Parterre beds have been watered.

At eight-thirty the house steward, Henry Taylor, mounts the stairs to his master's bedroom, where Baron Ferdinand Rothschild is already awake. The housemaids, with jugs of hot water, and footmen with a trolley of tea, coffee, and peaches begin their round of the bedrooms, starting at the east end of the house, with Baron Ferdinand's sister Alice de Rothschild. There are eight guests: Princess Louise, a grand-daughter of Queen Victoria, and her husband, the Duke of Fife, Lady Dorothy Nevill, Lord

and Lady Carrington, Miss Sophie Macnamara, and Lord and Lady Gosford. The maids and valets they have brought with them finish their breakfasts in the servants' hall, and go upstairs to help their masters and mistresses to dress. A little after nine Ferdinand is downstairs, has walked quickly through the main rooms with Taylor, and meets Alice in the small Dining Room to discuss plans for the day.

By ten-thirty, breakfast is over, and people begin to disperse: Ferdinand to his sitting room, and Alice to hers, the rest mainly to the West Gallery to read newspapers and write letters. The small Dining Room is cleared, and the footmen and the under-butler, William Hambrook, start to set the table in the Dining Room. The chef, Auguste Chalanger, has begun work in the kitchen and the confectioner, Arthur Chategner, is busy in the stillroom. A landau arrives with more visitors—E.C.Vernon Harcourt, W.V. Harcourt, Henry Chaplin, and Seymour Wynne Finch, who have all travelled up from London by train to Aylesbury, six miles away. They are followed by another carriage, which sets down their bags and four menservants at the luggage entrance in the east wing. Taylor greets the

After lunch, Ferdinand and the other men smoke cigars and discuss politics in comfortable armchairs set out on Turkish carpets in a striped tent on the front lawn, while the women are changing for the afternoon. A trap drawn by two small ponies, Bella and Comet, collects Alice from the front door, to take her to her pavilion at Eythrope, two miles away on the neighbouring estate, where the party is to be given tea; she uses the pavilion only during the day, as its low-lying site close to the River Thame is thought to be a risk to her health. At three-thirty four landaus draw up outside Waddesdon to take the guests to Eythrope. There they are greeted by Alice, who leads them through her

guests at the front door and takes them up to their rooms in the Bachelors' Wing. No sooner have they arrived, than another carriage appears, bringing Ferdinand and Alice's cousin Constance Flower and her husband, Cyril Flower, from their house at nearby Aston Clinton.

At eleven-thirty the guests, with Ferdinand and Alice (accompanied by Ferdinand's poodle Poupon), assemble in the West Gallery for a tour of the grounds. At the Aviary, the parrots and other birds have been brought out onto stands dotted about the lawn, to be inspected and fed. From there, the party moves on to the pens containing mountain goats, deer and llamas. They then walk slowly down the hill to the enormous range of glasshouses. At the entrance they are met by the head gardener, John Jaques, who escorts them on an inspection of the orchid and carnation houses before they continue their tour through the Water Garden to the bottom of the hill. Here Ferdinand has his half-timbered model Dairy, where they are invited to sample some fresh cream and strawberries. The party then begins their promenade back to the house, pausing briefly at the stables.

PRELUDE

gardens down to the Thame, where they board a miniature steam launch crewed by boatmen in straw hats banded with the Rothschilds' racing colours, blue and yellow. The boat glides along the curving path of the river to a summer house, where a table is laid for tea.

By six-thirty in the evening, the guests are back at Waddesdon and ready to change for dinner; every female guest is provided with orchids from the glasshouses for her corsage. The housemaids carry hot water to the bedrooms, while the footmen tour the downstairs rooms, lighting candles, setting out lamps, closing the shutters, and drawing the curtains. The final touches are made to the dining table, banked high with Malmaison carnations grown at Waddesdon. Dinner, at eight, begins with consommé

and crayfish, followed by pullet, veal and beef, and concludes with early apricots and peaches from the garden; champagne is served throughout, except to Ferdinand, who drinks nothing but water, and waves most of the dishes away. After dinner, the men linger only briefly in the Dining Room before smoking cigars in the Conservatory and then joining the ladies in the Grey Drawing Room. Ferdinand then conducts them through his private sitting room, where two of his latest purchases, Gainsborough's portraits of the 10th Duke of Hamilton and Lord Archibald Douglas, are standing on easels, and into the Tower Room, lined with vitrines filled with Renaissance silver and silver-gilt, Venetian glass and Limoges enamels. Here he shows them his latest treasure, an Elizabethan miniature in a jewelled case.

By midnight, most guests are in bed, although a few men are lingering over the billiard table in the Bachelors' Wing. Susan Smith, having checked that the scullery man, Sam Syrett, and his staff have finished their work, tours the kitchen, turning down the gas and bolting the windows. As the clock strikes, the porter and nightwatchman, Thomas Trimby, begins his night-time tours of the corridors; two policemen hired from the local force have already collected their lamps for their patrols of the grounds. As the moon rises, Waddesdon is enveloped by silence, broken only by the call of a nightjar from his perch amid the lofty towers.

FOREWORD

Towards the end of his life, Baron Ferdinand Rothschild became increasingly concerned about the future of Waddesdon Manor, the huge, idiosyncratic French Renaissance-style château (his *grand projet*) which he had embarked upon in 1874, shortly after the death of his father Anselm. The creation of Waddesdon Manor, the Collections and the Gardens was to become his life's work. He wrote about it in his Red Book—privately printed for his friends—and his essay ends on a somewhat pessimistic note:

> "A future generation may reap the chief benefit of a work which to me has been a labour of love, though I fear Waddesdon will share the fate of most properties whose owners have no descendants, and fall into decay. May the day be yet distant when weeds will spread over the gardens, the terraces crumble into dust, the pictures and the cabinets cross the Atlantic and the melancholy cry of the nightjar sound from the deserted towers."

Today, against all odds, Waddesdon moves into the 21st century with a flourish and a future which has been guaranteed by the National Trust in perpetuity. The Manor, Collections and the Gardens have never looked better and are being enjoyed by visitors from all over the world. It is indeed a tribute to that vitality that only seven years since it was first published, this book should merit a second edition, to record the new acquisitions and developments both inside and out which ensure that there is always something to surprise and delight at Waddesdon.

It is an extraordinary and unlikely story of survival. Three generations of the Rothschild family who lived at Waddesdon were childless. Baron Ferdinand did not remarry after the death of his wife Evelina, who lost the child they were expecting. His sister Alice never married.

To their great sadness, James and his wife Dorothy (my cousins Jimmy and Dollie) were childless. After the war, Jimmy saw little future for the Manor in private ownership and therefore left the property to the National Trust.

Miraculously, the property has survived two World Wars, the Great Depression in the 1930s and taxation levelled at 98% on income and 83% on Death Duties in the period after the Second World War.

Not surprisingly, Waddesdon Manor is a most un-English house, for the founder of the dynasty, Mayer Amschel, had lived in the ghetto in Frankfurt and his five sons would establish themselves throughout Europe. Three of these branches have been deeply involved in Waddesdon: first the Austrian, then the French and more recently the English. Ferdinand, the creator, was born in France of an Austrian father and English mother and was brought up in Germany and Austria, but he much preferred England, and eventually married his English cousin Evelina. He saw the potential of Lodge Hill, which had not been built upon, and has splendid views across the Vale of Aylesbury to the Chiltern Hills on the Waddesdon Estate, acquired from the Duke of Marlborough in 1874. While it took him no less than 15 years to realise his vision of a Loire château, it has taken the present generation, a century later, two decades to review the huge and complex roof, to rediscover and enhance the High Victorian garden and to give the Manor and its Collections a renewed vitality.

Most of the 42 houses built by the Rothschild family across Europe during the 19th century have not survived in family ownership. Perhaps of those that remain, Waddesdon continues to express best the Rothschild attributes of an eye for country, a taste for art and entertaining and a "characteristic boldness and originality" as *Country Life* described Waddesdon in its first article in 1898.

Celebrated today as a unique evocation of 18th-century French interior design, Waddesdon can be ranked with the collections at Windsor Castle and Hertford House as an extraordinary and eclectic expression of its period. It was created as a setting for Ferdinand's house parties. Furnished with superlative French furniture and porcelain, its luxurious interiors are enhanced by superb English portraits and beautiful textiles. It became and remains an astonishing example of 'le style Rothschild' which influenced the great American collectors of the late 19th and 20th century, such as Morgan, Frick, Vanderbilt, Huntington and Astor.

Ferdinand, a hospitable man and a generous host, cared passionately about pleasing his guests and his pursuit of excellence—whether in his patisseries, his exotic birds and specimen trees or the music played during dinner—is a tradition which has recently been revived at Waddesdon to the delight of its many current visitors.

Each generation has played its part. Miss Alice's formidable housekeeping rules, based on her strict upbringing in Frankfurt, have become standard for the National Trust. She not only preserved her brother's creation but also added the arms and armour to the Collections and furniture and paintings which complemented her brother's taste. Her French great-nephew James de Rothschild and his English wife Dorothy inherited Waddesdon at a time (the 1920s) when admiration for Victorian eclecticism was at a low point. My cousin Jimmy's first love was racing and he added the Stud to the Waddesdon Estate. He also, however, commissioned the Bakst paintings of the Rothschild family in the *Sleeping Beauty* and both he and Dollie loved and cherished every aspect of Waddesdon. Through inheritance, Jimmy was to enhance the Collections in the 1930s when furniture, drawings, paintings and works or art were left to him by his parents, Baron and Baronne Edmond. It was also Jimmy who decided to leave Waddesdon Manor in his Will to the National Trust, together with an endowment fund. As a result, the future of Waddesdon Manor was assured in perpetuity, together with many of its contents. My cousin Dollie dedicated herself to this new chapter in the history of Waddesdon. She chaired the Management Committee and was responsible for the publication of the meticulous and scholarly series of catalogues which record and illustrate the collection. This process of accumulation and reflection of each generation of the family continues today, whether through the addition of significant works of art to the Collection, the annual exhibition programme or a major restoration project in the Gardens.

These too go from strength to strength. My daughter Beth, a keen and talented gardener, continues the family tradition of innovation and love of gardening. The subtle colours of carpet bedding, the restored Water Garden at the Dairy and the additions of contemporary sculpture which contribute so much to the character of Waddesdon are captured in the superb photography of John Bigelow Taylor and Dianne Dubler.

Drawing on unpublished research, Michael Hall has created a fascinating and lively account of this Rothschild house which I hope will give you as much pleasure perusing its pages as I have had during my long association with Waddesdon.

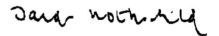

FOREWORD

WADDESDON MANOR

I

FERDINAND ROTHSCHILD
and HIS FAMILY

In 1897 Baron Ferdinand Rothschild began to write his memoirs. Although he was not old—he would turn 58 on December 17 of that year—and could not have known that he had only a year to live, he evidently felt the need to sum up his life to that point and explain how his great achievement, Waddesdon Manor, had been created. Two revealing chapters on his childhood and his collecting remain in typescript, but a third, on the construction of his house and the layout of its grounds, was privately printed and illustrated with photographs of the building and its collections. Bound in red morocco, which has given it the name of *The Red Book,* it was kept in the house—where it still remains—for the interest of Ferdinand's visitors, who often asked him for information about Waddesdon's history. Such questions have been posed ever since. How is that he came to build a house of such magnificence on this high, lonely hill in the heart of Buckinghamshire? Who was Ferdinand Rothschild?

Such curiosity is often satisfied simply by his surname. He was a member of one of the most celebrated families of his age, the owners of what was throughout his life the biggest private bank in the world. Although that is not sufficient to understand him, it is the essential starting point, for he owed his position and great wealth entirely to his family. The fortunes of the house of Rothschild can be traced back to the career of Ferdinand's great-grandfather Mayer Amschel Rothschild, who had been born in 1743 or 1744 in Frankfurt am Main, then an independent imperial city. His family, who

View through the house from the entrance hall to the garden.

derived their name from the house of a 16th-century ancestor, *Zum roten Schild*—'At the Red Shield'—had been involved in the textile trade, but Mayer specialised in antique dealing, and ran a mail-order business in coins and other antiquities. The capital he accumulated from this enterprise, and the links it gave him with princely collectors, notably the ruler of a neighbouring state, the Landgrave of Hesse-Kassel, enabled him to branch into banking. By the 1790s he was one of the richest men in Frankfurt, and was doing business in Amsterdam, Vienna, Paris and London, as well as all over Germany.

This was achieved despite the severe constraints on his life in Frankfurt. Like all the city's Jewish community, the Rothschilds were confined to a walled ghetto, the Judengasse, little more than a single, narrow, insanitary street. In 1770 Mayer made a good marriage to Gutle Schnapper, daughter of the court agent to the Prince of Saxe-Meiningen. They had 19 children, of whom ten survived to adulthood, all raised in a house which was substantial by the standards of the ghetto, but at just 14 feet wide must have been desperately cramped. It had so few rooms that Mayer and Gutle's five sons, who one day would be the wealthiest men in the world, slept together in a single attic room. The Rothschilds never forgot, nor sought to conceal, their origins, which, as Ferdinand recalled, were in such sharp contrast to the plutocratic splendour in which he had been raised. Gutle, who survived her husband by 37 years, never moved out of the house in the Judengasse, where she died in 1849 at the age of 96. One of Ferdinand's childhood memories was of being taken to visit her in that 'small, dingy dwelling': 'I can still see her, resting on a couch in her dark little sitting room, folded in a thick, white shawl, her deeply-furrowed face enclosed in a full and heavily-ribboned white cap, and a genial smile beaming from her bright eyes as she bade me partake of some favourite small, aniseed cakes'. When the remains of the Judengasse were finally swept away in 1884, the family had their original home preserved, as a monument to their extraordinary history.

The deep loyalties engendered by ghetto life were to be the foundation of the Rothschilds' international triumphs, for although Mayer despatched four of his five sons abroad, they always worked closely together in their endeavours to build up a multi-national merchant bank. The eldest, Amschel, stayed at home with his father; the second son, Salomon, moved to Vienna; the third, Nathan, went to Manchester; the fourth, Carl, was sent to Naples, then capital of the Kingdom of the Two Sicilies; and the youngest, Jakob, was established in Paris, where he was known as James. The most dynamic of the brothers was Nathan, who soon moved on from overseeing his father's business interests in Lancashire—then the manufacturing heart of the industrial world—to running a bank in London, which became his home in 1811. Nathan took the lead in seizing the commercial opportunities offered by the Napoleonic Wars, which forced governments to raise unprecedented sums of money from banks in order to finance their campaigns. In 1818 he masterminded an enormous loan to Prussia, which was raised in sterling, rather than *thaler*, and so was available to British investors. This was the beginning of the international bond market which was the principal focus of the family's financial interests for the rest of the century. By 1825, Nathan had sufficient reserves to bail out the Bank of England in a crisis. It was no wonder that only two years earlier Lord Byron had enquired in *Don Juan*, 'Who hold the balance of the world? . . . Who keep the world, both old and new, in pain or pleasure? . . . Jew Rothschild, and his fellow Christian Baring.'

To which the Rothschilds might have replied that by 1828, when the family's capital reserve was very nearly £4.4 million, the Barings, the second greatest banking family in the City of London, were worth less than a tenth of that. The main reason for the Rothschilds' eclipse of their rivals, beyond their commercial acumen and energy, was their belief in ploughing back profits into the firm, a policy that was reinforced by endogamy: Rothschilds tended to marry their cousins. This kept the money in the family. As yet, they were

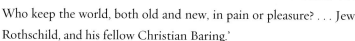

FERDINAND ROTHSCHILD AND HIS FAMILY

not known as great spenders, but the family tradition of antique dealing, together with the need to ease their way with attractive and expensive gifts, began to turn their attention to collecting, just at the time that the benefits of cultivating the politically powerful, both as clients and as suppliers of commercially useful information, were encouraging the family to invest in expensive houses and estates where they could entertain.

The Rothschild brothers were now dealing with aristocratic clients almost as social equals: in 1816 they were granted noble status by the Emperor of Austria, which entitled them to prefix their surname with 'von' or 'de'; in 1822 they were raised by the Emperor to the hereditary rank of *Freiherr*, or baron. (Yet it was not until 1887 that the Imperial household finally declared the family *hoffähig*—acceptable to be received at court and in society.) The arms they chose included a shield bearing arrows symbolising the brothers—four until 1818, when Nathan, who rather despised the whole business of aristocratic status, was granted the right to bear arms, and the arrows became five. However, unlike many of their Jewish contemporaries who converted to Christianity to help their social advancement—Benjamin Disraeli's family being the best-known example—the Rothschilds never wavered in their loyalty to their (Ashkenazi) Judaism, and were fiercely opposed to marriage with Christians—another factor that encouraged their offspring to marry each other. It was a loyalty that puzzled even sympathetic Christian acquaintances, few of whom could entirely shake off the 19th century's endemic antisemitism: in 1898 William Gladstone's private secretary Edward Hamilton recalled that his old friend Ferdinand 'was proud of his race and his family and liked talking about his predecessors as if he had an illustrious ancestry of the bluest of bloods'.

In 1836 the family successfully weathered its first great internal crisis, when Nathan died unexpectedly at the age of only 59. Leadership of the family passed to his youngest brother, James, the one who came closest to matching his dynamism and daring. By the time of Nathan's death, links between the English and other Rothschild houses had been well cemented by marriage. Nathan had married Hannah Cohen, daughter of a prosperous London merchant; they had seven children, four of whom married Rothschild cousins.

ABOVE: *Ferdinand's father, Anselm Salomon (1803–1874), son of Salomon Mayer, founder of the Viennese branch of the bank. Anselm was a notable collector. This oil sketch of 1831 is by Joseph Karl Stieler.*

OPPOSITE: *Ferdinand's mother, Charlotte (1807–1859), daughter of Nathan Mayer, founder of the London branch of the bank. This portrait of 1827, by Ary Scheffer, was treasured by Ferdinand throughout his life.*

The eldest, born in 1807, was Charlotte, who in 1826 had married Anselm, four years her senior and the only son of Salomon, head of the Viennese branch. Although Salomon's business interests were centred on Austria, he was unable, as a Jew, to own property there, and so maintained a town house in Paris and a villa at Suresnes, on the north-west edge of the city, as well as an establishment of his own

in Frankfurt. It was in Paris that Anselm and Charlotte settled, and began their family. Their first child, Mayer, died when only a year old, but all seven of their other children lived to adulthood: Julie (1830), Hannah (1832), Sara (1834), Nathaniel (1836), Ferdinand (1839), Salomon Albert (known to his family as 'Salbert', 1844), and Alice (1847). Ferdinand's name was a tribute to the Emperor Ferdinand of Austria, who in 1835 had given Salomon permission to undertake the first railway line financed by the Rothschilds, the Kaiser-Ferdinands-Nordbahn, between Vienna and Bochnia, the first section of which was opened in the year of Ferdinand's birth.

Although their marriage appears to have been relatively happy, Anselm and Charlotte lived increasingly separate lives. Anselm spent most of his time in Vienna after 1848, when the year of revolutions precipitated a crisis in the Viennese bank which he had to sort out, and he moved there permanently in 1855, when his father died. He was rarely accompanied by his wife, who disliked the city. This geographical distance between the couple was reinforced by their very different attitudes to their offspring, as recalled by Ferdinand. 'My Father', he wrote, 'was a high-minded and cultivated man, devoted to his work, a keen sportsman, fond of literature and art, of good talk and whist; but . . . he took only a feeble interest in his children'. Ferdinand's closest link with his father was their shared love of art and collecting, a side of Anselm's personality that he kept well hidden from the world for most of his life. According to his colleague Hermann Goldschmidt, he 'lived the life of an immigrant and a miser. He was averse to any outward displays of wealth, travelled only by hansom cab and never had his own coach-and-four'. He had various discreet liaisons, but unlike many of his cousins seems never to have maintained a mistress. In contrast to her husband, Charlotte was devoted to her children and they to her: 'All my love went to my mother . . . I could hardly bear to be out of her sight', wrote Ferdinand: 'my happiest moments were when I was recovering from an illness and she nursed me and stayed at my bedside, telling me stories of which I never tired. My Mother was my guardian angel, the one being around whom my existence revolved.' Even as a child, Ferdinand shared his mother's interest in interior decoration and gardening. He recalled happy evenings nestling at her feet 'while she worked on some tapestry chairs. I still have a settee made by her hands, in the designing of which she consulted me.'

Ferdinand's aesthetic outlook was undoubtedly shaped by his childhood homes. Of his grandfather Salomon's houses, he could only dimly recall Suresnes, famous for its garden, since it was ransacked in the revolution of 1848, but he knew the Paris *hôtel* well: here he had been

born. It was in the rue Laffitte, next door to that of Salomon's youngest brother, James (the Rothschilds tended to cluster together in cities), and, like his, was decorated in the style of the French Renaissance. According to the duchesse de Dino, 'the luxury of it beggars belief, but it is tasteful, pure Renaissance, without any admixture of other styles'. This choice of the Renaissance for the decorative schemes was criticized by Count Apponyi, the Austrian ambassador to France, whose comment that it was more appropriate for a château than a town house embodies a belief in stylistic decorum that would influence Ferdinand's choice of style for Waddesdon some 40 years later.

Salomon was also the first member of the family to have a house in Frankfurt outside the ghetto: he moved to the Schafergasse in 1807. Because of the restrictions on Jews owning property in Aus-

OPPOSITE: *Ferdinand Rothschild as a child. Ferdinand was named after the Emperor rather than a family member, because his birth in June 1839 coincided with the opening of the Vienna to Brno Imperial railway, in which his father and grandfather had invested. Watercolour by J. F. Nielmann, 1849.*

ABOVE: *Anselm Salomon sitting to his wife Charlotte, with their children Nathaniel and Julie and the children's nanny. The interior, probably their Paris house, includes family portraits and a cabinet of Anselm's collection. Oil painting by Charlotte de Rothschild, 1838.*

RIGHT: *Ferdinand's Baby Set: fork, knife, spoon, and cup.*

FERDINAND ROTHSCHILD AND HIS FAMILY

ABOVE: *Ferdinand Rothschild (1839–1898) in about 1860,*
the year he left Vienna to settle in England.

RIGHT ABOVE: *Ferdinand's third sister, Sara (1834–1924),*
who married an Italian industrialist, Baron Raimondo Franchetti.

RIGHT BELOW: *Ferdinand's youngest sister, Alice (1847–1922),*
photographed in about 1870.

ABOVE LEFT AND RIGHT: *Ferdinand's two brothers, Salomon Albert, known as 'Salbert'
(1844–1911) and Nathaniel (1836–1905), both photographed in about 1860.
Ferdinand had an affectionate but competitive relationship with both.*

LEFT: *Ferdinand's eldest sister, Julie (1830–1907), who married Adolph Carl,
son of the founder of the Neapolitan branch of the bank.*

ABOVE: *The entrance façade of Schillersdorf, Ferdinand's family Schloss near Raciborz, now Czech Republic, in an anonymous watercolour of 1848.*

OPPOSITE ABOVE: *Schillersdorf's garden front. Pencil and watercolour on paper by Alice de Rothschild, about 1860.*

OPPOSITE BELOW: Maison de Portier, Schillersdorf, *May 1864. Pencil on paper by Alice de Rothschild. This is one of the lodges built by Ferdinand's parents in a markedly English style.*

tria, his house on the Renngasse in Vienna was only rented, until the Emperor granted him a special exemption to buy it, which he took up in 1847; shortly afterwards he purchased a large estate at Koritschau in Moravia. He already owned the schloss at Schillersdorf in Silesia, a former monastery near Ratibor (now Raciborz), in the Carpathian mountains, which he had bought in 1842. When Salomon died in 1855, Schillersdorf was inherited by Anselm, who with his wife's assistance devoted much time to laying out gardens, planting the grounds and building estate cottages on the English model, in an English Tudor style. He rarely entertained there, and after his wife's death preferred living in a small house on the estate rather than in the schloss, but his children enjoyed their annual autumn holidays at Schillersdorf. 'It was an oasis in the wilderness', recalled Ferdinand, 'being provided with every British comfort and French luxury. The whole estate was a game preserve and we were able to shoot five days a week for three months . . . We led a thoroughly seigniorial life, heedless of the cares and the bustle of the outer world.' Watercolours by his sister Alice show the house flanked by formal gardens with fountains, looking out from a high hill across a wide landscape.

However, the family home that Ferdinand loved most was quite different. In 1835 Amschel, Salomon's eldest brother, had bought a small country estate at Grüneburg, just outside Frankfurt. Salomon seems not to have encouraged Anselm to acquire property in or near Frankfurt, no doubt wanting him to concentrate on his Austrian inheritance, so it was Amschel who in 1844 offered his nephew some land at Grüneburg where he could build 'a garden house' for

ABOVE: *The villa at Grüneburg, near Frankfurt, the favourite home of Ferdinand's childhood. Built for Anselm and Charlotte between 1845 and 1851, and destroyed in 1944, it is shown here in a watercolour of about 1870.*

OPPOSITE: *Salon Louis XVI, Château de Ferrières, Seine-et-Marne, France. Watercolour by Eugène Lami, about 1865. Bought by James de Rothschild in 1829, it was rebuilt by Joseph Paxton and G.H. Stokes between 1853 and 1865.*

himself and his family. Charlotte wrote to her eldest brother, Lionel, asking him to recommend an English architect: 'she wants some of the Gothic, Elizabethan and all sorts', reported Lionel: 'Not a palace but a good sized house.' In the end, Anselm seems to have overruled his wife, and the house, completed in 1847, was designed by a French architect, M. Bellanger, who is so obscure that even his first name is not recorded. The style finally chosen for the house can best be described as Franco-German Renaissance. Architectural historians have been reminded of Loire châteaux, but according to Ferdinand the model was 'the Duke of Nassau's castle at Biebrich on the Rhine'; he thought Grüneburg was 'the first private house in that style—since then it has been copied by the score'.

Equally original, in Ferdinand's eyes, was the choice of style for the interiors: 'Internally it was decorated in the Louis XV manner, then an altogether new departure from the fashion of the day; an innovation, too, which was soon repeatedly imitated. My Mother had taken the idea from a Pompadour bed she had seen in Paris.' Grüneburg's garden was Charlotte's special responsibility: 'My Mother who was a great adept at gardening took no small pleasure and pride in laying out the grounds, planting young chestnut trees on each side of the road which led from the farm past our gates towards the town. The twenty acres were made into flower gardens and orchards, with an aviary, and a pond which was stocked with carp and adorned with ducks. There was a mound which we called "the mountain" in a remote corner containing the ice-house, and close by were enclosures for a wild antelope and a tame deer which my father had brought from Egypt. It was all on a small scale but to us it seemed enormous.' In addition, Grüneburg had model stables and a dairy, with a dairymaid imported from Devon.

Even after his father's move to Vienna, the family spent every summer at Grüneburg. Yet Ferdinand had no other happy memories of Frankfurt. Somewhat surprisingly, his parents decided not to educate him privately, but sent him to the city's public *Gymnasium*, and when they moved to Vienna he was sent not to the Theresianum, with the sons of the aristocracy, but to the middle-class Schotten-Kloster: 'unlike Harrovians and Etonians I have the most unpleasant recollections of my schooldays', he wrote, and he regretted the fact that he never attended university. Ever afterwards, he had a strong urge to tutor himself, and frequently asked friends for advice about the books he should read in order to make up for the deficiencies of his education. He envied his English cousins the social ease which he believed had been granted by their public-school and university education, contrasting it with his own solitary bookishness as a child: 'romances and novels . . . increased the dreaminess of my disposition, which lasted until I was well into my teens'. He largely took for granted the wide intellectual horizons he inherited through being born into a

cosmopolitan family, which brought with it a familiarity with life in France, England, Germany and Austria, as well as fluency in three languages (although he spoke English and French with a pronounced Austrian accent).

By the time he was a young man, the family lead in terms of architecture and decoration had been taken by his great-uncle James, who had built not only his magnificent *hôtel* in Paris, but also the greatest country house of his generation of Rothschilds, Ferrières, just out-

side Paris, completed in 1860. Once more, the style was Renaissance, but this time strongly influenced by England, since James was building in conscious rivalry with his English nephews. That explains his choice of an English architectural team, Joseph Paxton and his son-in-law George Henry Stokes, and an English builder, George Myers, although the interiors were the responsibility of a French artist and stage designer, Eugène Lami. Ferdinand never ceased to be impressed by the beauty and magnificence of Ferrières, writing to his friend Lord Rosebery in 1878 that 'the grounds are kept like a drawing room, and the house or rather the palace, is a museum and a most comfortable residence in one'. However, it was to what he called 'old' England rather than France that he felt most drawn: 'In my earliest childhood',

he wrote, 'England was already the land of my dreams, the goal to which tended my conception of all earthly bliss.'

As a child, he had been taken by his mother on long visits to her parents' home, Gunnersbury Park, in west London. In origin a modest Regency villa on the site of the summer residence of Princess Amelia, it had been greatly extended for Nathan by the architect Sydney Smirke in 1835. Here Ferdinand recalled that he 'was spoilt beyond all measure, not by my Grandmother only but by my Uncles and Aunts.' He remembered also joining in at the age of five with the rescue of his small cousin Evelina, who had fallen into the lake, and how 'to my indescribable terror' one of his grandmother's llamas had chased him round the park. The English bank was then run by three of Nathan's four sons, Lionel (Evelina's father), Anthony, and Mayer; all had married cousins. A fourth son, Nathaniel, worked in France with James.

Ferdinand's decision to move to England was prompted by the tragically early death of his mother in 1859, at the age of only 52, when he was still 19. He shared her dislike of Vienna, where his father was living as a virtual recluse, entirely bound up in the business of the bank, and he was deeply influenced by her happy memories of her childhood in England. Ferdinand's three elder sisters were by then married, two to Rothschild cousins, Sara to an Italian Jewish industrialist, Baron Raimondo Franchetti: 'my younger Sister and Brother were children, and my elder Brother was arriving at an age when my pursuits were no longer his and his were not yet mine', wrote Ferdinand. As a result, it seemed to him there was nothing to keep him in Austria: 'being denationalised, so to speak, on the one hand, and not renationalised on the other . . . I severed the slender ties that bound me to the countries I had hitherto lived in, and when chance took me shortly afterwards on a visit to England, the land of my dreams, I prolonged that visit, repeated it for some years, and finally made England my permanent abode.' Once he had settled in his new country, he dropped the 'de' before his surname; as Hamilton later commented 'properly speaking, he ought also to have dropped the foreign title of Baron', but he did not, probably because he believed that the royal permission granted to his English cousins to use the title applied to him also.

Part of the attraction of England to Ferdinand was the readymade social circle provided by his extensive network of cousins, who supplied the family warmth he missed at home and offered friendships

The garden front at Gunnersbury Park, Ealing, Middlesex, England, in about 1860. Bought and remodelled by Nathan Rothschild in 1835, it was Evelina's childhood home.

FERDINAND ROTHSCHILD AND HIS FAMILY

of a type he had missed in childhood, when 'I really only cared for my own belongings'. His closest contemporaries were Lionel's five children, whom he regarded with admiring yearning: 'our English cousins who were physically and mentally far in advance of their years, were accomplished, good looking and high spirited, and realized in my eyes the very ideal of perfection'. This esteem was not entirely reciprocated by his male English cousins, partly because he made the mistake of trying too hard to fit in; temperamentally, he was also very different from his eldest cousin, the bluff and sporty Nathaniel, usually called Natty, the future first Lord Rothschild: he enjoyed teasing the shy, nervous Ferdinand, who rarely appreciated the joke. Nonetheless, their friendship was cordial on the surface and was greatly helped by the dawning relationship between Ferdinand and Nathaniel's sister Evelina, who had memorably fallen into the lake at Gunnersbury. She had grown up to be so beautiful that, according to her mother, idlers followed her in the street in admiration.

Ferdinand's marriage to Evelina in 1865 was greeted with rapture by their parents, who saw it as a renewal of the relationship between the English and Austrian branches of the family. The wedding breakfast, at her father's London house, 148 Piccadilly, was attended by Disraeli, who made a speech, and by the Austrian and French ambassadors. At the ball that followed, the guest of honour was one of the Queen's cousins, the Duke of Cambridge, whose wife was a daughter of the Rothschilds' first major client, the Landgrave of Hesse-Kassel. Evelina's mother, Charlotte, was amused by the excited attention Ferdinand paid to the wedding presents, as she wrote to her son Leopold: 'Ferdy's ambition is that Evy's jewels should surpass all others in the family in purity of taste and beauty—Though we cannot help smiling at his fastidious taste—I suppose perfection ought to be aimed at in all things.' He was equally concerned that Evelina should not put on weight, and forbade her to eat cakes. The couple embarked on a long Continental honeymoon, ending at Schillersdorf, where they planned to establish a home for part of the year, spending the rest of their time at Ferdinand's new London house, 143 Piccadilly. Evelina's long series of letters written to her mother during her honeymoon convey something of the sparkle that made her such a

favourite in the family. Her eye for the absurd not infrequently rested on her new husband, for all that he was 'a dear old duck & does all that he can to make me happy and comfortable': she could not resist recounting that while Ferdinand was out shooting with his brothers 'he trod on a poor hare, who was fast asleep, & he all but fell on his nose'. Even the reclusive Anselm was won over by her charm, and while the young men played billiards, he entertained her with 'stories & anecdotes about his curiosities & antiquities'. In September she wrote to her mother that 'Uncle Anselm is very busy at present . . . 100 labourers are digging at the end of the park, where a huge pond is to be arranged for wild duck shooting; he delights in alterations & improvements & stands for hours & hours in the same spot, watching his workpeople. Now that we have heard all Uncle Anselm's antiquity anecdotes & improper little stories, we spend our evenings in playing at draughts till it is time to go to bed.' They did not return to England until December, bringing with them such souvenirs as a pietra-dura slab, which was mounted onto a table for them by the London firm of Hatfields. Now in the Bedroom Corridor at Waddesdon, it is a touch-

OPPOSITE: *Evelina, painted around the time of her marriage in 1865, by James Sant.*

RIGHT: *Pietra dura slab bought by Ferdinand and Evelina on their Italian honeymoon in 1865. Incorporated into a table by Hatfields of London, it is now in the Bedroom Corridor at Waddesdon.*

FERDINAND ROTHSCHILD AND HIS FAMILY

ing relic of the couple's shared enthusiasm for 'curiosity hunting'.

The idyll was short-lived: after only 18 months of marriage, Evelina died in childbirth on December 4, 1866, while Ferdinand was in Vienna, helping out at the bank in the chaos following Austria's defeat in the war with Prussia. Her family was stricken; the following day, her cousin Constance, Anthony's eldest daughter, recorded in her diary a visit to Evelina's deathbed: 'the sight of the mourners— oh, it went to my heart. Saw the bedroom, that gay, bright room with the motionless form on the bed, with the poor, tiny baby on the sofa. Oh, what a sight.' Ferdinand was inconsolable. 'Mine is a loss which years cannot repair', he wrote to Leopold, 'Ever since my childhood I was attached to her.' He commissioned from the architect Matthew Digby Wyatt a Neoclassical mausoleum for her burial place in the Jewish cemetery in West Ham in east London: on it he inscribed in English and Hebrew words derived from the Psalms and Proverbs: 'She opened her lips with wisdom/And in her speech was the law of kindness/My darling wife.' Her memory is further commemorated in his charitable benefactions: at first he considered building a maternity hospital, but finally settled on a children's hospital, the Evelina, built at his expense in the New Kent Road, south London, and supported with annual payments of £2,000 to the end of his life.

The following eight years in Ferdinand's life are somewhat of a blank. He travelled a great deal, spending time in Russia and journeying as far east as Persia. At home, he devoted himself to country sports, and rented Leighton House in Leighton Buzzard, near the border of Bedfordshire and Buckinghamshire, from which he hunted with the Whaddon Chase and the Rothschild staghounds. Here he was joined by his youngest sister, Alice, then just 20, who was also an enthusiast for the sport. In due course, she too decided to settle in England. She was able to buy 142 Piccadilly, the house next door to his, and as Dorothy de Rothschild recalled in her book on Waddesdon, 'they pierced a communicating door between the two houses, thus establishing the future pattern of their lives, separate but together'. Ferdinand spent his time pursuing his interest in art, less by collecting himself than by attending sales or inspecting works of art on behalf of his uncles or cousins, who rapidly came to trust his judgment. He dallied with literature, publishing a romance entitled *Vroni* in German in 1878; another work of fiction, which remains in manuscript, is entitled *Lady Glendale*: the story of a beautiful young woman who decides to remain faithful to her elderly husband despite falling in love with a handsome suitor, it does not suggest Ferdinand had the potential to be a novelist, but it may partly have been an exercise

in written English. By the end of his life, Ferdinand had become an accomplished author, with a fluent and pithy style. There was little pressure on him to interrupt his agreeably dilettantish life with work: although he might be called on by his father in a crisis, it was clear that he had no desire for a business career: 'it is an odd thing', he wrote in 1872, 'but whenever I sell any stock it is sure to rise and if I buy any it generally falls.' He was a member of the first generation of male Rothschilds who were free to break from the business world and had no need to seek an alternative career. However, although Ferdinand's allowance was adequate to keep him in comfort, he lacked money for large-scale building or collecting.

Hunting brought Ferdinand and Alice into close contact with their cousins' lives as country-house owners. The Rothschilds had established their connection with central Buckinghamshire in 1833, when Nathan had rented the 17th-century house at Tring for the summer. His four sons all developed a taste for hunting. Sport was encouraged by their mother as good exercise, but it also provided an entrée into landed society. At first, the brothers were coolly received, partly no doubt for reasons of snobbery or antisemitism, but largely because of political differences: the Rothschilds were Liberals whereas the dominant landed interest in the area, the Duke of Buckingham at nearby Stowe, was a Tory and staunchly opposed the Liberal policy of free trade. As a result, the Rothschilds preferred to hunt their own pack of staghounds rather than join one of the established hunts. Nathan's widow was the first to buy land in the area, at Mentmore, a few miles north-east of Aylesbury, the county town. This may have begun simply as a financial investment—land prices were falling because of agricultural recession—but it was the nucleus of a large estate around Mentmore and Wing which was built up piecemeal by her youngest son, Mayer, in the 1840s.

In 1848 the Duke of Buckingham went spectacularly bankrupt, and a year later another large local landowner, Sir John Dashwood, died, leaving substantial debts. These events brought over 50,000 acres onto the market and the Rothschilds seized their opportunity. Their agent in Buckinghamshire was James James, a solicitor and partner in the Aylesbury firm of James & Horwood. A far-sighted man of business (and a pioneering collector of 18th-century English furniture), he advised the brothers to concentrate their landholdings in one area as much as possible, in order to strengthen their political influence in the county. As a result, Anthony bought the Aston Clinton estate from the Duke of Buckingham in 1851 and two years later Lionel acquired the Halton estate from Dashwood's heir. Both estates

were just to the east of Aylesbury and so an easy ride from Mentmore. Moreover, all could be quickly reached from London by railway. The Rothschilds became some of the first commuters: Lionel even found it possible to travel up by rail from London for a morning's hunting and then return for the day's parliamentary session.

At Aston Clinton and Halton, Anthony and Lionel contented themselves with enlarging the existing houses, but at Mentmore their youngest brother Mayer built for himself one of the great houses of the age, which set new standards for the Rothschilds throughout Europe. Work began on it in 1851, the year of the Great Exhibition, and Mayer's architect was none other than the designer of the Crystal Palace, Sir Joseph Paxton, who had been a family friend since the 1840s. Mentmore's mighty towers are flamboyantly Elizabethan in style—the principal model was Wollaton Hall in Nottinghamshire— but it was the emphasis on luxury and technological innovation that most impressed contemporaries. Paxton may have been employed as architect because Mayer knew he would be confident about designing the glass-and-iron-roofed central hall that rises the full height of the building. This was the setting for an eye-catching collection of French and Italian furniture, Gobelin tapestries and a mighty black marble chimneypiece said to have come from Rubens's house in Antwerp.

The entrance front of Mentmore, Buckinghamshire, in an oil painting of about 1855. Designed in 1850 by Joseph Paxton and G.H. Stokes for Mayer Amschel Rothschild (1818–1874), son of Nathan Mayer, the founder of the London branch of the bank, it set new standards of opulence for the Rothschilds' country houses.

Most of the furnishings and works of art were bought with the assistance of the dealer Alexander Barker, whom Mayer consulted closely about the arrangement and decoration of the house.

Mentmore, like its Rothschild neighbours, was designed as an assertion of status and a backdrop for entertaining on the grandest scale. These houses marked the family's social advance into country life and local office, as justices of the peace, magistrates, lord lieutenants and eventually members of parliament: in 1847 Lionel became the first practising Jew to be elected an MP, although it was another 11 years before he was able to take his seat, when the requirement for MPs to swear a Christian oath of allegiance was finally abolished. In 1859 Mayer joined him in the House of Commons, and in 1865 Lionel's eldest son, Natty, was elected MP for Aylesbury.

In the early 1870s, Ferdinand's uncles and cousins embarked on a further round of estate purchasing. In 1872, Lionel acquired (for £240,000) the 4,000-acre Tring estate, just over the county border,

FERDINAND ROTHSCHILD AND HIS FAMILY

in Hertfordshire, and in 1873 Mayer bought 90 acres at Ascott, two miles north of Mentmore, which came with a small house. Ascott was given to Lionel's son Leopold, who added substantially to the estate and enlarged the house. With Mentmore and Aston Clinton, these were the houses that Ferdinand and Alice would have known when they joined their cousins for hunting. Not surprisingly, Ferdinand hankered for something similar. In the summer of 1872, his father-in-law suggested to him that he might persuade Anselm to buy for him the Earl of Southampton's estate at Whittlebury in Northamptonshire, which had just come on to the market after its house had been badly damaged by fire. Ferdinand replied that 'it seems to me the very place I should like to have and I shall certainly write about it to my father. Unfortunately I am perfectly certain that he will never for one moment entertain the notion of purchasing it. Oddly enough, he was never partial to buying land . . . I only wish you could devise some means for me to find the money in some way or other and buy the place!' His prediction was correct, for on August 20 Anselm responded witheringly: 'What a nice fairy tale! I shall invest in English soil, yielding 3% while I have offers in the neighbourhood here of excellent grounds yielding at least $4^{1}/_{2}$ %.'

However, within two years Ferdinand's circumstances had been transformed, for on July 27, 1874, his father died. Contemporaries were struck by the contrast between the modest funeral Anselm had requested—he was buried in Frankfurt with no more ceremony than would be accorded 'a poor Jew', in the words of *The Times*—and his immense wealth: he bequeathed more than 50 million *thalers*—approximately £7.3 million. In his will, Anselm recognised that his sons Nathaniel and Ferdinand were not going to join the bank, and alluded affectionately to Ferdinand's interest in art. The two were left the greater part of his property and art collection: Schillersdorf went to Nathaniel, together with the house in Vienna; Ferdinand was given his London house, which had been bought with a loan from his father. Salbert, the only son to show any business aptitude, was bequeathed principally his father's share of the family partnership, so forcing him into the bank; he was not pleased. Alice was left the house on the Grüneburg estate, and land in Austria, a tacit recognition that, at 27, she was unlikely to marry. This gave Ferdinand the opportunity he had been waiting for: he and Nathaniel asked to withdraw their legacies from the bank. The partners drew up a new contract, completed in 1875, in which £8 million was deducted from the partnership's total assets of some £35.5 million; part of this was to allow Nathaniel and Ferdinand to be paid off.

Anselm's legacy coincided with a great opportunity: in May 1874, the Duke of Marlborough, prompted by the high price land was fetching, had put his estate at Winchendon in Buckinghamshire on the market. His family had never possessed an income to match their exalted status, and by the 1870s the Duke was struggling to maintain Blenheim Palace on an income of barely £40,000 a year; this sale of land was the beginning of a dispersal of assets that led over the next 12 years to Blenheim's gems, books and paintings being auctioned off—sales from which Ferdinand and other Rothschilds benefitted. About six miles north-west of Aylesbury, the Duke's Buckinghamshire estate consisted of 2,700 acres in the parishes of Waddesdon, Upper Winchendon, and Cuddington, described in the sale particulars as 'one of the finest dairy districts in the County. The lands are all thoroughly drained and in the best heart and condition.' No Duke of Marlborough

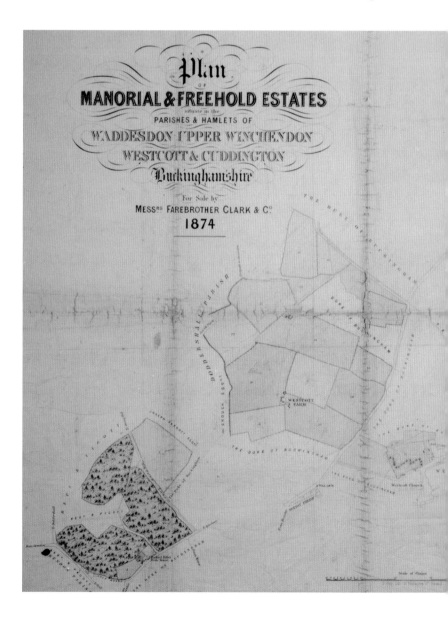

had ever lived there: the estate had been purchased as an investment in 1725. In the late 17th century, it had been the home of the first Marquess of Wharton, who had remodelled the medieval house at Winchendon and laid out a celebrated formal garden, of which traces remain visible. However, his house was demolished by the 2nd Duke of Marlborough, leaving only a fragment of the service wing, which still survives on Winchendon Hill, as a house now known as The Wilderness. Despite the agent's claim that 'great improvements have been carried out under the immediate inspection of the agent to the noble owner, by the erection of new homesteads on the most approved principles of modern farming', the estate presented a neglected appearance by the 1870s and produced a rental income of barely £6,000 a year. Ferdinand was well aware of its deficiencies, but the opportunity to buy so much land in Buckinghamshire was not to be missed. He would have preferred an

estate with a house on it, 'and could I have obtained one I should not have acquired this property', he recorded in his *Red Book*, 'which was all farm land, arable chiefly, with neither a house nor a park, and, although comparatively near London, was at a distance of six miles from Aylesbury, the nearest railway station. But there was none other to be had; there was not even the prospect of one coming onto the market, and I was loath to wait on the chance ... This much could be said in its favour: it had a bracing and salubrious air, pleasant scenery, excellent hunting, and was untainted by factories and villadom.'

Ferdinand moved quickly. Winchendon had come up at auction at Aylesbury on July 7, but was bought in at £170,000, since the

This plan of the estate, which was part of the 1874 sale particulars, shows Lodge Hill, the future site of Waddesdon Manor, at top centre.

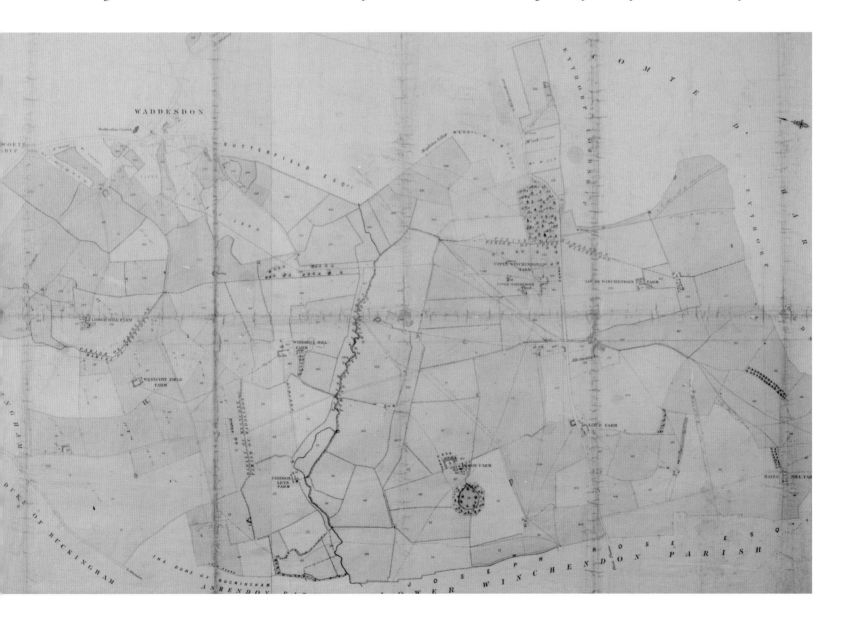

FERDINAND ROTHSCHILD AND HIS FAMILY

reserve had not been reached. Within days of his father's death, while he was still in Austria, Ferdinand was in negotiation with the Duke's agent. He completed the purchase quickly, with the aid of a loan from his uncle James, since it would be some time before his father's legacies would be paid. According to the *Buckinghamshire Herald*, which announced the sale on August 22, the price was 'about £200,000'. This seems to be accurate: at about this time Anthony wrote to his brother Lionel from Homburg that 'James has orders to purchase Waddesdon for 200000£ plus . . . for Ferdy'; there may, however, have been additional payments for the timber. On August 15, Ferdinand wrote to Lionel that 'I should have been glad to have [heard] from you whether you approved of the purchase and of the price I paid for it. Uncle Anthony tells me he does not consider it dear.'

It came naturally to the Rothschilds to think of their purchases as investments, as was shown by Anselm's refusal to buy land for Ferdinand: in 1844 Lionel had told his brothers that he expected 'a fair rate of interest' from his new land in Buckinghamshire. There

seems little doubt that he got it, for he and his brothers were buying during a slump and prices recovered dramatically during the next 30 years. Ferdinand, in contrast, was buying at the top of the market and the £74 an acre he gave for Waddesdon was a very high price. To take a near-contemporary comparison, when the glove manufacturer J. D. Allcroft bought the Stokesay estate in Shropshire from the Earl of Craven in 1869 he paid just over £40 an acre; the estate, although twice the acreage of Waddesdon, was otherwise closely comparable in lacking a house of any size and deriving only a modest income from mixed dairy and arable farming. The difference must largely be accounted for in terms of geography: Ferdinand had to pay more because the estate was nearer London. It seems unlikely he paid more than the market value—the rental was three percent of the capital value of the estate—but, as he soon realised, his timing had not been good: the price of agricultural land in the south of England declined sharply after 1875, largely because of competition from cheap imports of American grain. As the *Manchester Guardian* wrote after his death,

'the Baron used to say that he had bought a bare hill because at the moment when he wanted a country house there were no ready-made places in the market. If he had waited two years, the bad times would have set in and he would have been able to buy a wooded estate and plant his new house among old trees.' Even so, Ferdinand would probably have been surprised to realise that, taking inflation into account, his land would not recover its value until the 1960s, following the post-war agricultural boom.

Yet it is unlikely that he cared too deeply, for to him Waddesdon was not an economic asset, it was his life's work. It is notable that although the estate had always been known as Upper Winchendon, the name under which it was advertised for sale, Ferdinand and his family called it Waddesdon from the start, for he quickly decided that he would make his home not on the site of the old house, on Winchendon Hill, but on the even taller Lodge Hill, which rises above the little village of Waddesdon. On September 1, he wrote to his uncle Lionel that 'I have just come from a long ride over the Waddesdon property, and I hasten to tell you that I am very much pleased with it. I think it a lovely tract of land, beautiful soil, a few capital covers and very pretty scenery. The only thing it seems to be deficient in is timber. It strikes me that there is but one site for a house, and that is Lodge Hill just behind the village of Waddesdon; only the boundary of the estate would be rather too near the house.'

In *The Red Book* Ferdinand recalled at greater length the reasons for this initial decision: 'Lodge Hill, as the small but steep hill on which [the house] stands is called—its highest point being 614 feet above sea-level—commands a panoramic view over several counties. On the north is the long range of the Chiltern Hills; on the south-west the Malvern Hills loom in the far distance; on the west is Wotton, the former abode of the Grenvilles, a corner of which peeps out of a dense mass of woodland. Towards the north the eye travels over a boundless expanse of grass-land, and on the east the Vale of Aylesbury winds along. Lodge Hill when first taken in hand was a misshapen cone with a farmhouse on its top, to which a rough track for carts led direct from the village. Often when hunting I had noticed its triangular formation—the result probably of a volcanic eruption—and its fine hedgerow timber. When it came into my possession nearly all the timber had vanished, and but for a few hollies round the farmhouse there was not a bush to be seen, nor was there a bird to be heard; but luxuriant crops of wheat and beet told of the richness of the soil.'

The challenge Ferdinand had taken on—to turn round a neglected estate and build a house and lay out a garden on top of a bare hill—surprised his family. In December 1874 he and Alice took their cousin Constance to the future site of the house. 'The place under that grey wintry sky did not look attractive', Constance recalled, 'and the roads were certainly not adapted for wheel travelling, excepting for that of farm carts. As we began to mount the hill our horse felt what would be required of him and sagaciously slackened speed, at last refusing to go any further; and this was not astonishing, as the wheels of the carriage were sticking fast in the mud. So we dismounted, and youth being on our side, we managed to struggle on for awhile, gaining some idea of the view to be obtained from the top of the hill, without actually arriving at its summit. Tired and somewhat disappointed, I exclaimed at last, "And is it here, Ferdie, that you intend building your palace? And is this to be the site of your future park?"' Ferdinand was not to be deterred, and he belied his years of idle leisure by the speed and resolution with which he set to work. The bare, muddy fields which so dismayed his cousin were the blank canvas on which he would give physical shape to an artistic vision.

OPPOSITE: *The site of Waddesdon Manor on Lodge Hill was a treeless expanse of heavy clay in 1874. The Duke of Marlborough, indebted and forced to sell, had stripped the estate of its saleable timber.*

FERDINAND ROTHSCHILD AND HIS FAMILY

2

BUILDING the HOUSE

To Ferdinand's contemporaries, it was little short of a miracle that within five years of that initial expedition with Alice and Constance, an empty landscape had been transformed into the setting for a great house. This achievement was a tribute not only to Ferdinand's unexpected reserves of inherited energy and determination but also to the care with which he had chosen the men who realised his vision. Money was, of course, no obstacle, but that in itself was no guarantee of an artistically successful result or even of an efficiently accomplished building programme. Ferdinand had some important decisions to make at the outset, for he felt himself unable to follow his family's lead in his choice of architect and the obvious contractor was no longer available.

The Rothschilds tended to share architects: Paxton and Stokes, who had designed Mentmore and Ferrières in the 1850s, as well as working on Aston Clinton, had been replaced in the following decade by George Devey, who became Anthony's architect at Aston Clinton and Lionel's at Tring. He was also much employed at Mentmore by Mayer to design estate buildings. Devey was a London architect who had made a name for work on a modest scale in a revived vernacular idiom. He had numerous commissions from Liberal landowners and in the mid 1860s moved on from estate cottages and remodellings of old houses to a busy and prosperous practice designing new country houses. When Anselm wanted a new dairy on the Schillersdorf estate, he went to Devey: in August 1868 Ferdinand wrote to his uncles in England that he had been with his father to inspect the building, 'which

Aerial view of Waddesdon Manor, a view which emphasises the narrowness of the house,
designed to give all the main rooms a view south across the Parterre.

was built after Devey's plans ordered this year in London by Alice. It will be very pretty when finished, and none the worse for some china ornaments and implements we are to forward from London on our return.'

Perhaps as a result of this success, Devey was given an important commission by Alice in England. In August 1875, the 1400-acre Eythrope estate, which marched with Waddesdon, came onto the market for £130,000. It was snapped up by Ferdinand on Alice's behalf. Like Waddesdon, it had no big house: Eythrope House, the medieval seat of the Dormer family, remodelled in the mid 18th century by Thomas Harris and Isaac Ware for Sir William Stanhope, had been demolished in 1810–11. Alice commissioned a new house from Devey, but since she had been advised that her chosen site close to the River Thame could exacerbate her tendency to rheumatic fever, the building was designed solely as a pavilion for entertainment, and had no bedrooms, since she planned to spend the nights in the healthier air of her brother's house on the hill. Devey may have been disappointed not to have been given the far bigger commission for Waddesdon itself, but he was never employed by Ferdinand (although a small payment in 1879 may have been for work on his Piccadilly house). If Ferdinand had wanted an Englishman to design Waddesdon, Devey would most probably have been his choice, but he decided instead to search for a French one, since he had resolved to build his house in a French style. His eye soon lit on one of the most fashionable architects of the day, Gabriel-Hippolyte Destailleur.

'It may be asked', wrote Ferdinand in the *Red Book*—and clearly he was asked this quite often—'what induced me to employ foreign instead of native talent of which there was no lack at hand? My reply is, that having been greatly impressed by the ancient Châteaux of the Valois during a tour I once made in the Touraine, I determined to build my house in the same style, and considered it safer to get the designs made by a French architect who was familiar with the work, than by an English one whose knowledge and experience of the architecture of that period could be less thoroughly trusted. The French sixteenth century style, on which I had long set my heart, was particularly suitable to the surroundings of the site I had selected, and more uncommon than the Tudor, Jacobean, or Adams, of which the country affords so many and such unique specimens.'

This bland statement deserves further analysis. English 19th-century patrons had for long admired the decorative arts, interiors and to a lesser extent the buildings of 18th-century France, but interest in French Renaissance architecture was a more recent development. In visual terms, a cousin of the revived Elizabethan or Jacobean styles, it was used with aplomb by such architects as R.C. Carpenter, Benjamin Ferrey and Henry Clutton. Renaissance styles, whether English or French, appealed to patrons eager to respond to the busy aesthetic of the Gothic revival without calling in its overtones of medieval Christianity or the feudal past, which appealed so much to the Anglican church and the traditional landed interest. For that reason, the Renaissance revival was a popular choice for secular public buildings (such as hotels), for which Gothic was thought inappropriate for reasons of decorum, as well as for houses commissioned by new landowners. There had been several substantial new English houses in a French Renaissance style before Waddesdon, most notably perhaps E.M.Barry's Wykehurst in Sussex (1871–74) for Henry Huth (like Ferdinand, the son of a banking family and also a notable collector), and Impney Hall in Worcestershire, designed in 1869 by a Parisian architect, Auguste Tronquois (with Richard Phené Spiers as executant architect). The client was a wealthy salt manufacturer, John Corbett, whose wife was French, and the couple may have been directly influenced by the Rothschild taste for the French Renaissance evident in James and Salomon's Parisian *hôtels*.

There is little evidence that Ferdinand took much interest in contemporary architectural developments in England, except where they involved the Rothschilds. His main reason for adopting a French style was almost certainly the negative one of avoiding comparisons with country houses his family had already built. In 1880 he was consulted by his close friend Lord Rosebery about the most appropriate style for a London house Rosebery was thinking of asking Destailleur to design for him. 'The Italian Renaissance requires enormous proportions', Ferdinand replied. 'Louis XVI is the simplest and cheapest & I think as good as any for a town house. Louis XIV is grander & handsomer, but as my brother has just built one of that style & employed D[estailleur]—I should avoid running the risk of copying it. Louis Quinze is rather coarse & wld. not do for London I think—if you employ the frenchman I can give you several hints to prevent expense.' By choosing a French idiom Ferdinand avoided comparison with Mentmore and Ferrières, where an English Renaissance style had been so triumphantly adapted to the needs of the 19th century. His letter also suggests the competitive eye he kept on his brothers' building schemes in Austria. Nathaniel built an immense Renaissance palazzo on the Theresianumgasse in Vienna, designed by Jean Girette, and laid out a magnificent garden at his villa on the outskirts of the city, Hohe Warte. On Ferdinand's advice, Salbert had commisisoned his equally grand town palace from Destailleur, built on the Heugasse and begun in 1876. In addition, while Ferdinand was embarking on Waddesdon, both Nathaniel and Salbert were building new country houses—the Château Penelope at Reichenau for Nathaniel and Schloss Langau at Enzesfeld for Salbert.

In Destailleur Ferdinand found an architect perfectly suited to his needs. Born in 1822, he was the son of an architect, François-Hippolyte Destailleur, and his Irish wife, Eleonor O'Brien. The elder Destailleur had studied under Charles Percier and had had a busy practice designing Palladian townhouses and châteaux. Following his training at the Ecole des Beaux-Arts, the younger Destailleur worked with his father and in 1852 inherited his post as architect to the Ministère de Justice. He also continued to work for many of his father's most influential patrons, most notably—in Ferdinand's eyes—the family of the duc d'Orléans. A passionate belief in the need to create a national style for the 19th century led him to form an unparalleled collection of books and prints illustrating the history of French architecture and design and he published immensely influential facsimiles of historic French architectural and ornamental treatises, most notably (in 1868) Jacques Androuet DuCerceau's 1577–79 *Plus Excellens Bastimens*, which illustrates many of France's greatest Renaissance châteaux.

These activities would have been enough to bring Destailleur to Ferdinand's attention, but he may also have encountered his work in Paris, where he had designed several *hôtels* in a variety of styles, and had a reputation for remodelling the interiors of existing houses to bring them up to date, often with a shot of Rococo glamour. Destailleur may have appealed because his scholarly antiquarianism was in distinct contrast to the gaudy classicism of the recently extinguished Second Empire: Ferdinand certainly thought the most celebrated Parisian monument of the age, Charles Garnier's Opéra, then nearing completion, was 'frightfully overdone', as he wrote to Lionel in 1874. Although it is true that the French Rothschilds had tended to flourish more easily under the Bourbon than the imperial regimes, and so may as a result have favoured the nationalistic Gothic or Renaissance styles associated with the former, the choice of an architect such as Destailleur was more probably influenced by Ferdinand's indifference to any style that might be thought of as modern. He wanted instead a house that both inside and out was as careful a recreation of past styles as possible.

Moreover, Destailleur's potential as a designer of country houses was then being made evident at the *Schloss* at Pless (now Pszczyna) in Silesia, where in 1872 he was given the commission to remodel the rambling seat of Hans Heinrich XI von Pless. The result is an immense Louis XV château with interiors fitted out with *boiseries*, tapestries and

Gabriel-Hippolyte Destailleur (1822–1893), the French architect commissioned by Ferdinand Rothschild in 1874 to design Waddesdon Manor. Much of Ferdinand's library of books on topography, architecture and ornament was bought at the sale of Destailleur's library, which followed the architect's death.

new plasterwork designed by Destailleur on French historical models in an ensemble which parallels the architect's work at Waddesdon. Ferdinand does not mention Pless in *The Red Book* but he probably knew the house, which is a close neighbour of Schillersdorf. He certainly knew the Pless palace on Wilhelmstrasse in Vienna, also designed by Destailleur, and Prince Heinrich's lively English daughter-in-law, Princess Daisy of Pless, stayed with Ferdinand at Waddesdon. Another of Destailleur's earlier commissions which Ferdinand does mention may have had a direct influence on the conception of Waddesdon. This was the remodelling of the enormous château de Mouchy, near Beauvais, for successive ducs de Mouchy, a task which Destailleur had inherited from his father and was to occupy him on and off for the rest of his life. The spectacular site of this great turreted 16th-century château (now demolished), perched on the edge of a high ridge, may have influenced Ferdinand's

Chateau de Mouchy, Oise, France, in a late-nineteenth-century photograph. Destailleur worked for much of his life on the restoration of Mouchy for the ducs de Mouchy, and the chimney stacks and ornamental stonework find parallels at Waddesdon.

wish to build Waddesdon on a prominent hill; there is no doubt that details of Mouchy, from decorative motifs to the profile of the dormer windows, were directly copied at Waddesdon.

Ferdinand had a remarkably untroubled relationship with Destailleur, whom he summed up as 'a man of the highest capacity in his profession. He was a purist in style, painstaking, conscientious, and of the most scrupulous honesty. During the eighteen years of my relations with him there was never the smallest difference between us.' Nonetheless, he found the busy, scholarly architect dilatory, as well as more interested in questions of style than of convenience. As Ferdinand recalled, 'He had not the faintest conception of the needs of a large establishment, sacrificed the most urgent household requirements to external architectural features, and had the most supreme contempt for ventilation, light, air, and all internal conveniences. This, perhaps, need not have surprised me, for he and his numerous family lived huddled together in a small and musty house in a dingy back street which I never entered without a shudder.' Although Ferdinand does not say so, one drawback of this equable relationship was that the client too often got his way; Ferdinand was so sure of what he wanted that he did not always listen to the advice of his experienced architect, with results that he sometimes regretted. Destailleur did not record his views of Ferdinand, but his son, Walter André d'Estailleur (who followed the family's 18th-century spelling of its name) wrote an unpublished memoir of his life, in which he recalled Ferdinand in words that probably reflect his father's opinions: '*un homme grand et plutot maigre, assez aimable, sans plus, extrêmement autoritaire et curieux. Il etait cependant une des figures marquantes de la fin du siècle dernier*' ['a tall and rather spare man, kindly enough but no more, extremely authoritarian and inquisitive. He was, nevertheless, one of the outstanding figures of the end of the last century.']. The measured tone of this judgment is an indication of how much Waddesdon was a realisation of Ferdinand's vision, not its architect's.

Destailleur first visited the site of the future house in the autumn of 1874, and drew up a design at once. None of the many letters that must have passed between him and Ferdinand have survived, but the evolution of the design over the next few months can be traced, thanks to the survival of numerous drawings in the records of Destailleur's practice, which are now divided between the Archives Nationales in Paris

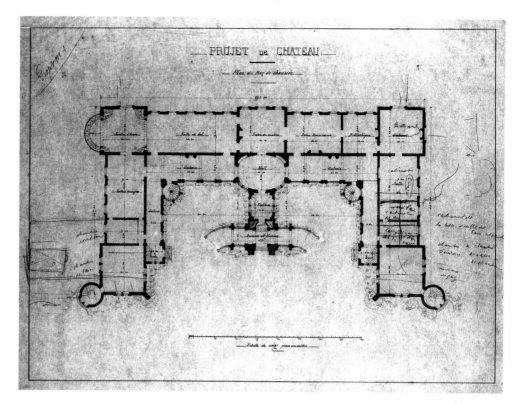

Destailleur's first proposal for Waddesdon, designed shortly after his first visit to the site in the autumn of 1874. Modelled closely on the plan of Schillersdorf, it is much larger than the final house. No service wing is shown; Destailleur may have intended to place the service rooms in a raised basement.

and the Kunstbibliothek in Berlin. The surprisingly complex story they tell, which has been analysed by Bruno Pons, shows the impact of English ideas of convenience and propriety on French domestic traditions.

Destailleur's first proposal, for which plans but no elevations survive, was in the form of a large, open and rigidly symmetrical rectangle, in which a monumental south-facing garden façade nearly 255 feet (77 metres) in length was linked to long wings which ran north to create a spacious entrance courtyard. These wings terminated in circular towers. Visitors would have arrived via a curved carriage ramp at a *porte cochère* and then passed through a rectangular vestibule into an oval hall and from there into a square 'Salon du Matin'. That sequence, which derives ultimately from 17th-century French town houses, was retained right through to the final design, and indeed the main block changed comparatively little in its layout through all the subsequent revisions: it was long and narrow, with a single enfilade of rooms overlooking the garden—the first idea was to make them (from east to west) a conservatory, a ballroom, the Salon du Matin, a 'Salon Renaissance', a library and a billiard room. On the courtyard side were galleries leading to the dining room in the east wing and a 'Cabinet' in the west wing. As in the final design, the principal staircases are modestly sized circular stairs at the junction of the wings with the main block. To a striking degree, this layout is modelled on Schillersdorf and it is revealing that a plan of that house survives in Destailleur's papers; it was probably supplied by Ferdinand as a model for his architect to imitate.

Although the layout of English houses was becoming less complex in the late 1860s, partly as a result of the move away from courtyard-plans of the type of Mentmore, Destailleur's initial proposal would have looked radically simple to an English architect, especially in the narrowness and axial formality of the central block. In planning, it owed far more to French than to English precedents—such details as a billiard room forming part of the main sequence of ground-floor rooms would have seemed odd to the English, who usually placed the billiard room, with a smoking room, in a suite set aside for male visitors; there are also no instances of a spiral stair in a principal position in an English house at this date. The design included no large hall, of the sort popular in contemporary houses as a place for guests to meet. Although such enormous spaces as Mentmore's central hall had fallen from fashion by the early 1870s, Ferdinand was eventually to regret doing away with one altogether. The approach to the front door by means of steps or a carriage ramp indicates that Destailleur originally planned to raise the house on a basement; since the initial design does not show a service wing it is possible that he proposed putting the services there. This was still acceptable practice in France but was by then virtually unknown in English country houses, which, in contrast to their French equivalents, had a long tradition of enforcing rigid separation between families and their servants. There was also a strong dislike of any aspect of the house's practical functions, from cooking smells to the sight of laundry, impinging on its public face.

This drawback to the initial design was no doubt pointed out to Ferdinand: on Destailleur's plan, somebody has scribbled in pencil a proposal for the location of a service wing, roughly where the Bachelors' Wing was eventually built. In December 1874 Destailleur produced revised drawings, showing a separate wing to the east for services and guest accommodation, connected to the main house by a passage. The carriage ramp and steps have been eliminated, suggesting that it was at this stage that the house acquired the comparatively low proportions that distinguish it from its 16th-century French models,

Destailleur's revised plan for the house, dated December 1874, now shows the Bachelors' Wing, which incorporates service accommodation, at the northeast corner. Ferdinand asked Destailleur to remove the projecting wings.

ROJET DE CHATEAU

Plan du rez de chaussée

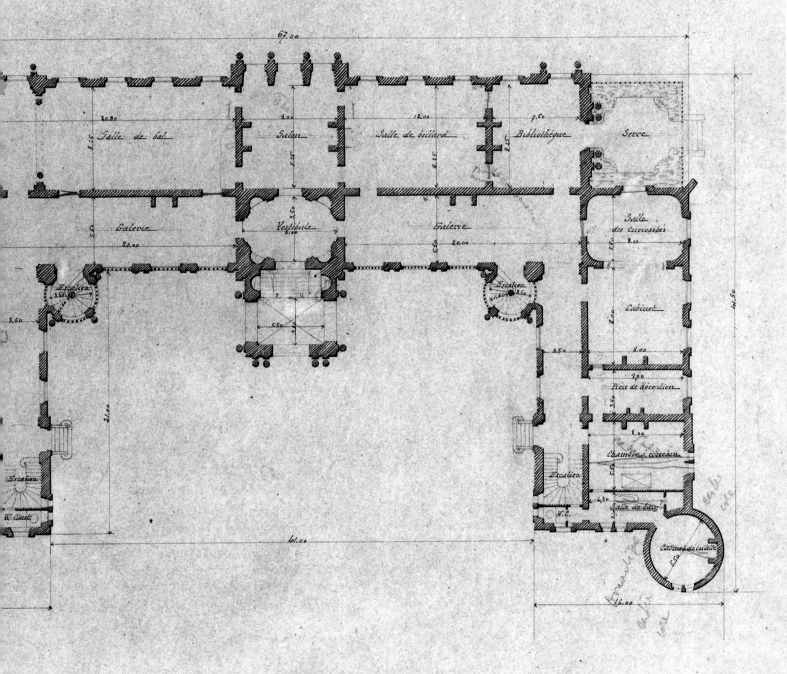

Salle de bal   Salon   Salle de billard   Bibliothèque   Serre

Galerie   Vestibule   Galerie

Salle des curiosités

Escalier   Escalier

Cabinet

Pièce de réception

Chambre à coucher

Escalier   Escalier

W.C.   W.C.   Salle de bain

Cabinet de toilette

Dressé par l'architecte soussigné.
Paris le 10 X.ᵇʳᵉ 1874 —

Echelle de 0.005 pour un mètre.

which were invariably raised on a high basement. Ferdinand must also have asked Destailleur to reduce the size of the house, since the length of the garden façade has been cut by 33 feet (10 metres); an elevation of this façade suggests that the original proposals for the exterior were decoratively simpler than they became. Destailleur also worked out in more detail the arrangement of the west wing, which was to function as a private apartment for Ferdinand, a widower's equivalent of the family wing which was a familiar feature of contemporary country houses. Originally, he proposed putting all Ferdinand's private rooms, including his bedroom, on the ground floor: principal bedrooms in this position were still not uncommon in France, but in England they were no longer found in new houses. Ferdinand soon

changed his mind about that, and his bedroom, bathroom and dressing room were moved up to the first floor, linked to his ground-floor sitting rooms by a small, private spiral stair. The numerous changes to the designs for his suite—there were no fewer than four further revisions of the arrangement of the rooms between December 1874 and March 1875—may have been the origin of Ferdinand's impatience with Destailleur's indifference to matters of domestic comfort. The architect certainly had no special gift for planning: one obvious failing in the plan that would have been criticised in contemporary manuals on house design is the long and awkward route between the kitchen and the dining room, which meant the food had to be conveyed across a service staircase.

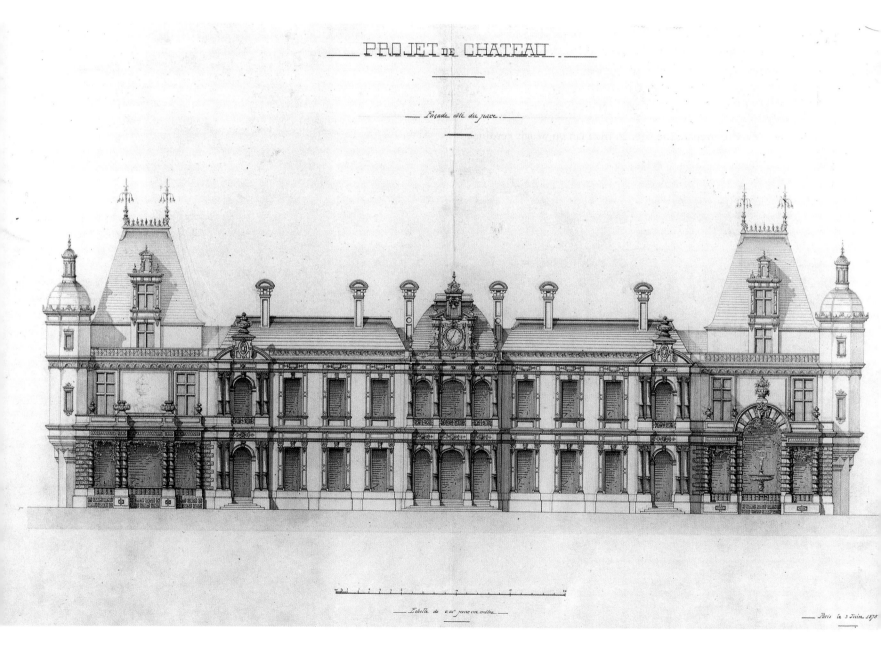

It would be interesting to know whether it was Ferdinand or Destailleur who was responsible for the idea of the principal bedrooms on the first floor being arranged as separate suites, each with its own lobby and bathroom as well as bedroom and dressing room. This was a novel idea, and as late as 1910 such an arrangement in other houses was a matter of interested comment in the architectural press, when it was assumed to be an American innovation. Destailleur's plan shows that the origin of such schemes was French, a source that might have been credited at the time if the main bedroom floor at Waddesdon had been laid out as originally devised, but the clarity and spaciousness of its initial design was one of many sacrifices made to Ferdinand's decision to simplify and reduce Destailleur's proposals.

Bruno Pons has traced five separate schemes drawn up in less than six months after the first proposals, but only the last of these, dated 11–12 March 1875, marks a radical departure, in that the wings are drastically reduced in size. It is tantalising that no evidence remains of the discussions that led to the final design, completed in 1877, after a two-year gap caused largely by the immense effort necessary to prepare the site. In the plan on which Ferdinand finally settled, the house is now a long, shallow central block 154 feet (48 metres) long, flanked by two square pavilions taking the place of the vanished wings, although only that on the east retains the circular tower which terminated them; the block on the west has been given a much larger circular tower facing the garden. The loss of floor space has in part been compensated for by the addition of an attic storey with prominent dormer windows. The result is a design far more compact, upright, and picturesquely asymmetrical than Destailleur's initial proposals. Unchanged in all these revisions is the shallowness of the main block, which makes the house almost transparently open to the landscape. Every principal ground-floor room has a garden view, a reminder that Waddesdon was designed primarily as a place of summer entertainment.

Externally, as Anthony Blunt observed, the selection of French Renaissance motifs eschews Mannerist detail, of the sort familiar from Fontainebleau, and exhibits 'a definite preference for the moderate and the classical as opposed to the ornate and the fanciful'. Yet it is much busier in detail than was originally planned, partly because the decorative schemes have been compressed rather than simplified. On the broad, flat garden front this is perhaps an improvement; but on the entrance façade the proliferation of motifs, yet further enriched by the addition of dormers, produces a dense, clotted rhythm. 'By the side of the great châteaux of the Touraine', wrote Ferdinand in *The Red*

OPPOSITE: *Design for the garden or south façade, 3 June 1875. The symmetrical end bays were replaced by a more picturesque round tower to the west and by a Conservatory to the east.*

ABOVE: *A drawing by Destailleur for the pediment on the south front. Ferdinand's 'F' echoes the monogram of Francis I at Fontainebleau, France.*

Book, 'Waddesdon would appear a pigmy. The Castle of Chambord, for example, contains 450 rooms, the smallest of which would dwarf the largest of Waddesdon. But its main features are borrowed from them: its towers from Maintenon, the Château of the Duc de Noailles, and its external staircases from Blois, though the latter, which are unglazed and open to the weather, are much more ornate. Though far from being the realisation of a dream in stone and mortar like Chenonceaux, M. Destailleur's work has fairly fulfilled my expectations.'

Critics and historians have further elaborated Ferdinand's analysis of Destailleur's sources: the staircases clearly owe more to Chambord than they do to Blois and the towers more to Chaumont

than to Maintenon; the richly crested dormers derive from Azay-le-Rideau and Chenonceau; the mighty chimneys look back to DuCerceau's depictions of the 16th-century Louvre. There are more than a few ingredients from the 17th century stirred into this predominantly Renaissance mix: the square dome over the centre of the house evidently derives from the Pavillon de l'Horloge at the Louvre and the columns flanking the entrance recall François Mansart's suave Classicism at Château de Maisons, an influence continued into the oval entrance hall. Enjoyable although it is to spot these sources, it is perhaps a criticism of Waddesdon that the motifs Destailleur has collaged together so skilfully are more compelling than the whole. It is only in distant views, which emphasise the romantic profile of its turrets, that the composition achieves authoritative coherence. There are few informed contemporary reactions to the house, but the response of the architect Eustace Balfour, who visited the house shortly after its completion, may have been typical: having greatly admired the interior, he wrote to his wife that 'outside the house is not quite so successful though very clever. It is an adaptation by a French architect, of Blois'. Ferdinand's relatively cool comment, that Destailleur had 'fairly fulfilled my expectations', suggests he may have agreed with this assessment of the relative merits of interior and exterior, but he cannot have complained that he had not been given what he wanted. As he later reflected, his reduction of Destailleur's initial plan had gone too far: "'You will regret your decision," he said to me at the time, *"one always builds too small."'*

  Once the foundations were complete, the building of Waddesdon was accomplished with remarkable swiftness and efficiency. This may have been thanks in part to having an experienced executant architect and surveyor on site to realise Destailleur's designs (Edward H. Burnell, who was based in London), but in Ferdinand's mind the greatest tribute was due to his contractor, Edward Conder, although he would probably not have been his first choice had Waddesdon been begun a few years earlier. George Myers, now best remembered for his long association with A.W.N.Pugin, had been the builder responsible for Ferrières as well as for virtually all the Rothschilds' major projects in England since he won the contract for Mentmore in 1851, including Evelina's mausoleum at West Ham and

OPPOSITE: *The West Tower, overlooking the Parterre. It was built to serve as Ferdinand's private apartment. Below the balcony is the window of his former bedroom, now the Bakst Room. Above (formerly a servant's room), is the Drawings Room, created in 1999.*

ABOVE: *Detail of the upper floors at the west end of the house, which provided bedroom accommodation for guests and servants. The strapwork pilasters and pinnacled dormer windows are derived from early-sixteenth-century models.*

OVERLEAF: *View of the Vale of Aylesbury from above the central pavilion of the house. The crisp carving of acanthus, animal heads and corbels is striking.*

the refurbishment of Ferdinand's London house. However, Myers had retired in 1873, and his firm had closed after his death in January 1875. Conder, whose firm, Edward Conder and Son, was based at Baltic Wharf in Kingsland Road, Shoreditch, east London, was a more than adequate substitute—'I have never met a more trustworthy man of business' wrote Ferdinand in *The Red Book*. The regard in which he is held is demonstrated by an inscription recording his role in the building which is carved on the east flank of the main block.

Use of a principal contractor was a practice adapted from the commercial construction world: the customary method of building country houses before the early 19th century had been to employ direct labour through a clerk-of-works who was usually a member of the estate staff. This was still the approach favoured by some patrons who felt that use of a contractor was too constricting. When in 1884 Ferdinand's friend Lord Windsor embarked on building Hewell Grange in Worcestershire, a house close in scale to Waddesdon, he resolved to employ all the labour himself: 'Though this plan may not have been an economical one, it was unquestionably the best', he wrote, 'as it enabled us to make any alterations as the work proceeded, and it saved us from the disappointing feeling that if we had had more time to consider details we should have done them differently.' Ferdinand may have understood the argument—Hewell Grange is the only modern English house he is said to have envied—but the advantage of his chosen method in terms of speed was enormous. It took only three years from the laying of the foundation stone for Waddesdon to be ready for occupation, whereas the building of Hewell took almost seven, even though there were none of the problems Ferdinand had brought on himself by his choice of site.

His first practical difficulty was that there was no adequate source of water on Lodge Hill. He entered into a contract with the Chiltern Hills Water Company for a supply which involved laying nearly 11 miles of pipes between Aylesbury and Waddesdon at his

OPPOSITE: *The Morning Room bay window with a glimpse of* Thais *by Sir Joshua Reynolds.*

ABOVE: *This design by Destailleur for the coffering in the ceiling of the Oval Hall reveals his painstaking attention to ornamental detail. It was simplified in execution.*

expense and the construction of a large storage tank in the grounds. Here must have been the first realisation that Ferdinand's arrival promised to revitalise the neighbourhood: in October 1875, the water company's chairman was able to tell his shareholders with some satisfaction that 'they hoped to have a large increase of customers from the extension of the pipes, which included Eythrope, Hartwell, Winchendon, Lodge Hill, and Westcott, besides Waddesdon. So large an extension of course implied a large expenditure of money, but happily the Company would not have to pay, though they hoped to have the profit of it.' Three taps were opened for public use in Waddesdon village. The house's water storage facilities proved inadequate in hot weather, and one summer the supply failed altogether: 'but for the manager's energy, who sat up all night at the Works sending us up water', remembered Ferdinand, 'we should have been compelled to leave the next day. To obviate the recurrence of a similar difficulty another and a larger tank was constructed.' The result was an underground reservoir below the Aviary which is so large it requires a dinghy to cross it.

A second difficulty was the supply of materials. Although the nearest station was at Aylesbury, six miles away (the extension of the Metropolitan railway to Waddesdon which Ferdinand believed to be imminent when he bought the estate did not occur until 1897), he was able to benefit from the private goods tramway constructed in 1871 at the expense of the 3rd Duke of Buckingham to link his estate at Wotton with the railway line at Quainton. It had a station known as Rag Hall—in effect little more than a siding—at Hall Farm just outside Waddesdon, and at Ferdinand's instigation two small branches were built: the first led to a depot at the foot of Lodge Hill, where a cable tramway was built up to the summit of the hill; this was the method of transporting building materials to the site of the house. Some joists in the roof still bear labels 'E. Conder, Waddesdon siding'. A second branch track was built to allow coal to be taken to a new gasworks at Westcott, opened in 1883, which was to supply the house. The gash in the hillside made for the construction of the cable tramway was retained after the completion of the house, and was later converted into a picturesque valley spanned by the Tay Bridge, an ornamental garden feature. 'Other materials for the building', wrote Ferdinand, 'as well as for the farmsteads, cottages and lodges, and the trees and shrubs, had to be carted some miles by road. Percheron mares were imported from Normandy for this purpose, and they proved most serviceable, for though less enduring they travelled faster over the ground and were much cheaper than Shire horses. They have since doubled in price. When worn out they went to stud.' He no doubt got the idea of using Percherons from Schillersdorf, where Anselm had used them for carrying out his landscaping projects.

There is a story that when Benjamin Disraeli—who had an estate at Hughenden in the south of the county—was taken to see Waddesdon under construction he observed that the Almighty would have completed the creation of the world in less than seven days if he had had the assistance of the Rothschilds. By the autumn of 1875 there were 100 workmen on site. It was a formidable task to lay out roads winding up to the top of the hill, which had to be levelled to create a platform for the house, once the existing farmhouse and cottages had been swept away. According to the *Gardeners' Chronicle* in 1885, soil to an average depth of nine feet was carried away from a ten-acre site at the top of the hill. This work was entrusted to a London engineer, George Alexander, who followed a scheme prepared by a Parisian landscape designer, Elie Lainé. Employing a Frenchman to lay out the landscape and gardens was even more unexpected than Ferdinand's use of a French architect, especially as Lainé was nowhere near as well known as Destailleur. Ferdinand explained that he had approached Lainé only after William Broderick Thomas, 'the then most eminent English landscape gardener, had declined to lay out the grounds for reasons he did not divulge'. In his history of Waddesdon's gardens, Brent Elliott has suggested that the reason for Thomas's refusal was that he

ABOVE: *Lodge Hill was so steep that extensive digging and levelling were necessary in order to create an entrance drive with an easy gradient. A temporary tram line was constructed to move stone, brick and wood from the railway to the site. Percheron mares, which Ferdinand considered less enduring, but faster and cheaper than Shire horses, were imported from Normandy to move materials.*

OPPOSITE ABOVE: *Excavations for the drive at Waddesdon Manor.*

OPPOSITE BELOW: *Cutting the carriage drive, which spirals two and a quarter miles around Lodge Hill up to Waddesdon Manor.*

had just started work on remodelling the grounds at Sandringham for the Prince of Wales.

Lainé designed the two-and-a-quarter-mile carriage drive which spirals around the hill up to the house, and was from the beginning one of Waddesdon's most admired features: 'the approach winds around the hill as it goes up in great sweeping curves', wrote Eustace Balfour to his wife: 'the whole is in wonderfully good taste and the views are magnificent'. However, this effortless elegance was the result of strenuous and tedious labour: 'slowest and most irksome of all', recalled Ferdinand, 'was the progress of the roads, on which the available labourers of the neighbourhood were engaged, supplemented by a gang of navvies . . . The steepness of the hill necessitated an endless amount of digging and levelling to give an easy gradient to the roads and a natural appearance to the banks and slopes. Landslips constantly occurred. Cutting into the hill interfered with the natural drainage and, despite the elaborate precautions we had taken, the water often forced its way out of some unexpected place after a spell of wet weather, tearing down great masses of earth. Like Sisyphus, we had repeatedly to take up the same task, though fortunately with a more permanent result.'

Further difficulties were experienced with the foundations of the house itself. 'The part of the hill we had selected for its site consists of sand', explained Ferdinand, 'and the foundation having been proceeded with for some months proved not to have been set deep enough, as they suddenly gave way. The whole of the brick-work had then to be removed and thirty feet of sand excavated until a firm bottom of clay was reached.' Perhaps not surprisingly, Ferdinand became depressed by the initial lack of progress, and although he had made the old fragment of Winchendon Manor, The Wilderness, a home for himself during the building work, he hardly used it between 1874 and 1877, when Waddesdon at last began to rise with some rapidity, preferring instead to come over when necessary from Leighton

Château de Waddesdon, pendant les trav...

LEFT TO RIGHT: *After the laying of the foundation stone on August 18, 1877, the Manor started to rise more rapidly. These photographs show the south front and West Tower; the north front under construction; the north front complete; and the south side of the Bachelors' Wing. Note the tramway for bringing materials to the site.*

House, which he had purchased in 1875. His agent on site was his bailiff George Sims, who was to be employed by the estate for half a century. There are many gloomy references to the slowness of the work in Ferdinand's letters: on February 2, 1875 he wrote to his uncle Lionel from Leighton that he had just spent the day at Waddesdon, where 'I was pleased with the plantations but appalled at the amount of work which has to be got through. I was six hours there today, and I shall have to be there all day tomorrow. W[addesdon] is not better than a wilderness and a quagmire at present.'

His optimism had been fully recovered once the foundation stone was laid on August 18, 1877 and the construction of the house was under way. Waddesdon is built of brick faced with Bath stone, of which two varieties were used, a fine-grained one from Box Ground for the lower walls and a harder, more shelly stone from Stoke Ground for the upper parts of the house, which are more exposed to

the weather. Most of the major ornamental carving on the exterior was executed by French masons under the supervision of a Parisian sculptor, M. Doumassy, who also worked with Destailleur at Mouchy. Both their names are inscribed, with the date 1879, on the central pavilion overlooking the garden at Waddesdon. The honey colour of the stonework, achieved by a century's weathering, which is now such an attractive aspect of the house, was there from the beginning, for in order to disguise the whiteness of the new stone, Ferdinand had the entire building washed with an artificial colour. Inside, the principal floor joists are steel beams, chosen because they are fireproof but also because they can span greater widths than wooden beams, so allowing for large, uninterrupted spaces in the reception rooms. Steel beams are also stronger than wooden ones, a fact exploited by Destailleur in the way that the first-floor layout does not correspond to the ground floor, as would have been essential in a house of traditional construction, where a wall cannot be built above a void on the floor below.

As this suggests, the house was up-to-the minute in its technology. It was originally lit by gas from its own gas works; houses were not designed with electricity in mind until the mid 1880s (Alfred de Rothschild's Halton, begun in 1883, had it from the start, and even

had arc-lamps on the roof to illumine the garden). When Ferdinand extended the house in 1889 he took the opportunity to convert it to electricity. It was centrally heated with hot air piped through grilles around the edges of the rooms on the ground and first floors (radiators were used on the top floor) and was kept draughtproof by a method described by Peter Inskip, the architect who supervised the restoration of the house in the 1990s: the large, plate-glass casement windows have a single lock which, when turned, not only bolts the window at top and bottom but also causes a metal bar to rise along the bottom of the window as a draught-stop. Waddesdon became famous for this attention to detail: after Ferdinand's death *The Westminster Gazette* claimed that on his orders 'a vast quantity of cork was even mixed with the mortar to preclude the possibility of echoes being developed by the lofty and spacious rooms and galleries'. Fire prevention was another concern, and there are outlets for water hoses in the walls of the bedroom corridor and service wing.

By the standards of the day, the house was well equipped with lavatories and bathrooms, although it seems odd to modern sensibilities that more were not provided in place of the sluices which were supplied at intervals in the upper two floors for housemaids to

empty the contents of chamber pots; even Alice appears not to have had her own bathroom and to the end of her life preferred a hip bath. Sufficient water pressure was achieved by placing tanks at either end of the building, one on the top floor of the west range and one in the top storey of the circular tower in the east block. There are no plans showing the house as completed for Ferdinand; the earliest surviving show it at Alice's death in 1922. On the first floor there were then nine lavatories but only three bathrooms (two ensuite), which served not just the eight principal bedrooms (including Ferdinand's) but also four rooms for ladies' maids; there were another three bathrooms (one ensuite) and four lavatories serving the nine guest bedrooms in the Bachelors' Wing. The second floors of the main house and the Bachelors' Wing had 32 bedrooms between them, presumably mostly for the staff and for visiting servants: they had to share just two bathrooms and five lavatories.

The east block of the main house incorporates a mezzanine floor providing access to the first floor of the service wing, always known as the Bachelors' Wing, as its first-floor bedrooms were designed for single male guests. Such a mezzanine was more commonly found in French houses than in English; as in French houses, it principally con-

BUILDING THE HOUSE

tained servants' accommodation—four bedrooms for visiting ladies' maids, and one for a housemaid, together with a bathroom and sitting room for their use. The Bachelors' Wing was extended and altered in the early 1890s, so it is not entirely clear how the service rooms on its ground and basement floors were originally laid out; the 1922 plans, which presumably record the arrangement at the time of Ferdinand's death, show a central courtyard, round which were grouped accommodation for the housekeeper and the steward, together with the kitchen, scullery, still room, servants' hall and linen room. Rooms in the basement were set aside for a bake house, vegetable store, a butcher's shop, knife room, coal cellar, boot room, drying room, brushing room, cellars for beer and wine (to which access was provided by a carriage ramp), a glass store and a 'mat room' (possibly for storing or cleaning rugs and carpets). By the standards of the time this was ample but by no means exceptional service accommodation.

While the house was going up, rapid progress was being made with the gardens and grounds. Destailleur had limited influence on the immediate surroundings of the house, although he was asked to supply designs for balustrading and for plinths for statues. As late as 1886 he was making proposals for the terrace on the south side of the house which would have involved a great ornamental basin and grotto set into its retaining wall, from which seven jets of water would have sprung, like the fountain at Vaux-le-Vicomte. Ferdinand does not, however, seem to have wanted such elaborate and formal architectural features, preferring instead much softer transitions between the house and its terrace, the garden and the park, so that it is hard to tell where artifice gives way to nature.

An aerial view of the house today shows Lodge Hill rising up like a wooded island in a sea of fields. As the still bare slopes of the hills at nearby Ashendon, Brill and Quainton suggest, those woods are all Ferdinand's doing: his clothing of the hill in mature trees astonished his contemporaries as much as the building of the house on this apparently inconvenient site, and rapidly entered local legend. A successful method of transplanting trees had been pioneered in the 1830s by William Barron, head gardener at Elvaston Castle in Derbyshire, who had such success that by the 1860s he and his family firm were offering transplantation as a commercial service. Ferdinand did not employ Barron, preferring to have his own garden staff adapt his

This 1877 photograph shows an army of stonemasons preparing the Bath stone, which encases the brick structure of the Manor. It was later colour-washed to tone down its whiteness.

methods, unfortunately without Barron's high success rate. The trees were transported—some from as far away as Kent—in specially made carts, each pulled by a team of 16 of the specially imported Percheron mares; the size of the trees meant that telegraph wires had to be temporarily taken down to allow them to pass. Ferdinand noted that 'if I may venture to proffer a word of advice to any one who might feel inclined to follow my example—it is to abstain from transplanting old trees, limes and chestnuts perhaps excepted, and even these should not be more than thirty or forty years old. Older trees, however great may be the experience and skill of the men engaged in the process, rarely recover the injury to their roots, or bear the change from the soil and the climatic conditions in which they have been grown. Young trees try your patience at first, but they soon catch up the old ones and make better timber and foliage.' The most notable failures were in the double avenue of red oaks that led up to the entrance front.

Despite having a French landscape designer, there was little that was foreign in the layout or planting of the grounds; Ferdinand, his bailiff, George Sims, and the head gardener, Arthur Bradshaw, decided all the details. New trees formed shelter belts, largely of red horse chestnut, along the north side of the estate. Many conifers were planted, notably Austrian pines, which framed the views along the drives. Contemporaries were struck by the careful attention that had been paid to colour effects in the combination of trees and shrubs, something that was newly fashionable in the 1870s: the Waddesdon landscape glowed with the 'brilliantly effective' colours of 'snowy hawthorns, scarlet and white Chestnuts, clumps of double scarlet and white Thorns, Lilacs, golden yews', wrote *The Gardeners' Chronicle* in 1886; golden yew was used so prominently that it became particularly associated with Waddesdon.

Another novelty that attracted comment in the gardening press was the use of artificial stone to create landscape features. On the west side of the avenue leading up to the entrance front is a rockwork cave which combines limestone spoil from the digging of the house's foundations with an artificial stone made of Portland cement which was known as Pulhamite. It was made and installed by James Pulham & Son of Broxbourne in Hertfordshire, whose showpiece at Waddesdon was the rockwork for the water garden which lies beyond the stables. In the mid 1870s Pulham was employed at Sandringham for the Prince of Wales, who may have drawn Ferdinand's attention to the firm's work; his 'stone' was also used for features in the Rothschilds' garden at Gunnersbury. The rockwork cave next to Waddesdon's entrance avenue was originally designed for a group of mountain

goats, part of the extensive menagerie Ferdinand kept in the gardens, but their smell soon led to them being moved further away and the cave was converted to a tool store.

It is possible that Ferdinand's instant garden was intended to be accompanied by instant wildlife. According to Fred Cripps, an old friend of Ferdinand's great-nephew James de Rothschild, while the trees were being planted, Ferdinand 'introduced every form of bird life, the birds being acclimatized in cages all over the garden and their wants administered to by keepers in velveteens. They were then finally released before the official opening of the house.' This is not totally implausible, but there is undoubtedly an element of the apocryphal in Cripps's account of what happened next: 'Among the guests on this occasion was the late Lord de Grey, probably the greatest shot in the recorded history of the sport. Ferdinand de Rothschild had to go to London for the day of the opening. On his return he was met by Lord de Grey, who took him with great pride to show him rows of little birds—chaffinches, bullfinches, linnets—the cocks in one row, the hens in the other, just as game would be laid out after a day's covert shooting. His name does not appear again in the visitors' book.' In fact. Lord de Grey was a regular visitor throughout the 1880s, so if the story is true he must have been forgiven.

Ferdinand's fondness for birdlife is commemorated by Waddesdon's most notable garden building, the elaborate cast-iron Aviary to the west of the house, completed in 1889. Its Rococo forms imitate aviaries erected at Versailles and Chantilly in the 18th century, but the immediate model may have been the aviary at Ferdinand's childhood home at Grüneburg, which was an inspiration for so much at Waddesdon. It is similar to one built by Ferdinand's sister Julie at Pregny, near Geneva, on the estate of their cousin Adolph (one of Carl's sons), whom Julie had married in 1850. Further to the west are the stables, ranged around three sides of a courtyard: they were not built until 1884, before which horses and carriages were accommodated in tents and in the village's inns. Destailleur was responsible for the 17th-century French façades of the stables, of brick dressed with stone, but the plans were made by Ferdinand and his stud groom, working with Conder. Behind the stables was an extensive Water Garden leading down to the half-timbered Dairy, laid out on the scale of a model farm and in style closer to rural Normandy than England.

On a level plateau between the stables and the Water Garden were the seven-acre kitchen garden (four acres of which were walled) and the extraordinarily ambitious complex of glasshouses. In 1882 Ferdinand signed a contract with George Berry for glasshouses to be

Landscaping the park at Waddesdon.

erected under the supervision of his agent Henry Wyatt of Aylesbury; by 1884 there were already 40. Most of the glasshouses were made by the celebrated firm of R. Halliday & Company of Middleton in Lancashire, who remained responsible for their upkeep until well after the Second World War; they also built glasshouses at Pregny for Adolph and Julie de Rothschild. A solitary photograph is all that survives to record the breathtaking scale of Waddesdon's, based around a large domed house designed principally for show, with ornamental planting and sculpture. The glasshouses incorporated an ornamental bridge spanning cascades which sprang from a grotto of Pulham's stone planted with ferns, creating what *The Gardeners' Chronicle* in 1885 described as 'a scene quite fairy-like in its character'.

Although Destailleur designed at least one lodge for the house (the beautiful pavilion in Louis XVI style on the main road between Aylesbury and Waddesdon, for which his drawings are dated 1882) and was presumably responsible for the handsome wrought-iron gates at the principal entrances, he had nothing to do with the village landscape through which the house is approached. It was achieved with some difficulty. As Ferdinand observed at the outset, one disadvantage of his chosen site for the house was that it was too close to the edge of the estate. To secure privacy and to preserve the immediate views from the house he set about acquiring more land, which eventually amounted to an additional 500 acres: 'small properties that ran into the estate on all sides had to be obtained from a variety of owners, of whom some were unwilling to sell, others held their land by a complicated title, and others again had let it on long leases. Tenants had to be dispossessed and otherwise provided for; a large silk factory and three public-houses had to be acquired; the dilapidated homesteads pulled down and rebuilt

elsewhere; over 150 cottages and a huge flour-mill purchased and demolished to make room for the proposed improvements and then rebuilt further off.

Ferdinand's architect for the remodelling of the village was a local man, William Taylor, originally based in Bierton, and subsequently in Aylesbury, where from 1894 he worked in partnership with his son Frederick. One of Taylor's partners was the builder John Durley, who had worked with Devey on estate buildings at Mentmore and on the remodelling of Ascott, and Taylor's work shows that he had a sophisticated understanding of Devey's approach to vernacular design. The centre of the village forms an exceptionally attractive and complete ensemble, achieved by the Rothschilds' rebuildings of cottages and by the additions of estate amenities, such as the club and reading room (built in 1883) and the village hall, added in 1897. Taylor's best-known building is the Five Arrows Inn, built in 1887 to replace the Marlborough Arms, one of eight pubs in the village in the late 19th century. Like most of Taylor's work at Waddesdon it is picturesquely half-timbered and gabled to an almost Tyrolean degree. Tile-hanging, *sgraffito* decoration and elaborate ironwork in an Arts-and-Crafts manner complete a picture-book model village that can be compared not only with the work of other Rothschilds in the county but also with such celebrated achievements as John Douglas's buildings on the Duke of Westminster's Cheshire estates, where this sort of picturesque old-English manner, pioneered by Devey, was elaborated in the 1870s and 1880s.

However, Ferdinand's remodelling of the estate was not whole-heartedly welcomed by the inhabitants of Waddesdon. After his death, *Lloyd's Weekly News* recalled that the village before his arrival was 'about as bad a specimen of an English rural community as could very well be found', but added that 'Baron de Rothschild's improvements upset the old order of things to an extent which caused many hard things to be said of him. The villagers saw cottage after cottage disappear, and they resented the interference with their old habits of life by . . . a taciturn, unpopular man'. Ferdinand's foreign origins and Jewishness probably did not help. He was aware of having stirred up bad feeling. In August 1878 he gave a dinner for his and Alice's ten-

This is the only known photograph of the glasshouse ranges at Waddesdon, built between 1882 and 1884. They were believed to be the largest at any private house in England. Here, prize-winning orchids were cultivated by Ferdinand, and vegetables, fruit and flowers were grown for the house. The glasshouses were closed in 1962 and most were demolished in 1975.

BUILDING THE HOUSE

Five Arrows Hotel,
Waddesdon,
Aylesbury

ants in a marquee erected in the grounds of the Wilderness, where he delivered a speech, reported by the *Buckinghamshire Herald*, in which he apologised for the inconveniences caused by his alterations to the estate 'but as he had purchased it for residential purposes, they would see that those alterations became in consequence absolutely necessary'. Although it was not until the 1880s, and his entry into public life as a member of parliament, that Ferdinand became more confident in his dealings with his tenantry, and as a consequence more popular, most inhabitants of Waddesdon must soon have realised that they would benefit from his presence, if only because, as *Lloyd's Weekly News* put it, 'work on the estate could be had for the asking', something which was increasingly valued as English agriculture entered a long period of recession from the mid 1870s onwards.

In his well-informed *Recollections of Old Country Life* (1894), J. K. Fowler, an old friend of the Rothschilds' local solicitor, James James, recalled that when his brother visited Waddesdon in about 1892 to advise Ferdinand about the Dairy 'he expressed himself astonished at the magnificence that he saw both inside and outside the house. The Baron said, "Yes, it ought to be a good property, for it cost me over two millions of money."' This story does not entirely ring true, since Ferdinand was known to dislike questions about his expenditure, and so would probably not have volunteered information on the subject, but is this a reasonable estimate of what was actually spent? Although there is plenty of information available about Ferdinand's financial circumstances, it is not easy to form a total picture of what he spent on Waddesdon, since although he drew substantial sums from his capital, his income was so large (it seems to have fluctuated between about £80,000 and £100,000 a year) that he was able to pay for a considerable amount of building work out of it, and the records of such payments do not fully survive. Fowler is our source for the contract price for the house, which James told him was £87,000. To that James added 'to take off the top of the hill, to

prepare it for building and to make the roads up to it, cost £55,000'. These sums seem plausible. Analysis of payments from Ferdinand's account with N.M.Rothschild indicate that the cost of the house had risen to £160,000 by 1880; the stables and other ancillary buildings amounted to £40,000. This suggests that up to 1880, when Ferdinand first slept at Waddesdon, the landscaping and building works had cost him at least £255,000; it is not possible to calculate what the decoration of the house cost, but it could easily have brought the total to over £300,000. To take the contemporary comparison mentioned in the previous chapter, at Stokesay Court in Shropshire, also built by Edward Conder, a large new house, outbuildings and extensive estate improvements were achieved in 1889–92 for £155,000. Ferdinand could therefore have built two sizeable country houses—and remodelled their estates—for the money he lavished on Waddesdon alone.

From 1882 onwards, Ferdinand kept notes about his expenditure on Waddesdon, covering not only land purchase, building work and decoration but also wages and maintenance. These reveal that between 1882 and 1892, when he supposedly had that conversation with Fowler's brother, he spent £743,504. If to that is added both the £200,000 he paid for the estate and the building and furnishing costs of some £300,000, the total expenditure on the estate between 1874 and 1892 must have amounted to nearly £1.5 million, and the payments which can be traced are undoubtedly less than the total; perhaps 'two millions of money' was not such an exaggeration after all. This figure appears all the more remarkable when it is recalled that Ferdinand's calculations almost certainly did not include the element for which the house is best known and has always been most admired: its collections.

OPPOSITE: *Ferdinand revitalised the village at Waddesdon with the building of The Five Arrows Hotel, seen here in a photograph of about 1900, above, and the Reading Room, below, in a postcard of about 1908, where reading, indoor games and non-alcoholic drinks could be enjoyed by the villagers.*

3

BUILDING the COLLECTIONS

One of Ferdinand's most treasured memories was of being allowed as a child to help pack up his father's art collection 'as soon as the swallows made their appearance', when the family moved to its villa at Grüneburg for the summer: 'It was my privilege on these occasions to place some of the smaller articles in their old leather cases, and then again in the winter to assist in unpacking them and rearranging them in their places. Merely to touch them sent a thrill of delight through my small frame.' Ferdinand's intense response to works of art was shaped by these early experiences: he remembered spending hours 'learning under my mother's tuition to distinguish a Teniers from an Ostade or a Wouvermans from a Both. I had a particular fancy, however, for a head of a girl by Greuze.' It is touching to recall these words when seeing some of the pictures bought by his parents in the Morning Room and West Hall at Waddesdon today—*A Hawking Party* by Philips Wouverman and Adriaen van Ostade's *The Musicians*. The Greuze, however, although also at Waddesdon, was discovered to be a copy and Ferdinand relegated it to a bedroom.

Despite the austerity of his daily life, Anselm was an indefatigable collector and he often exhausted his sons when they accompanied him on one of his tours of 'curiosity shops'. Ferdinand recalled that 'he used to rise at 6 o'clock and remain on his legs until dusk ... shopping and sight-seeing.—I wish he had handed his constitution down to his sons'. He recalled the 'museum', the room for displaying works of art which Anselm added to his Vienna house, 'where he spent many a happy

The Musicians, *by Adriaen van Ostade.*

hour, puffing away at his cigar, and making the catalogue of his collection in the company of one Plach, an Austrian dealer.' This catalogue, illustrated with photographs, was eventually completed by Franz Schestag and privately published; it reveals Anselm's interest in medieval and Renaissance gold and silver plate, in Dutch 17th-century paintings and in 18th-century gold boxes, all of which were to become enthusiasms of Ferdinand. His inheritance in 1874 of a substantial number of his father's works of art was the centrepiece, as well as the foundation, of his own collections. That is often forgotten, since most of the pieces he inherited from Anselm, together with his own collection of medieval and Renaissance works of art, were bequeathed by Ferdinand to the British Museum, and so have left Waddesdon.

Anselm's and Ferdinand's tastes were characteristic of what by the 1850s had become a clearly defined Rothschild tradition of collecting. Distinguished by an interest in precious materials and excellence of craftsmanship, it had its origins in the *Schatzkammer* of royal or aristocratic tradition. Such collections were made up of the sort of rare or precious objects supplied by Anselm's grandfather, Mayer Amschel, in his antique business in the Frankfurt ghetto. To some degree, the Rothschilds always considered their collecting as an investment and so tended to limit themselves to works with a clearly ascertainable market value. Ferdinand recalled that in his childhood even the most precious Renaissance plate bought by his family was valued by dealers according to its weight; in painting, the Rothschilds sought solely the best and most characteristic works by acknowledged masters whose value a connoisseur could assess at a glance. Since they were Jewish, they naturally tended to prefer secular pictures and they had a special fondness for the detailed and highly finished art of the Dutch Golden Age, a favourite of French collectors since the mid 18th century and of the English since the early 1800s. None of the family showed much interest in acquiring contemporary art, since, as Ferdinand observed, 'modern art when it happens to be entirely original loses much of its value because of the facility with which it can be obtained'.

These tastes were enlarged by the need to furnish the houses which, from the 1830s onwards, became a visible assertion of the Rothschilds' wealth and status. Although, as described in chapter one, in the 1840s they had commissioned decorative schemes in Renaissance styles, perhaps inspired by their collecting enthusiasms, by the time Ferdinand came to build Waddesdon, educated taste favoured interiors that were authentic, in the sense of being composed of genuine fittings and furniture of the past, not modern imitations of them. When, for example, Ferdinand visited Alnwick Castle in 1864, recently recast for the Duke

of Northumberland by Anthony Salvin in a mighty Gothic form, but with interiors in the style of the Italian High Renaissance, he wrote to his English cousins that 'I cannot say I found the decorations of the rooms very tasteful though they are extremely gorgeous . . . everything is modern including the furniture and I think that you will agree with me in not much admiring entire new sets of boule and marquetrie chairs'. His objection was not to the choice of style for the interiors—which had provoked disapproving comment from English critics, for whom the Renaissance was then deeply unfashionable—it was the Duke's use of reproduction period furniture and fittings he disliked. Such a prejudice was new: one of Ferdinand's greatest predecessors as a collector of French 18th-century furniture, the 4th Marquess of Hertford, who died in 1870, had spent large sums on reproductions of such pieces which were specially made for him. This was something of no interest to Ferdinand, whose purchases of modern copies were limited to minor items of furnishing, such as fire-dogs and wall-lights: 'a copy, at its best', he wrote 'is but an excellent imitation or a clever forgery'. He was part of a younger generation that was making a cult of what would soon be called 'antiques', although that was a term he never used: with studied carelessness, like many collectors of the time, he called his expensively acquired trophies 'curiosities' or 'bric-à-brac'.

A preference for the authentic furniture and fittings of the past narrowed the field for interior decoration considerably, for there was insufficient material available to equip a whole house with genuine furnishings of a medieval or Renaissance date, and they would not in any case have satisfied contemporary ideas of comfort and convenience. As Ferdinand put it, 'a general adoption of the art of the Renaissance, so that its feeling could pervade our everyday existence, would be out of keeping with all the essentials of modern life'. The chosen style tended, therefore, to be 18th-century, since there was a flourishing market for furniture and decorative arts of the period and because, in Ferdinand's words, it possessed 'that adaptability which more ancient art lacks'. There was no doubt in the connoisseur's mind that 18th-century interior decoration meant France, the source of the most admired furniture, bronzes, porcelain, textiles and panelling. There were clear precedents for Waddesdon in Ferdinand's childhood home in Grüneburg, where a Renaissance architectural style of international origins was combined with French 18th-century interiors derived from an interest in the furniture of the period. Ferdinand believed that this was a taste pioneered by his family: 'Whether it is to the credit of my family or not may be a matter of opinion, but the fact remains that they first revived the decoration of the eighteenth

century in its purity, reconstructing their rooms out of old material, reproducing them as they had been during the reign of the Louis, while at the same time adapting them to modern requirements. In England as yet this new departure has not struck root so deeply as on the Continent.' In fact, revived 18th-century styles in interior decoration using 'old material' were well established in England as well as France by the time work had begun on Waddesdon, but Ferdinand was right in thinking that by the end of the century this approach to interiors had become associated in the public mind with his family, partly because of their fame but also because they did it more comprehensively, or at least more expensively, than anybody had done before.

Before he acquired independent wealth on his father's death in 1874, Ferdinand had trained his eye and developed his enthusiasms by acting virtually as an agent for his family as they exploited their international contacts in the pursuit of works of art. It was not easy, however, to persuade his father to open his purse strings: he might, Ferdinand later wrote, 'have formed a matchless collection, for he lived in a country where for years old works of art were deemed worthless, and he had the Austrian market all to himself. But his taste was limited to a small range as he cared for minute articles only, besides which his time was too much occupied with business to enable him to devote much of it to other pursuits. When I left Vienna for London in 1860 I had many opportunities of offering him works of art, but he rarely availed himself of them.' Although Anselm lived austerely, and did not appreciate his family's enthusiasm for smart French interiors, he shared their competitive spirit, and was delighted when he outwitted the keenest collector of them all, his uncle James, head of the French branch of the family, by buying under his nose a boxwood figure signed by Dürer which he had spotted while they were on a joint tour of the 'curiosity shops' of Vienna. In contrast to his father, other members of the family were only too glad to use Ferdinand to scout for them. One letter of 1865 from Paris to his uncle Lionel in England is typical: 'This morning I took a walk with one of my curiosity friends. He showed me a pretty little pair of Louis XVI lights which I bought; and accompanied me to the Pourtales collection . . . I could only find the porphyry column and not the green one. The first is very thick and might fetch £250. Let me bring to your notice a large porphyry antique vase (without mountings but with cover). I think it would look very well on your mantelpiece . . . It is about the same size as your pair. They tell me it cost the late Count frcs. 30/m and will fetch frcs. 20/m.'

The remarkable unity of the family's taste that this letter implies was highlighted on the occasions when they collaborated to acquire collections that came onto the market, which they then divided amongst themselves. The best-known example was the sale of the Willem van Loon collection of 82 Dutch and Flemish pictures in Amsterdam in 1878, acquired *en bloc* by the English and French Rothschilds. Two pictures from this collection, by Gabriel Metsu and Willem van de Velde the younger, are now at Waddesdon. However, by the time Ferdinand began collecting, in the 1860s, certain national differences had begun to emerge in the Rothschilds' collecting traditions. The old fascination with Renaissance gold and silver plate was strongest in Germany and Austria, with Mayer Carl and Anselm, for example, whereas James in France made some adventurous purchases of Old Masters of a sort that had not previously appealed to his family, including not only Rembrandt, Van Dyck, and Rubens, but also Van Eyck and Petrus Christus. In England, Ferdinand's uncle Lionel followed this lead with acquisitions of works by Domenichino and Andrea del Sarto, but, more surprisingly, in the 1850s he also began to buy 18th-century English portraits, one of the very few areas in which the Rothschilds were pioneers—indeed, the rapid rise in the value of pictures by Gainsborough and Reynolds in the mid 19th century was prompted in part by the family's entry into the market. This is a taste that can largely be explained by the way the Rothschilds modelled their collections on those around them: as Lionel's mother, Hannah, wrote to her youngest son in May 1838, about the decoration of a room at their home in Gunnersbury, 'You, dear Mayer, will know if the style is good. Having seen many of the best finished country houses, your judgment must be good.' Many of those 'best finished' houses, most notably Stowe, the greatest neighbour of the Rothschilds in Buckinghamshire, presented a persuasive model of English paintings combined with French (or French-inspired) furniture and porcelain. Lionel's tastes, with his collections, were inherited by his three sons, Nathaniel, Alfred and Leopold, whose collecting proceeded simultaneously and often in rivalry with Ferdinand's.

All these themes—north European gold and silver plate of the 16th and 17th centuries and French decorative arts and English painting of the 18th century—flowed into Ferdinand's collecting, yet even for a Rothschild he was restricted in his tastes, especially in the fine arts. It is almost as though by keeping his focus narrow, he sought to make it easier to guarantee the quality of what he bought. As was true of all his family, he preferred the furniture and porcelain of the middle of the 18th century, which connoisseurs regarded as a high point of decorative accomplishment between earlier simplicity and later floridity. There is, for example, no early or late Sèvres at

Waddesdon. However, his taste was by no means always predictable, especially in furniture, where he had an individual appreciation of bold and sometimes challenging forms. He followed Lionel's interest in English portraits, which he described as 'unrivalled in charm', but whereas Lionel's collection ranged from Hogarth to Hoppner and Beechey, Ferdinand limited himself exclusively to Gainsborough, Reynolds, and Romney. He was known in society as a connoisseur, as is suggested by H.J.Brook's once-famous conversation piece, *Private View of the Old Masters Exhibition, Royal Academy 1888*, painted in 1889, which depicts Ferdinand as a prominent figure in the Victorian art world. However, he bought almost no Old Masters outside the Dutch and Flemish schools he was brought up with, although, like his cousins, his interests had moved on to include a somewhat later generation than had appealed to his parents, with major acquisitions of such painters as Meindert Hobbema and Aelbert Cuyp. His most significant purchase at the sale of the Blenheim Palace paintings was *The Garden of the Hesperides*, then thought to be by Rubens, for which he paid £26,250. Towards the end of his life, according to the obituary published by *The Times*, 'he used to confess that the longer he studied art, the more his taste went back to the *primitifs*, to the men who lived before our modern conventions had come in and swamped originality', and, according to the same source, he is said to have coveted Jan van Eyck's portrait of Jan Arnolfini and his wife more than any other picture in the National Gallery. This is unlikely to have much to do with a Ruskinian enthusiasm for the early Renaissance: it surely owes more to the family's taste for highly wrought decorative objects of the period, but, unlike his uncle James, Ferdinand never bought early Netherlandish art.

Like most English collectors of his time, he showed no great interest in acquiring continental 18th-century painting. He acquired no Watteaus or Fragonards for Waddesdon, to accompany its French furniture of that period, although paintings by both artists were bought by James for Ferrières and by Mayer for Mentmore. Ferdinand was by no means indifferent to 18th-century French painting, for he greatly admired Lord Hertford's spectacular purchases in this field. Moreover, in 1864 Sir Dudley Coutts Marjoribanks told him that he might have to sell a newly acquired set of Bouchers as there

OVERLEAF: Private View of the Old Masters Exhibition, Royal Academy 1888, *by H.J. Brooks, 1889. Oil on canvas. Ferdinand stands in the group on the left with Sir John E Millais, Sir John Pender, the Marchioness of Granby, Humphry Ward (art collector and journalist for 'The Times'), and the painter George Richmond.*

BUILDING THE COLLECTIONS

H. Jamyn Brooks

was no place for them in his London home, Brook House, then under construction. 'My heart fluttered wildly, I already saw the Bouchers on my wall', Ferdinand recalled, 'but my hopes were short-lived, as Mr. Wyatt, the architect of Brook House, provided for the canvases.' Ferdinand did possess a Fragonard, which he bequeathed to his sister Hannah, but it was hung at 143 Piccadilly; he also bought some overdoors by Boucher or in his manner, both for Waddesdon and for London, together with *fêtes galantes* by Pater and Lancret and a group of Venetian views by Francesco Guardi. These now seem minor ventures. His only unquestionably significant purchase in this field would be the pair of enormous canvases of Venetian scenes by Guardi, bought in 1877, which line the East Gallery at Waddesdon, but even

here there is a sense that they are as much architectural fittings as works of art. Ferdinand shared his family's intense enthusiasm for Greuze's sentimental girls, so incomprehensible to modern taste, but he bought few French 18th-century portraits. Among them are Elisabeth Vigée-Lebrun's *Duchesse de Polignac*, which is still at Waddesdon and Boucher's 1756 *Madame de Pompadour*, which he kept in London and bequeathed to his brother Nathaniel. Both were clearly chosen for the sake of the sitter as much as the artist. Here is one of several major contrasts between Ferdinand and his cousin Alfred, whose building and furnishing of his country house at Halton followed the example of Waddesdon in so many ways. At Halton, Alfred's notable collection of French 18th-century art (which included eight Bouch-

ers) suited the flamboyant and slightly risqué personality of its owner. Ferdinand's lack of enthusiasm for buying French painting for Waddesdon was closer to conventional late-Victorian tastes: the great Rococo painters were less in favour with his generation than they had been with Lord Hertford's, partly perhaps because of moral queasiness. There are plenty of paintings of pretty women at Waddesdon, but nothing that could reasonably be described as erotic.

Ferdinand was a typical Rothschild in his lack of interest in collecting modern art. Although he was acquainted with a number of contemporary artists, including John Everett Millais, William Wetmore Story, Lord Leighton and J.L.Meissonier, and was a friend of the Austrian-born sculptor Joseph Edgar Boehm (whose father had

OPPOSITE: Le repas de Noces de Village, by Nicolas Lancret, about 1735–37. Oil on wood. This light-hearted scene of music, dancing and eating appealed to Ferdinand's taste for depictions of festivity, which characterizes his collection of paintings and books.

ABOVE: The Bacino di S Marco with the Molo and the Doge's Palace. This detail encompasses the Libreria, the Campanile, the Piazzetta with the Torre dell'Orologio and St Mark's, and the Doge's Palace, and captures the vibrancy of life on the Venetian waterways.

OVERLEAF: The East Gallery, dominated by the largest-known works by Francesco Guardi, about 1755–60. Oil on canvas. These enormous panoramic views of Venice depict, on the left of the fireplace, The Bacino di S Marco with the Molo and the Doge's Palace, and on the right, The Bacino di S Marco with S Giorgio and the Salute.

BUILDING THE COLLECTIONS

The Duchesse de Polignac, *by Elisabeth Louise Vigée-Lebrun, 1783.
It was bought in 1883 from the Comtesse de Clermont-Tonnerre by
Ferdinand, attracted by the royal associations of the artist, portrait painter to
Marie-Antoinette, and the sitter, a friend of Marie-Antoinette.*

Baron had given the mighty sum he must have disbursed for his gold vase, to secure the best work in gold that the present age can produce, he would have done more for art than in transferring Cellini's work from one storehouse of treasures to another . . . Raffaelles are not produced by giving £70,000 for a Raffaelle'. This was undeniable, but it is not clear that Ferdinand would have understood the argument, since collecting was for him an element in the creation of a new work of art—Waddesdon itself. (Ironically, the gold mounts of that vase, one of five supposedly Renaissance mounted hardstone vessels he acquired in 1897 from the 8th Duke of Devonshire, were actually made in the early 19th century.)

Although his tastes were fully formed by the 1860s, Ferdinand began to collect on his own account with some hesitancy. He recalled in particular being shown Princess Galitzin's collection in St Petersburg in 1867, when he was offered the first refusal of anything he chose: 'I alas! was still very inexperienced, moreover I was bewildered and hustled . . . For myself I bought only a very inferior picture of the school of Snyders'. However, by then he had made the purchase that initiated his serious collecting. From Alexander Barker, the dealer who had advised his uncle Mayer on the interiors at Mentmore, he bought a Sèvres turquoise potpourri vase in the form of a ship. He agreed to such a high price that he had to make payments to Barker in instalments, and he kept the ship out of sight of his uncles, in fear of being scolded for his extravagance. It was, however, a well-informed purchase: dated 1761, it is one of only eleven known examples of this model (remarkably, Ferdinand was to acquire no fewer than three of them; all are now at Waddesdon). He does not record the price, but we know that in 1874 one of Ferdinand's great rivals in the pursuit of Sèvres, the Earl of Dudley, paid £10,500 at Christie's for another example, together with a pair of jardinières. When Ferdinand started collecting in earnest in the 1870s, he was buying at a period of rapidly escalating prices. In 1870, for example, he paid £6,800 at the Demid-off sale for a damascened shield by George de Gys, which had fetched only £250 when previously sold in 1842. Such outlays dismayed even some of the Rothschilds: when Ferdinand was furnishing 143 Piccadilly, his mother-in-law commented that 'the prices asked for everything and readily obtained are truly fabulous; they make one smile and almost shudder; many men consider themselves lucky if they obtain an appointment that yields five hundred a year—the sum which the Bond Street dealers unblushingly demand for a clock or a pair of lights.'

Ferdinand did not collect only for Waddesdon, and one of the great gaps in our knowledge of his tastes is that there are no pho-

been known to Anselm), the only modern paintings or sculpture he bought were portraits—even the bronze stallion by Boehm in the stables courtyard at Waddesdon is thought to be a study of Ferdinand's favourite hunter, Gorse. When he made a special effort in 1884 to see Ary Scheffer's then-celebrated *Dante and Beatrice* while it was in London, he was prompted by the fact that Scheffer had painted a portrait of Ferdinand's mother in 1827 which he greatly treasured, rather than any known enthusiasm for Scheffer's work. His apparent indifference to modern art was criticised after his death by *The Spectator*, which wrote scornfully of the enormous sum he had supposedly paid the Duke of Devonshire for a vase attributed to Benvenuto Cellini: 'If the

Ferdinand's three Sèvres pot-pourri vases in the shape of ships, 1761. This is the rarest Sèvres form, admired for its delicacy and complexity.

tographs of the interiors of his Piccadilly house, the contents of which were dispersed after his death. Moreover, only the smallest fragments, in the shape of a few bills and some notes in his personal account books, remain as a documentary record of his collecting. Presumably, everything else was destroyed with his private papers after his death. However, it is also possible that he did not keep such records: surprisingly few collectors do, perhaps because, for many, the total ensemble is what matters rather than the individual items. That loss makes it difficult to judge whether Ferdinand's tastes changed during his creation of Waddesdon. There is some evidence, for example, that he was becoming increasingly interested in Neoclassical design towards the end of his life, but in the absence of secure dates for most of his purchases, it is impossible to be sure, and our picture of his taste is inevitably, therefore, a static one. Unlike his father, he did not attempt to produce a catalogue

of his collection, apart from his books, and the scrappiness of the notes made by Alice when she attempted a few years after her brother's death to list the provenances of works of art at Waddesdon suggests that he rarely discussed his collecting in detail even with her; when she records a price, it is only because it was of anecdotal interest, such as the £8 given at a sale in Maidenhead for a pair of wall lights made for Marie-Antoinette's apartment at Compiègne. Dorothy de Rothschild, whose husband, James, inherited Waddesdon in 1922, recalled her father-in-law, Edmond de Rothschild, telling her that he had once interrupted Ferdinand's enthusiastic account of a new acquisition to ask where it had come from, 'and at once he shut up like a clam'. Yet Ferdinand had a remarkably articulate interest in both the history of collecting and in collecting as a contemporary social phenomenon, which prompted not only a lively chapter, 'Bric-à-Brac', in his unpublished memoirs but also

BUILDING THE COLLECTIONS

an article in *The Nineteenth Century*. This makes it a little surprising that he covered his own tracks as a collector so well.

Discretion certainly counted for a lot: he acquired many pieces from private collections, and knew—like any dealer—that he had a greater chance of success if he kept such negotiations secret, partly to keep rivals at bay and partly because a reputation for respecting a vendor's privacy would encourage more to approach him. As Ferdinand wrote, 'many a gentleman's pride suffers grievously when he sees his grandmother's portrait, perhaps, handled by unfeeling strangers, or subjected to the cruel stare of an idle throng, while the reasons which compel him to barter it away are being canvassed and made known to the world at large.' His sources were not necessarily the great aristocratic collections. Among the scraps of Ferdinand's correspondence that have survived are some undated letters from B.L. Johnstone, vicar of Maids Moreton in Buckinghamshire, offering Ferdinand a Romney valued at 700 guineas: 'it is a portrait of my wife's great aunt Miss Aubrey . . . it has been in her Family since it was painted . . . An expert informed Mrs Johnstone that he believed it was one of Romney's *early* Portraits it was so highly finished'. Ferdinand had the picture sent over to Waddesdon and within a few days a price of £600 had been agreed upon. It is regrettable that there is no similar documentation for other private sales

ABOVE AND OPPOSITE: *This massive cylinder-top desk, veneered with tulipwood, mahogany and purplewood, was possibly made by Jean-François Leleu around 1781. It belonged to Pierre-Augustin Caron de Beaumarchais (1732–1799). Its marquetry depiction of a pamphlet,* Considérations sur L'Independence de L'Amérique, *recalls his memorandum of 1776 to Louis XVI about the rebelling American colonies.*

from English collections, which brought him such treasures as the monumental desk which had belonged to Caron de Beaumarchais, acquired from the 6th Duke of Buccleuch, or the Riesener roll-top desk perhaps made for Louis XV's daughter Marie-Adélaïde, which he bought from Sir Henry Hoare's collection at Stourhead.

Luckily, however, a very full set of letters concerning one of Ferdinand's most famous Continental acquisitions does survive. In

his account in 'Bric-à-Brac' of the fates of the great European art collections, he mentions that 'until the beginning of the present century Holland was rich in private collections of the old masters of the Dutch school, but the only one of these collections that still survives is that of Baron Six Von Winter, and even that has been shorn of some of its gems.' Rather oddly, he does not record that those gems were by then hanging on his walls. The Six family's collection in Amsterdam—described by *The Times* as 'the one *intacta virgo* among the old collections of Europe'—had largely been formed in the 17th century by the burgomaster Jan Six, a close friend and patron of Rembrandt. Its magnificent array of family portraits, most famously Rembrandt's depiction of Jan Six, and its representative display of masterpieces of the Dutch Golden Age had long been hungrily eyed by collectors. In 1896 the family at last guardedly encouraged an approach by L. Auerbach, an agent used by the Rothschilds. Ferdinand was almost certainly the instigator of this, since he was on the lookout for paintings that would be suitable for his new morning room at Waddesdon. Presumably to secure his anonymity, the negotiations were carried out on his behalf by his cousin Alfred. It was a tricky purchase, as the Sixes had never before sold any paintings and they had an inflated idea of their value: as Auerbach wrote to Alfred, 'it is not very likely that the family will make concessions . . . for this is the first time since the family has been in possession of the pictures that they have not refused point-blank to enter into any negotiations'. The letters allow us to trace the offers and counteroffers between January and March 1897 which eventually secured three major paintings, by Aelbert Cuyp, Gerard ter Borch and Gerard Dou. The price was 780,000 guilders (the family had initially asked for a million), secured in competition with other dealers, one of whom made an offer of three

ABOVE: A Landing Party on the Maas at Dordrecht, *by Aelbert Cuyp,*
late 1650s. This late addition to the assemblage of Dutch paintings in the Morning Room
was acquired by Ferdinand from the Six Collection in Amsterdam.

OPPOSITE: *A detail of the Morning Room's centrepiece, a massive and complex secre-*
taire, made by Jacques Dubois and Jean Goyer in about 1770, for a Prussian or Russian
patron. Made of oak, with Japanese and European lacquer and veneered with tulipwood,
purplewood and mahogany, it was in England by 1782.

million guilders for the entire collection—turned down, according to
Auerbach, only 'because it included the two Rembrandts, which latter
will not be sold under any circumstances, as they are family portraits'.

Auerbach was concerned to keep the negotiations secret,
insisting, for example, that insurance for the pictures, once they had
been sold, should be taken out in London, since if he arranged insurance in Amsterdam, 'the sale of the pictures could not remain a secret
here, and the affair would certainly become generally known through
the newspapers'. There was considerable public curiosity about the
sources of Ferdinand's acquisitions and the prices he paid. For example,
the remarkable French drop-front secretaire of princely scale, which he
acquired for the Morning Room in about 1890, was sold to him in conditions of great secrecy by the Hon George Fitzwilliam, who needed
cash in an emergency after a friend had defaulted on a loan for which
Fitzwilliam was guarantor. As part of the deal, Ferdinand commissioned
a replica to take the place of the original at Milton Hall, near Peter-

borough. Nonetheless, news of the purchase leaked out, and there was excited
speculation in the press that Ferdinand
had paid as much as £40,000 for the
secretaire—the precise amount was still
being debated by his obituarists eight
years later. *The Graphic* recorded after
his death that 'it was a peculiarity of the
late Baron Ferdinand that few things
annoyed him more than being asked
how much he had paid for this or that
treasure which he possessed', although
that was surely not so surprising.

This interest in secrecy meant
that Ferdinand never bought works in
his own name at auction. Rothschilds
always preferred to use agents to bid
anonymously for them, but Ferdinand
was exceptional in making this his invariable rule; even Alice bought
under her own name occasionally. His agents were usually the dealers
who played an important part in his collecting, but there is no evidence
that he relied on any one in particular to help him build his collection
or furnish Waddesdon, as his uncle Mayer had employed Alexander
Barker at Mentmore, nor did he employ a single dealer to act as his agent
to the extent that Lord Hertford had used Samuel Mawson of Berners
Street. Yet he appreciated the way dealers made life easier for him by
turning collecting into shopping: in a letter of September 1867 from
Russia he describes to his uncle Lionel how 'Davis the dealer called on
me this evening. He has purchased some splendid things, candelabras,
cabinets etc, and perhaps you will like to see some of his so-called treasures which are already on their way to Bond St before they are offered
to Sir Dudley Marjoribanks.' Lionel obviously thought this a lazy way
to acquire a collection, for Ferdinand goes on to defend himself: 'you
will say that we might pick up some good things just as well as Mr Davis.
I do not doubt it either, but we begrudge the time it entails and we
prefer admiring what is easily viewed and accessible to the irksome and
unprofitable labour and moreover very tiring work of running into the
country . . . and meeting many disappointments to bring home what
we can purchase in Bond Street with every ease, facility and comfort'.
'Mr Davis' was either Frederick Davis or his son Charles, who had a
shop in Pall Mall and who were both so closely involved with Alfred de
Rothschild's collecting that Charles Davis catalogued his collection. As

well as selling directly to Ferdinand they occasionally acted as his agent: for example, in 1870 they bought at Christie's on his behalf an 18th-century Italian commode with especially magnificent marquetry which is now at Waddesdon; it came from the collection of Sir Dudley Coutts Marjoribanks (later Lord Tweedmouth), the banking millionaire mentioned in Ferdinand's letter who had once so tantalised him with the prospect of some Bouchers.

Other dealers whose names recur in the history of Ferdinand's collecting include Agnew's of Old Bond Street, for pictures, and the Wertheimer family of New Bond Street and Norfolk Street, principally for *objets d'art*. Records at Agnew—then run by William Agnew—reveal that Ferdinand began buying in earnest in 1879 when Waddesdon was being furnished, although his first purchase (Gainsborough's *The Pink Boy*, which cost him £5,512.10s) was hung at his London house. He bought from Agnew's fairly regularly up to 1891, but then stopped, probably because he was beginning to run out of space, although in 1896 he bought a group of 13 inexpensive topographical and marine paintings, now in the East Hall, presumably to furnish his new steam yacht, *The Rona*. Ferdinand made it clear to Agnew's what sort of pictures he wanted: in 1888 he wrote to Sir William that 'I should much like to see the Lady & child by Sir Joshua on my return—I do not care abt. children by themselves, but as accompaniments to a good looking mother I would willingly accept them.—I can do with several more busts as well as 3/4—but all female portraits'. This sort of sweet-toothed taste for a pretty face was characteristic of the time—even Lord Hertford would turn down a

BELOW: Commode, attributed to Pietro Piffetti, a Turin-based court ébéniste, of about 1735–40. The curvaceous carcase is decorated in tortoise-shell and ivory with boys at play, taken from Jacques Stella's Les Jeux et Plaisirs de l'Enfance, *Paris, 1657. Ferdinand aquired it from the Marjoribanks Collection in 1870.*

OPPOSITE: A corner of the Morning Room, showing a portrait of Ferdinand on an easel in front of his much loved Gainsborough, The Pink Boy, *of about 1785. During Ferdinand's lifetime, it was hung in his Piccadilly dining room; it came to Waddesdon as a bequest from his niece, Baroness Edmond.*

WADDESDON MANOR

Rembrandt if the subject was an old man. Ferdinand's indifference to portraits of children was overcome if the picture on offer was a celebrated trophy, such as Reynolds's portrait of his great-niece Theophila Gwatkin, which became famous in the 19th century under the name *Simplicity*, thanks to a popular engraving.

The records of Samuel Wertheimer and his two sons, Asher and Charles, have been lost, but a chance survival of a group of bills at Waddesdon shows the sort of expensive items they supplied for Ferdinand. In January and February 1893, for example, he acquired from Asher Wertheimer four gold boxes, an 'enamelled gold Flacon the top formed as a negress', a piqué table-case, a French barometer mounted with Sèvres plaques, a bust attributed to Lemoyne, a pair of Louis XV candlesticks, a gold enamelled *souvenir* and a pair of overdoors and a ceiling panel attributed to Boucher; all this cost him £10,700. Meticulous details about provenance are supplied. A comparison of these bills with Agnew's records makes it clear that the parts of the collection that now attract most attention are not necessarily those which cost the most. For example, in March 1893 Ferdinand paid Charles Wertheimer £2,250 for a gold box with miniatures signed by Van Blarenberghe; only 12 of the 32 pictures he bought through Agnew's cost more. Samuel Wertheimer acted as buying agent for Ferdinand, Alice, and several of their cousins, most notably at Christie's celebrated sale in 1882 of works from the Duke of Hamilton's collection. His close relationship with the family was revealed at his death in 1892, when Alfred and Leopold Rothschild were his executors; Ferdinand stood as godson to one of his children.

Ferdinand's network of dealers extended well beyond London. He was a regular customer at Heilbronner at 3 rue du Vieux-Colombier in Paris and, like many Rothschilds, he also bought through the leading Parisian dealer Charles Mannheim, whose shop was at the rue de la Paix. Mannheim is now best remembered for having been the model for Elie Magus, the Jewish dealer in Balzac's *Le Cousin Pons*, published in 1847, which is such a perceptive account of a collector interested in 18th-century French decorative arts. Ferdinand was fascinated by the phenomenon of the dealers who themselves became plutocrats, recalling how Alexander Barker, who had begun life as an apprentice to a bootmaker, surrounded himself with objects of the greatest luxury, and 'ate his cutlets from Sèvres china, [and] sipped his '48 claret from Venetian glass'. But even this was eclipsed by the dealer Frédéric Spitzer, who lived in great magnificence in a hotel built for him in the rue de Villejuste. Although Anselm had many dealings with Spitzer, Ferdinand never bought anything from him, but he was well aware of the caution with which he had to be approached: 'It will, perhaps, be

ABOVE: Miss Theophila Gwatkin, *by Sir Joshua Reynolds, painted about 1788. This is one of thirteen paintings by Reynolds at Waddesdon.*

OPPOSITE: *A French snuff-box (1778–79) with six depictions of Parisian low life, painted by Van Blarenberghe in 1762–63. Ferdinand bought it from Wertheimer in 1893.*

best to observe a discreet silence as to the operations which first brought grist to his mill . . . out of one fine old work of art he manufactured two or three'. In fact, as Ferdinand hints, Spitzer's career had a shadier element than that, for he worked hand-in-hand with the greatest of all 19th-century forgers, Reinhold Vasters of Aachen, a restorer of gold and silver antiquities who copied originals given him for restoration and sold the originals through Spitzer. As a result, almost every major collection of Renaissance gold and silver includes works of apparently impeccable provenance which are in fact fakes by Vasters—The Metropolitan Museum of Art in New York owns no fewer than 30. Although Ferdinand comments 'he was straight enough when it served his purpose', did Spitzer attempt to pass off fakes on Anselm? It seems possible, since the collection which Ferdinand inherited from his father includes at least two pieces by Vasters. Spitzer may also have sold stolen items to Anselm, if, as seems likely, he supplied one of the greatest trea-

*Part of Ferdinand's collection of Renaissance treasures, bequeathed to the
British Museum in 1898.* ABOVE: *The Holy Thorn Reliquary of Jean, Duc de Berry,
French, about 1405–10;* OPPOSITE: *a hand-bell by Wenzel Jamnitzer of Nuremberg,
about 1555–60. Its lizards, insects and flowers were cast from life in silver.*

sures Anselm bequeathed to Ferdinand, the gold and enamelled Holy
Thorn reliquary made in about 1405 for Jean, duc de Berry. This had
been stolen from the Geistliche Schatzkammer in Vienna in the 1860s,
when it was replaced by a copy made by another skilled forger, Salomon
Weininger. Neither Anselm nor Ferdinand was aware of the origins of
the reliquary, which became known only some years after it had entered
the British Museum, with the Waddesdon Bequest.

It is not surprising, therefore, that Ferdinand tended to regard
collecting as a battle of wits between dealer and collector. As his friend
Edward Hamilton recalled, 'he had a horror of being *done*'. Only the fact
that his father's collection had largely been formed in the 1830s and
1840s, when the forging of Renaissance gold and silver was still relatively
uncommon, explains why such a high percentage of it was authentic. 'In
my young days', wrote Ferdinand in *The Red Book*, 'I burnt my fingers
pretty often and severely, but experience taught me caution, and from
the time I seriously entered the lists as a collector, I have only acquired
works of art the genuineness of which has been well established.' The
best guarantee of authenticity was an impeccable provenance, and when
this was available, Ferdinand's additions to the collection matched his
father's triumphs. Perhaps the most romantic of all was his purchase at
the 1882 Hamilton Palace sale of the Lyte Jewel, a miniature of James
I and VI by Nicholas Hilliard mounted in an exquisite gold locket set
with diamonds. It had descended in the family of Thomas Lyte of Lytes
Cary in Somerset, to whom the king had presented it, until sold to the
11th Duke of Hamilton in the mid 19th century. However, provenance
even from famous collections was not always enough: for example, all five
of the Renaissance jewels bought by Ferdinand from the Countess of
Mount Charles came from the celebrated collection of Lady Coynygham,
mistress of George IV; all were modern.

Such difficulties were one reason for collectors moving into
the 18th century, where although copies and 'improved' objects were
far from unknown they were on the whole easier to spot. For example, virtually every 19th-century collection of Sèvres includes some of
the pieces that were made more desirable by dealers with the addition of gilding or decoration or by the overpainting of the grounds
in some rarer and therefore more expensive colour. At Waddesdon,
however, there are none. Ferdinand's one error in this field entered
family legend: in 1871 he sold to Samuel Wertheimer a pair of Sèvres
vases 'of inferior quality' which he had bought from Alexander Barker
about ten years before to accompany his remarkable 'ship' potpourri
vase; Wertheimer sold them on to one of Ferdinand's French cousins, Gustave de Rothschild, who was horrified when he turned one

RIGHT: *A carved agate vase with gold enamelled mounts and cover, formerly attributed to Cellini, which Ferdinand bought from the Duke of Devonshire in 1897.*

OPPOSITE: *The Lyte Jewel, set with 29 diamonds and containing a miniature by Nicholas Hilliard of James I, who presented the jewel to Thomas Lyte in 1610.*

over and saw Minton's trademark: its base was a modern replacement. Ferdinand does not reveal whether he thought Barker knew about the Minton mark, yet he was well aware of what the dealer got up to: 'he served his good customers honestly but as a rule he tampered with his goods, playing tricks with and "improving" them, often to their serious detriment but more often to the detriment of their purchasers'.

Ferdinand had an excellent visual memory: according to Alice, it was he, rather than the unrecorded dealer, who spotted that an unmarked late-18th-century writing table imitated the lower part of Oeben and Riesener's celebrated *bureau du roi* made for Louis XV's study at Versailles, which he had seen on exhibition at the Louvre. He bought the table, which proved to be one of his greatest coups: now known to have been designed by the sculptor Jean Hauré, it was made for Louis XVI in 1786 for his study at Versailles, and so was designed to be ensuite with the *bureau du roi*. Furniture history was then not even in its infancy, and the royal Garde Meuble's system of marking furniture had largely been forgotten; of the great French craftsmen of the ancien régime, only the names of Boulle, Riesener, and Gouthière had remained part of the popular consciousness. As Lord Hertford sardonically remarked about the optimistic descriptions of works of art he was offered by dealers, '*Bronzes, pendules et meubles, tout est de Reissner, ou de Boule, ou de Gouthière et tout a appartenu a Marie Antoinette, a Mme Du Barry, ou a Mme de Pompadour*'. That makes it all the more remarkable that Ferdinand secured so many pieces with a royal provenance. Thanks to his faultless eye for quality, Waddesdon possesses such entrancing treasures by J.-H. Riesener as the secretaire made for Louis XVI's study at the Petit Trianon and the rolltop desk made in 1763 for the comte de Provence, the future Louis XVIII.

It is not always clear how much Ferdinand knew about the provenance of his purchases (sale catalogues rarely provided such details), but where reliable information was available it encouraged him to buy. For example, his most famous purchase at the 1882 Hamilton Palace sale was the writing table made by Riesener for Marie-Antoinette's use at the Petit Trianon. The 'martyr queen' was by then the subject of a flourishing romantic cult, much encouraged by the Empress Eugénie, and any piece of furniture associated with her commanded a premium;

ABOVE: Mémoire sur la Réformation de la Police de France, by Guillaute, 1749. This book appealed to Ferdinand, not just because of its contents, but also because of its provenance and cover embossed with the coat-of-arms of Louis XV. The binding is by J.-A. Derome l'aîné and the illustrations are by Gabriel de Saint-Aubin. It was bought by Ferdinand from Baron Jérôme Pichon in 1897.

OPPOSITE: When invited to fancy dress balls, Ferdinand liked to dress as a Renaissance nobleman from Austria. This photograph was taken for an unknown occasion.

even so, the £6,300 paid by Ferdinand was thought to be an extraordinarily high price: 'If Juvenal had been present at the auction-rooms in King-street yesterday', commented *The Times*, 'he would have seen the man who gave six thousand sesterces for a mullet outdone by another who gave six thousand pounds sterling for a writing table'.

Ferdinand himself emphasised that the historical associations of an object were an important part of its attraction to him: 'Old works of art are not . . . desirable only for their rarity or beauty, but for their associations, for the memories they evoke, the trains of thought to which they lead, and the many ways they stimulate the imagination and realise our ideals'. For example, he was well informed about the lives of the sitters in his portraits and had a large collection of memoirs and biographies of 18th-century figures, both French and English. For Ferdinand, history was largely a matter of personalities and his delightful book *Personal Characteristics from French History*, published in 1896, is a sequence of pen portraits of the great names of French history, from the first monarchs to Robespierre. His library contained many books that had had famous owners, including Louis XV, Madame de Pompadour (he owned no fewer than 14 books from her library), Madame du Barry, Marie-Antoinette, and—a wry touch—Dr Guillotin. Waddesdon, therefore, reverberated with associations for Ferdinand that are often now missed. When he described in his book the personality of the maréchal duc de Richelieu, nephew of the great cardinal, as being an embodiment of the 18th century in 'its vices, its frivolity, its scandalous levity, its superstitions, and base corruption', he cannot have failed to remember that Waddesdon's breakfast room was panelled with *boiseries* from a house, the hôtel Dodun, which Ferdinand believed had belonged to the maréchal. His account of the man's depravities make it clear that Ferdinand's attitude to the 18th century was by no means one of simple nostalgia, as is sometimes assumed: in his mind, 'our ideals' were an advance on those of the past.

Such historical associations could also be more modern. A concern for provenance is, of course, one way of avoiding fakes, but Ferdinand's fascination with the great collectors and collections of the past went further than that—he clearly saw himself as part of a developing modern tradition of collecting. The collectors who interested him were naturally enough those who had shared his tastes: George IV, Lord Stuart de Rothesay, or Sir Robert Peel. Again, absence of documents makes it unclear how much he knew about the history of the various objects he bought, but he was certainly aware, for example, that his so-called 'Cellini bell' had come from Horace Walpole's collection, since it had been a highlight of the 1842 Strawberry Hill

sale. In 1883, this virtuoso piece of Renaissance silverwork, crawling with lifelike lizards, was still accepted as the work of Benvenuto Cellini, and was published as such by Eugène Plon in his book on the artist, although he states that Ferdinand himself thought the piece was German and possibly by the celebrated Nuremberg smith Wenzel Jamnitzer. There can have been little doubt in Ferdinand's mind, since three years earlier his father's cousin Mayer Carl had bought a standing cup in a strikingly similar style by Jamnitzer (for which he had paid 800,000 francs, then the highest price ever given for a work of art). Ferdinand's attribution of the bell to Jamnitzer is now universally accepted.

Although, with his sister Alice and cousin Edmond, Ferdinand bought major pieces of French furniture at the 12th Duke of Hamilton's sale in 1882—one of the most spectacular of the entire century—we do not know whether he was attracted by the connection with William Beckford's collection at Fonthill (Beckford's eldest daughter and heir was the wife of the 10th Duke). Although he acquired for his London house a magnificent pair of boulle armoires with a French royal provenance that had been in the Fonthill collection (for which he paid £12,075), he does not mention Beckford in his writings on collecting, perhaps because of the air of scandal that hung about the name, but his interest in the provenance of the Hamilton pieces is suggested by his purchase through Agnew's in 1891 of a pair of portraits by Gainsborough of the 10th Duke and his brother, which are still at Waddesdon. Ferdinand also owned books that had belonged to Beckford, among them a copy of Félibien's 1706 history of the abbey of St Denis, which contains annotations in Beckford's hand. Another volume brings together several strands in the history of collecting: Beckford's beautifully bound copy of the catalogue of the engraved gems owned by the duc d'Orléans, one of the greatest of all French collectors, which was acquired by Ferdinand at the sale of Destailleur's library. Other pieces at Waddesdon had scarcely less distinguished provenances. Ferdinand undoubtedly knew that Romney's portrait of Lady Stuart had been in Lord Stuart de Rothesay's collection at Highcliffe, since he acquired it from Stuart's daughter Louisa, Lady Waterford, in about 1890, together with a fine secretaire stamped by Jacques Dubois and a Savonnerie screen. Ferdinand also acquired several pieces that had been in the Demidoff family collections. The Russian-born Anatole Demidoff, known as the Prince of San Donato after his estate near Florence, died in 1870 after having spent a large part of his family's mining and armaments fortune on works of art of Rothschild quality. Much of his magnificent collection was sold in the year of his death, when Lord Hertford made his last major acquisitions. The core of what remained formed the nucleus of a collection formed by his nephew, Prince Paul Demidoff. In turn, this was dispersed in sales in the 1880s, at which Ferdinand made several further purchases. It is not known if Ferdinand knew the Demidoffs, but he was certainly acquainted with their greatest French rival in the salerooms, the duc d'Aumale, who was present at a dinner party Ferdinand gave in London in 1881 for the Prince of Wales to meet Sarah Bernhardt.

Yet the only collector to whom Waddesdon makes explicit tribute—apart perhaps from the 10th Duke of Hamilton—is George IV. Ferdinand regarded him, with some justice, as the most influential collector in England of the sort of objects pursued by the Rothschilds, from Renaissance gold and silver plate and Dutch pictures to French porcelain and furniture of the highest quality: 'the acclimatisation of French art might have been only temporary had not the Prince

ABOVE: Alexander, 10th Duke of Hamilton, *by Thomas Gainsborough, about 1785–90. Oil on canvas. Ferdinand owned several pieces from the Duke's celebrated collection, part of which had been inherited by the Duchess of Hamilton from her father, William Beckford.*

OPPOSITE: *The steel and rock crystal chandelier reflected in the Tower Drawing Room's mirror was made in France in the late seventeenth century. It was acquired by Ferdinand from the Demidoff collection. The terra-cotta figures are in the style of Clodion.*

Regent . . . settled its destiny in this country' wrote Ferdinand. 'He was endowed with the most exquisite taste, and availed himself of the unique opportunities of the time with a profusion that, however, was always tempered with good judgment . . . He made Windsor Castle and Buckingham Palace storehouses of art treasures, and trained a school of collectors who profited by his example.' Such praise explains the prominent position accorded by Ferdinand to Gainsborough's swaggering 1782 full-length portrait of George as Prince of Wales, which hangs in the Red Drawing Room, tellingly juxtaposed with a marble relief portrait of Louis XIV above the door as a genealogy of the taste that shaped Waddesdon.

Among the 'school of collectors' trained by the Prince Regent was his Vice-Chamberlain Lord Yarmouth, later the 3rd Marquess

of Hertford, who acted as the Prince's agent in buying works of art. He also formed a major collection which was inherited in 1842 by his son, the 4th Marquess, who was to be the greatest English rival of the Rothschilds as a collector in the mid 19th century. With an annual income of £250,000, he completely dominated the market and pursued Old Masters and French 18th-century decorative arts with an extravagant determination that astonished his contemporaries. Lord Hertford lived as a recluse in Paris, where Ferdinand saw him only once, at Prince Beauvau's sale in 1865: 'he possessed that certain unmistakable "something" which denoted the "somebody" and attracts attention. He was very un-English in appearance, having inherited the sallow complexion and bright dark eyes of his Italian mother, a lady of questionable notoriety'. Although they never seriously competed as collectors, since Lord Hertford died four years before Ferdinand's inheritance, Ferdinand was fascinated by him both as a collector and as a man, and he made great efforts to get to know Richard Wallace, to whom Hertford left his collections. They became good friends, although Wallace never confided to Ferdinand the fact that he was Lord Hertford's illegitimate son.

Ferdinand implicitly contrasted his collecting with Lord Hertford's when he wrote that 'it may be questioned whether his love of art did not degenerate into mania and whether he went on amassing pictures, furniture and china, for the pleasure their possession gave him in the artistic sense, or from less creditable motives. He never saw many of the objects his agents purchased as they were forwarded from the place they were bought direct to Manchester House [Hertford's London home], and for several years before his death he did not set foot in London; while of those he personally acquired a great number were at once piled up in a lumber room.' Ferdinand was very different. He was not an accumulator: it is inconceivable that Lord Hertford could have written to a dealer as Ferdinand did to Agnew's in 1888 about an unidentified painting, 'I find to my regret that I must give up all notion of purchasing the picture as it would or could not possibly be placed advantageously in any room of the house.' Collecting for Ferdinand was not an end in itself; he was not content to pile up furniture in storage, nor was he ever likely to have sent off an agent in pursuit of a picture which he had forgotten he already owned, as Lord Hertford was reputed to have done, much to Ferdinand's amusement. As with most of his family—and his collecting never moved beyond the boundaries laid down by family precedent—he bought works of art principally to furnish his houses. Where he outshone all his relatives, however, was in the personal care he took with the arrangement and display of the treasures he had brought together. Magnificent and valuable although its components are, at Waddesdon it is the ensemble which matters most.

OPPOSITE: *A corner of the Red Drawing Room, originally conceived as the Van Dyck Room, in which an equestrian portrait of* Prince Thomas of Savoy-Carignan *was to have been the centrepiece. This idea was abandoned in favour of an arrangement emphasising Ferdinand's inspiration and sources for Waddesdon: George IV, in a portrait by Thomas Gainsborough of 1784, and Louis XIV, in a marble relief by Antoine Coysevox above the doorway and personified as Apollo in the Savonnerie carpet.*

4

FURNISHING the HOUSE

SINCE WADDESDON IS NOW A MUSEUM, admired above all for the quality of its collections, it is easy to lose sight of the fact that Ferdinand saw it very differently. For one thing, he would not necessarily have regarded its furnishings as 'collections' at all. In the drawings for Destailleur's first revision of the designs, a small room in Ferdinand's private apartment in the west wing is labelled 'salle des curiosités'. This was for the display of those precious medieval and Renaissance objects which, as the Waddesdon Bequest, left the house for the British Museum at Ferdinand's death. This was for him 'the collection'. In the house as it was built, the 'salle des curiosités' was the circular Tower Room on the ground floor. Its appearance in the early 1880s was described by the architect Eustace Balfour in the letter to his wife which was quoted in chapter two: 'There was one room like the turrets at Inverary in shape, only bigger, hung entirely with magnificent Italian needlework, and quite full of old Venetian glass set in silver gilt, and other beautiful pieces of metal and gold plate.'

The furnishings in the rest of the house, despite their splendour, were treated in a different manner. The Rothschilds had never created galleries in the tradition of the great aristocratic collections; they arranged their pictures and furniture in domestic ensembles. Ferdinand's understanding of the interiors at Waddesdon can be deduced from the fact that of the 39 photographs in *The Red Book* devoted to works of art, 31 are of paintings; four are of groups of Renaissance objects; one is of a piece of sculpture; and only two are of furniture—the great Beaumarchais desk and a fall-front secretaire

Ferdinand Rothschild and Poupon, his favourite poodle, relaxing in the Baron's Room. He is surrounded by Sir Joshua Reynold's portraits
of Theophila Gwatkin and Mrs Scott of Danesfield, as well as by a Louis XVI tapestry fire screen, and five Mazarin blue Sèvres vases and covers.
This photograph was taken for The Red Book, *1897.*

mounted with Sèvres plaques, on which three pieces of Sèvres are displayed. In other words, the paintings were considered by Ferdinand to possess an interest independent of the interiors of which they formed a part; the furniture and porcelain, not to mention the textiles, were not, or at least not to a similar degree. That was typical of his family, although he would not have shared the emphatic views of his mother-in-law, Charlotte, who wrote to her son Leopold in April 1865 that she was very glad his father had made no bids at the Beauvau sale in Paris, since 'it is ridiculous to spend thousands of pounds upon mere trash; pictures and curiosities may be works of art; but bits of furniture are not'.

Ferdinand was furnishing Waddesdon at a mid-point in the history of attitudes to 18th-century decorative arts. As he explained, at the beginning of the 19th century, thanks to the French Revolution, 'an art that had so recently been a contemporary art had, without any warning or transition, become an art of the past'. That made it easy for the generation of the 1820s to make the jump from buying new furniture or porcelain to searching for older pieces, but they did not necessarily become collectors as a result. For example, in the two years after their marriage in August 1829, the 5th Duke and Duchess of Buccleuch spent a considerable amount of money on amassing Sèvres, but they never bought any more after that, since it had been acquired for use. Similarly, Ferdinand did not buy porcelain or furniture that he could not use or incorporate into his interiors, but around him men such as Lord Hertford and, later, Ferdinand's cousin Alfred de Rothschild, bought to collect: where Ferdinand had two complete Sèvres services, one for Waddesdon and one for London, Alfred had six.

Similarly, as pieces of the finest 18th-century furniture became rarer and more expensive, they were increasingly acquired solely as collectors' items. When, for example, William K. Vanderbilt and his wife, Alva, built their New York townhouse to designs by Richard Morris Hunt in 1879–82, they—like Ferdinand—matched a French Renaissance exterior to interiors in both Renaissance and 18th-century styles, but, although their financial resources exceeded even his, they made no effort to furnish their 18th-century rooms solely with 18th-century works of art, choosing instead a number of trophy objects, from portraits by Gainsborough and Reynolds to a Riesener bureau once owned by Marie-Antoinette, around which

they built interiors from modern furnishings in period styles. By the turn of the century, that was the customary approach to fashionable interiors, and every drawing room in Mayfair, Fifth Avenue, or on the boulevard St Germain respected a distinction between *chaises courantes*—chairs to admire—and *chaises meublantes*—chairs for sitting on, a distinction which, after all, had 18th-century precedents.

It had some force even at Waddesdon. Ferdinand's approach to the furniture of the past was not that of the Vanderbilts, for he eschewed modern reproductions, but there was nevertheless a clear hierarchy to Waddesdon's furnishings. At the top are the great collector's items, such as the Beaumarchais desk or Marie-Antoinette's writing table and other pieces by Riesener with a royal provenance. Below them is the 18th-century furniture that falls more evidently into the category of furnishings, either because it is comparatively modest or because it has been altered to appeal to 19th-century

BELOW: *The Grey Drawing Room in 1897, furnished with a mixture of French eighteenth-century textiles, including a Savonnerie carpet and chairs covered in Beauvais tapestry, as well as with more practical late-Victorian sofas and love-seats.*

OPPOSITE: *The Grey Drawing Room today, as set out for the National Trust by Dorothy de Rothschild with the comfortable late nineteenth-century furniture removed.*

tastes. Ferdinand was typical of his family and his generation in his admiration for decorative richness in furniture. As a result, dealers responded by 'improving' simple 18th-century pieces with embellishments, often themselves authentically 18th century, such as ormolu mounts, Sèvres plaques or panels of marquetry. New gilding commonly replaced painted decoration. The presence at Waddesdon of pieces altered in this way does not, however, mean that Ferdinand had been duped. For example, in the West Gallery at Waddesdon there is a pair of marble-topped and ormolu-mounted commodes in the manner of Charles Cressent; one has a 19th-century carcass but 18th-century mounts; the other has an 18th-century carcass but its mounts are modern. In other words, a single authentic commode by Cressent has been made up into a (much more desirable) pair: they had passed through Alexander Barker's hands, and he was probably responsible for this piece of fakery. When Ferdinand bought them through the dealer Charles Annoot at Christie's in 1874 he paid fairly low prices (£273 and £283 10s), suggesting that he knew what he was buying; presumably, he acquired them with the needs of a furnishing scheme in mind. The third tier in the hierarchy of furnishing consists of the new upholstered settees and chairs which were liberally interspersed among the 18th-century pieces, as revealed by photographs of the interiors before the house was bequeathed to the National Trust. This must have been the furniture that was actually used on a daily basis; it provided the comfort and convenience which Ferdinand saw as the great contribution of his age to the art of living.

That combination of the best of the past with the most convenient of the new was evident in the very structure of the house, built in accordance with the latest technology, but fitted out with panelling and chimneypieces of 18th-century date. It is perhaps surprising that there is no evidence that Ferdinand or Destailleur considered incorporating old architectural elements into the exterior of the house. There was after all a celebrated English precedent in the fragments of the medieval Normandy château of Les Andelys which, in 1830, Lord Stuart de Rothesay had built into his new Gothic house in Hampshire, Highcliffe Castle. In 1881, just as Waddesdon was being completed, the entire *cour d'honneur* of the château de Montal was dismantled and transported by train from Auvergne to Paris for sale. This was not the

sort of opportunity Ferdinand chose to exploit, despite his familiarity with the thriving French architectural salvage trade which brought him so many of the remarkable *boiseries* that form the settings for his furniture and works of art.

It is one of the long-standing Waddesdon myths that Ferdinand was able to acquire these fittings thanks to the large-scale demolitions in Paris ordered by Napoleon III to make way for the boulevards laid out in the 1850s and 1860s as part of the city improvement programme undertaken by Baron Haussmann. In fact, virtually every identifiable building from which he obtained his architectural fittings still stands today. The sale and reuse of second-hand panelling and other architectural elements was a business that owed little to Haussmann and can be traced back well into the 18th century, in England as well as France. Once the Napoleonic Wars were over, English clients eager to recreate the appearance of *ancien régime* interiors were well supplied with authentic material. On a shopping trip to Paris in 1824, the 5th Duke and Duchess of Rutland took the opportunity to buy (for 1,450 guineas) a job-lot of *boiseries* and furniture which had supposedly belonged to Madame de Maintenon and had been tracked down for them by the sculptor Matthew Cotes Wyatt, who was designing new interiors for them at Belvoir Castle, Rutland. The *boiseries* (actually of about 1735) were installed in the Elizabeth Saloon at Belvoir, where they had to be extended to fit the space with a specially made dado. This sort of adjustment, required to bridge the scale between 18th-century Parisian townhouses and 19th-century English country houses, was often to prove necessary at Waddesdon.

The Wyatts specialised in French interiors created from old materials. In 1826 Matthew's brother, Benjamin Dean Wyatt, was buying *boiseries* in Paris for the Duke of York's new London house, York House (now Lancaster House), and their cousin, Sir Jeffry Wyatville, designed the Grand Reception Room at Windsor Castle, created for George IV in the late 1820s, around a set of Louis XV *boiseries*. These had been acquired for £500 in July 1826 from a Parisian dealer, Delahante, who also supplied the Gobelin tapestries which they frame. Here the additional decorative details needed to scale up the *boiseries* were made in plaster by the firm of Bernasconi. They were just one of several decorating firms who became adept in the creation of the rococo detail that by the mid century had become virtually *de rigueur* for the feminine atmosphere of drawing rooms. It was a style that was more rarely seen outside that context, although between 1834 and 1839 Lord de Grey designed for himself an entire house for his Bedfordshire seat, Wrest Park, in a highly competent Louis XV style

Autumn and Winter: Detail of the panelling in the Ante-Room to the Morning Room. Carved in oak in about 1725–50, it is from the Hôtel Jacques-Samuel Bernard, rue du Bac, Paris.

derived from his careful study of J.-F.Blondel's *Maisons de Plaisance* and other French architectural treatises. De Grey's designs for *boiseries* were executed in plaster, possibly by Bernasconi. It was the Victorian enthusiasm for imitating carving in plaster or other moulded materials which led Ferdinand to insist that, in contrast, his interiors were built of 'old materials' (although he did, in fact, make use of grained plaster imitating wood for such details as the cornices in the west and east galleries and other places where it would not be apparent from the ground).

Finding 'those 'old materials' was becoming difficult, since by the time of the Second Empire, 18th-century *boiseries* had become as eagerly sought-after as good furniture of the period. When, for example, the château de Bercy, near Paris, was demolished in 1860, its rooms of Louis XIV panelling were divided among three distinguished buyers. The Empress Eugénie bought some for her house in the rue de l'Elysée, James de Rothschild took the library panelling for re-use at Ferrières, and Lord Hertford acquired the *boiseries* from the first-floor salon, which he then sold to William Strode for installation in the dining room at Camden Place in Chislehurst, Kent. In about 1852, the dealer Alexander Barker acquired the 1730s panelling, mirror frames and chimneypiece from the well-known gallery of the hôtel de Villars in Paris for Mayer de Rothschild to incorporate into the dining room at Mentmore. The fittings from the hôtel de Villars which Mayer did not require, principally additional mirror frames, were retained in Barker's stock and eventually sold by his nephew, Mr Roe, to Ferdinand for the Dining Room at Waddesdon.

By that time, museums had entered the market, following the foundation in 1868 of the Musée Carnavalet, the museum of the history of Paris. The South Kensington Museum's programme of acquisition of 'period rooms' began in 1869; somewhat surprisingly, its first purchase was not an Elizabethan oak parlour but (for the sizeable sum of £2,100) the Louis XVI boudoir of Madame de Sérilly, from the hôtel Sérilly in the Marais. This new interest on the part of museums may have prompted collectors to look at the panelling they bought with a more antiquarian eye, and begin to consider the scale and arrangement of the rooms from which they had come. It certainly encouraged evergreater competition, especially for the rarest and most sought-after type of *boiseries*, the richly carved examples of the period 1715–40 which dealers always called 'Louis XIV'. By the time that Ferdinand was contemplating Waddesdon, he was buying in competition with his French cousins, most notably Gustave, then busy with his new Paris *hôtel*: 'I have been to a good many shops but have not seen anything you would call a fine thing,' wrote Ferdinand to his uncle Lionel in December 1874, 'but there are plenty of pretty decorative articles about if one chooses to pay for them. I saw a very pretty Louis XVI mantelpiece for which I offered five thousand francs and which Gustave bought five minutes afterwards for twelve. I have heard indirectly that he is seriously contemplating the purchase of the well-known boiseries for which some fabulous sum was asked but which I believe are to be had for a more modest sum.' Ferdinand had the advantage of employing Destailleur, whose architectural work in Paris brought him opportunities for acquisitions on his client's behalf. For example, in 1859 he had been commissioned to build a convent on a site next to the former hôtel Peyrenc de Moras (now the Musée Rodin) in the rue de Varenne, which probably brought the *hôtel*'s superb *boiseries* to his attention; it is not known when those on the ground floor were removed, but they came into Destailleur's hands and were divided between the Grey Drawing Room at Waddesdon and the house he was designing for Ferdinand's brother Albert in Vienna.

Destailleur's major purchase for Ferdinand was the panelling from the hôtel Dodun in the rue de Richelieu—the one Ferdinand incorrectly believed had belonged to the maréchal-duc de Richelieu, who was supposed to have built a secret passage linking it to the home of his mistress. Ferdinand managed to acquire all the panelling from its first floor by 1875, when Destailleur refers to it in his designs for Waddesdon. Like most of the panelling bought by Ferdinand, it was stripped, stained and had its ornamental details picked out with gilding, thus giving the *boiseries*, which in the 18th century were almost invariably painted, a characteristically 19th-century look. This is enhanced by the way they are installed. The sort of richly carved panelling Ferdinand liked had been expensive to make and so was used sparingly in 18th-century interiors, where it was spaced out by plainer panels. Destailleur, by contrast, created entire rooms from carved panelling alone, giving Waddesdon's interiors a much richer look than was usual in the 18th century in rooms of this scale. Despite this, and despite the fact that this liberal use of carvings meant that in almost all the larger rooms at Waddesdon they had to use elements taken from more than one interior, Destailleur and Ferdinand believed they were following an archaeological approach, most clearly evident in the way they went to great trouble to make copies for Waddesdon of the plaster friezes of the rooms from which the panelling came.

Yet, as Bruno Pons explains in his catalogue of the *boiseries*, only two of Waddesdon's interiors can be understood as recreations of 18th-century rooms in their proportions and general appearance, and significantly these are the ones with painted panelling. The first is the Grey Drawing Room, a reconstruction of the layout of the salon in the hôtel Peyrenc de Moras, although its height has been raised, the forms of the windows are modern, and the room lacks its original overdoors. Its colour scheme may be 18th-century in derivation, since the room was originally painted *couleur d'eau*, a blue-grey. Even more convincingly archaeological—indeed, it could be called a 'period room'—is the Green Boudoir on the first floor, originally intended to be part of Alice's suite, but eventually converted into the dressing room for the State Bedroom. Here, the exceptionally delicate carving of the panelling with Chinese figures and monkeys seems to have encouraged Ferdinand to preserve as closely as possible the appearance of its source, the cabinet Chinois in the hôtel Dodun (including a version of the original green colour scheme), although the room's high, narrow proportions, determined by its cramped urban site, seem anomalous amid Waddesdon's ample modern spaciousness.

This interest in accurate recreation of 18th-century interiors puzzled some contemporary critics, as it seemed inconsistent with the choice of style for the house itself. 'The great defect of the house as a whole,' wrote the *Daily Telegraph* after Ferdinand's death in 1898, 'is that while the exterior successfully reproduces the features of the French Renaissance in its prime, the exquisite "boiserie" furniture, and decorations of the interior are for the most part—and apart from a few striking exceptions—in the finest French styles of the eighteenth century. To enshrine the marvels of the English and French schools of painting of that period which Baron Ferdinand by degrees brought together, a later and altogether different style of French architecture would have been preferable.' Such a judgment implies a late-19th-century preference for a museum-like consistency in a period recreation, based on the new scholarship of architectural and furniture history. Ferdinand came from a generation without such pedantic expectations, but it is true that originally he planned a greater variety of historical models for Waddesdon's interiors, perhaps taking cues from the collections of Renaissance objects as well as from the architecture. Destailleur's original proposal for the reception rooms included a 'Salon Renaissance', which presumably would have resembled the Renaissance interiors created by Salomon and James in Paris in the 1840s. Its intended flavour can be enjoyed at Waddesdon today in the Billiard Room, where a late-16th-century French chimneypiece, said to have come from Dijon, is combined with outstandingly fine 16th-century panelling, probably from the Montmorency château at Acquigny, near Louviers. It is not entirely clear when the Billiard Room was completed, since it may have been altered when the Bachelors' Wing was extended in 1891–92; by 1896 Ferdinand's collection of Renaissance works of art had been installed in the adjacent Smoking Room, which may explain this choice of style for the Billiard Room.

More surprisingly, Ferdinand's original plans for the Red Drawing Room were very different from the room as it appears today. This is the pivotal interior on the ground floor, as it stands on the short axis of the house between the entrance hall and the garden terrace, and also links the principal drawing room with the dining room. Ferdinand wanted Destailleur to design its interior round a full-length portrait by Van Dyck of Prince Thomas of Savoy which he had acquired in Genoa. He proposed fitting out the room with Spanish panelling, a suggestion which filled Destailleur with horror: '*L'Effet serait deplorable a Waddesdon. Les panneaux de Paris seront d'un meilleur goût.*' Ferdinand gave way, but not before he had commissioned an alternative design in a Renaissance style, with a coffered ceiling. Although

OPPOSITE: *The Green Boudoir, created for the hôtel Dodun, rue de Richelieu, Paris, France, about 1725–27. The delicacy of the frieze and panelling in this room, furnished as Ferdinand would have known it, is complemented by the Meissen candelabra and mantel clock, and the Venetian chandelier.*

ABOVE: *The intended centrepiece of the Red Drawing Room:* Prince Thomas of Savoy-Carignan, *after Sir Anthony Van Dyck. The original, painted in 1635, is in Turin.*

Destailleur won that argument, the room's walls are hung with red silk rather than lined with *boiseries*; it is also the only room with a painted ceiling. It may have been a change in Ferdinand's attitude to the painting that was decisive; since the Van Dyck was eventually hung in an obscure position upstairs, he may have come to recognise that it was only a copy.

Perhaps because the Red Drawing Room is the most frequently photographed of Waddesdon's interiors, there is a popular belief that the house is furnished in rich colours with much gilding. This impression of dark heaviness is heightened by the requirements of conservation, which mean that most of the rooms shown to the public are illuminated only by low-level artificial light. In fact, the house respects the traditional hierarchy, well understood by all 19th-century decorators as well as their 18th-century predecessors, which restricts decoration in the grand manner to the most important reception rooms. It is hard to imagine a greater contrast with the stately magnificence of the Red Drawing Room than the light, cheerful tones of the Low White Drawing Room, on the mezzanine floor which links the main house with the Bachelors' Wing. As Sir Geoffrey de Bellaigue points out in his catalogue of the furniture at Waddesdon, the arrangement of the interiors suggests an understanding of the division in the French royal palaces between the state apartments, where the king performed his public duties, and the private apartments, accessible only to the royal family and an inner circle of courtiers. The former were customarily hung with silk and had painted ceilings, like the Red Drawing Room; the latter were intimate, panelled spaces, like the Low White Drawing Room. This was a division much discussed in the memoirs of the period that were Ferdinand's favourite reading.

This raises the question of who was responsible for the decoration and arrangement of the interiors. Destailleur supplied drawings for the installation of the reused architectural fittings, and provided designs for new ones, such as chimneypieces. He was presumably also responsible for such important decorative details as the standard Waddesdon picture frame, used for all the paintings (surprisingly, perhaps, although Ferdinand removed the original frames, he did not throw them away, and many are still at Waddesdon). However, the controlling eye was undoubtedly Ferdinand's, and it does not seem that he relied on anybody else for assistance to the extent that Mayer had used Alexander Barker at Mentmore or James had employed the painter and stage designer Eugène Lami at Ferrières. Although the profession of interior decorator was still at an embryonic stage in the 1870s, the large decorating firms which had evolved out of 18th-century and Regency upholstery businesses acted as interior designers in a way that we understand today. Ferdinand undoubtedly employed professional upholsterers; it would have been impossible to have completed the fitting out of Waddesdon to such a high standard so quickly without the participation of such firms to help organise it for him.

The Billiard Room, lined with Renaissance boiseries and barrel-vaulted in late-fifteenth-century French style with nineteenth-century stamped and gilded leather between the ribs. The sixteenth-century chimneypiece is French.

The attention to detail which is one of Waddesdon's outstanding characteristics is exemplified in the choice of upholstery silks and passementerie. ABOVE LEFT: The silk Dining Room curtains have a design after Philippe de la Salle, of flowering rose branches hung with baskets of flowers. Note the hovering butterflies. ABOVE RIGHT: The Grey Drawing Room's French eighteenth-century tapestry lambrequins are designed to imitate festoon curtains. BELOW LEFT: The silk curtains of the State Bedroom have a ribbon and flower design, a French nineteenth-century reproduction of a pattern from about 1755–60. BELOW RIGHT: Passementerie from Waddesdon's collection. OPPOSITE: Detail of the trimmings of a silk pouffe of about 1880 in the Grey Drawing Room.

In his private account books, Ferdinand lists payments to unnamed upholsterers under separate headings for 'French' and 'English', with much larger sums going to the former. The only French name with a documented link to Waddesdon is Decour in 9 rue Copernic, Paris, whose label, marked 'Galerie des Guardi', remains attached to the crimson curtains in the East Gallery, which are made from what appears to be an 18th-century velvet. A firm such as Decour would certainly have been capable of drawing up schemes for entire interiors for Ferdinand, as well as simply supplying materials for him. Their presence at Waddesdon makes it tempting to assume that he used French firms for the luxury textiles, both historic and modern (which generally copy 18th-century designs), and English ones for the materials used to upholster the everyday furniture or to make such comparatively utilitarian items as case covers. It is certain, for example, that the grey silk damask used for wall hangings in the Morning Room was woven by Prelle of Lyons, who supplied it to Decour. The firm may well have been responsible also for the crimson silk damask in the Tower Drawing Room, which, as the textile historian Natalie Rothstein has pointed out, is a copy of an 18th-century brocaded silk. However, the set of seat furniture in the East Gallery, which consists of one 18th-century chair and another three chairs and two sofas copied from it in the 19th century, was upholstered with a French silk velvet of about 1730 by an English firm, Bertram & Sons of Dean Street, whose label has survived. Another London upholsterer with a documented link with Waddesdon is Howard & Sons of Berners Street. It was probably an English firm that produced the fitted crimson Axminster carpet used throughout most of the main rooms on the ground and first floors. It is unusual in being entirely plain, without the pattern or borders familiar from English fitted carpets of the period, presumably to avoid competition with the textiles used for curtains and upholstery.

OPPOSITE: *The French screen in a corner of the Baron's Room was created from eighteenth-century Beauvais tapestry panels, and the daybed is strewn with nineteenth-century satin-weave silk cushions. The carpet was rewoven in 1981, copying the late-nineteenth-century original.*

ABOVE: *The central feature of the carpet in the Red Drawing Room is Apollo's head, surrounded by flowers, palms and crowns. The god symbolises Louis XIV, who commissioned the set of carpets from the Savonnerie factory in 1663, for the Long Gallery of the Louvre, Paris.*

There was a lively market for old silks, tapestry work and embroidery that could be reused in modern interiors. When in Florence in 1875, Ferdinand spent a considerable sum on 'a fine lot of old velvet', as he described it in a letter to his uncle Lionel, and a firm such as Decour could have helped Ferdinand track down and reuse 18th-century textiles. Alice was also a discriminating collector of old textiles, most notably 17th and 18th-century embroidery, and Adélaïde de Rothschild, who married her cousin Edmond (James's youngest son), formed a notable collection, much of which is now at Waddesdon—although even that is eclipsed by the astonishing 700 tapestry and embroidered 18th-century French chair covers accumulated by Josephine Bowes in Paris at the same time, which are now in the collection of the Bowes Museum in County Durham. Ferdinand's eye for quality led him to make some spectacular purchases for himself in this field, most notably of carpets from the French royal Savonnerie factory. Waddesdon contains no fewer than three of the factory's most famous masterpieces, the 104 carpets woven on Louis XIV's orders from 1665 onwards for the long gallery of the Louvre. Two were bought by Ferdinand, for the Red Drawing Room and West Gallery, and another by Alice, for her sitting room. The refined luxuriousness of Waddesdon's interiors is perfectly exemplified by the hearth-rugs in the ground-floor rooms: they are Savonnerie stool covers ordered by Louis XIV for Versailles. Ferdinand also acquired for the Tower Drawing Room a well preserved Savonnerie carpet woven for the royal gallery in the chapel at Versailles. These carpets came through specialist dealers. A bill from one, G. Pluyette of 56 rue Perronet, has survived, dated December 25, 1893, although unfortunately it does not identify the Savonnerie for which Ferdinand paid 3,500 francs.

This weaving together of old and new textiles helps explain much of the subtlety of tone and colour in Waddesdon's interiors. Ferdinand was not of course alone in seeing how reusing old materials could soften the effect of grand new rooms, and the house suggests the influence not just of his family but also of aesthetically minded friends who applied a similar approach to their own houses. It would be intriguing to know, for example, how much he looked for advice to his close American friend Clarence King, who was noted for his skilful use of antique textiles. Best remembered now for his book *Mountaineering in the Sierra Nevada* (1872), King was a geologist by training and an adventurer by nature, who kept a secret black wife and family in Brooklyn. He had just the sort of raffish, extrovertly masculine personality that appealed most to Ferdinand. The novelist Henry James recalled King as 'charming, but a queer, incomplete unsatisfactory creature', able to charm 'all the bric-a-brac out of the shops', who enjoyed 'buying old silk tapestries or the petticoats of Madame de Pompadour to cover New York chairs . . . or philandering with Ferdinand de Rothschild, who appears to be unable to live without him'. James's dig at King for buying petticoats was sharper than he may have realised, for both King and Ferdinand re-used fine 18th-century dress silks for upholstery, which they had trimmed with new *passementerie*. The stools in the Red Drawing Room, for example, are covered in a dress fabric of 1735. Although this sounds an impractical use for a fragile textile, it was not uncommon: another of Ferdinand's friends, Lady Desborough, made up cushions and curtains from 18th-century dresses she had taken to pieces.

Lady Desborough was a member of that fashionable artistic and aristocratic circle known as the Souls, who included the Conservative prime minister Arthur Balfour, the Tennant sisters, Violet Granby, the Wyndham family, and Lord and Lady Windsor. Their close attachment to Ferdinand has surprised historians, who assume that such delicate aesthetic palettes would have choked on Waddesdon. Such an assessment underestimates the range of their tastes, which sought artistic quality rather than a particular style, as the new houses they built reveal. Waddesdon seems very remote from the Windsors' Hewell Grange, celebrated for its refined and original blend of Jacobean architecture with Italian *quattrocento* interiors, and it seems to have even less in common with the Wyndhams' Clouds in Wiltshire, Philip Webb's country-house masterpiece, where the white rooms were set off by bold Morris textiles. Yet Ferdinand's eye for tone and texture allows Waddesdon to be compared with any of

The Morning Room, furnished with Ferdinand's collection of Dutch paintings, chairs covered with Beauvais tapestry and Savonnerie carpets made for Louis XVI. Against the far wall is the great secretaire acquired by Ferdinand from the Fitzwilliam family.

these houses. To a certain degree, the effects that he chose have been lost, for some of the textiles have inevitably faded in over a century, and where they have been replaced or repaired, conservators have attempted to match the faded tones rather than return to the colours originally used, so that, for example, the curtains in the Ante-Room are now buff and pale yellow rather than their original duck-egg blue and primrose. It is clear, however, that Waddesdon's dominant colours are not crimson and gold, but blues, greys, pinks, clear greens, and soft yellows, the colours of its old silk and tapestry, which are echoed in the subtle shades of the marbles lining the entrance hall and dining room. They also pick up hints suggested by the pictures, from Lady Jane Halliday's silvery-grey dress in Reynolds's portrait in the Grey Drawing Room to the shimmering blue silk worn by Gainsborough's Lady Sheffield, which echoes the blue ground of the Red Drawing Room's Savonnerie carpet. It is still possible to see why the magazine *Country Life* claimed in 1902 that at Waddesdon 'there is no fear of brilliant colour, it is an eminently cheerful and inspiriting interior.'

It is rarely seen in such terms, in part perhaps because the Rothschilds' houses are usually analysed as economic rather than artistic phenomena. Since they were the homes of the *nouveaux riches*, historians have been more interested in what they cost than in what they looked like. It is arguable that by the 1880s the Rothschilds had ceased to be *nouveaux riches*, but in any case perceptive contemporary critics were no longer lumping all their houses together. Eustace Balfour, whose opinions of Waddesdon have already been quoted, embodied up-to-the-minute artistic taste, since he had trained as an architect under Basil Champneys, a brilliant pioneer of the Queen Anne movement, and, as Arthur Balfour's youngest brother, was a fringe member of the Souls. When he visited Halton, designed by William Rogers, the house architect of its builders, Cubitt, he was predictably horrified by Alfred's taste in interior decoration: 'I have seldom seen anything more terribly vulgar', he wrote to his wife. 'Oh! but the hideousness of everything, the showiness! . . . the coarse mouldings, the heavy gilding always in the wrong place, the colours of the silk hangings! Eye hath not seen nor pen can write the ghastly

Ferdinand's delight in rich and contrasting surfaces and textures is demonstrated in this group of objects. ABOVE LEFT: *A writing table of about 1775 by Martin Carlin with a stand made of Sèvres porcelain.* BELOW LEFT: *An Augsburg table top, inlaid with a view of a fantastic city created from mother-of-pearl, brass and tortoiseshell.* OPPOSITE: *Gleaming mother-of-pearl on a bronze coffer of about 1750 in the West Gallery, juxtaposed with a chair from a set upholstered in eighteenth-century needlework.*

ABOVE: *The Great Hall, Halton House, Buckinghamshire, 1881–83. Photograph by Bedford Lemere, 1884–92. The room is crammed with Louis XVI tables and Victorian upholstered chairs and sofas. It embodies the taste commonly attributed to the Rothschilds, but very different in its effect from the subtleties of Waddesdon.*

OPPOSITE: *Alfred Charles de Rothschild in a* Vanity Fair *watercolour by Spy.*

coarseness of the sight!' His reaction to Waddesdon could not have been more strikingly different: 'The panelling and the tapestries, the hangings and the marbles were all one more beautiful than another, and the whole in exquisite taste.' Although Balfour's assessment may well have been influenced by the very different personalities of Alfred and Ferdinand, the contrast he draws is a telling one. In the quality of their furnishings and works of art there was little to choose between the two houses: it was the arrangement of the rooms and their decorative finishes that made all the difference.

Again and again at Waddesdon, the eye is struck by felicities of arrangement—the positioning of the Beaumarchais desk so that the light falls on it in the way suggested by the shadows in its marquetry, for example, or the way that the 18th-century chimney backs have been chosen to harmonise with the decorative motifs of the panelling. A touch of wit can also be discerned in the positioning of Reynolds's full-length portrait of Emily Pott above the chimneypiece in the Morning Room, where a mirror might conventionally have been expected. Miss Pott is shown as Thaïs, the courtesan who urged Alexander the Great to burn the temple at Persepolis; she wields a flaming brand as though to light a fire in the grate below. Ferdinand was generally well informed about the biographies of the sitters in the portraits he bought, and so would have known that contemporary gossip suggested Reynolds intended to show Miss Pott, the mistress of several prominent men, setting fire to the temple of chastity. There is also what might be called an intellectual element in the arrangement of the works of art at Waddesdon, hinted at by the *Daily Telegraph* in 1898 when it commented that 'nowhere is it more difficult to decide the much-vexed question whether Sir Joshua Reynolds holds his own against his overpoweringly brilliant rival, Gainsborough, or succumbs to the magic of his brush'. It seems possible that this rivalry was intended to form a topic of conversation for Ferdinand's guests, some of whom would have enjoyed such mild art-historical debate.

This use of works of art and objects of curiosity as a backdrop to Waddesdon's social life was not limited to the interiors, for the house sat in a garden that had its own collections of art, of animals and birds, and, of course, of plants. Most notable, in artistic terms, is the 18th-century garden statuary. For example, the Parterre on the terrace below the south front of the house centres on an early-18th-century group, *Pluto and Proserpina*, part of a fountain made by Giuliano Mozani for the Farnese palace at Colorno, near Parma in northern Italy; at the corners of the terrace are other Italian sculptural groups arranged to suggest the four seasons, and the steps leading from the house to the

Parterre are flanked by six early-18th-century Flemish vases with mythological scenes from the workshop of Jan Pieter Baurscheit and his son. On the far side of the house, the north fountain incorporates figures of a triton and nereids, also from Mozani's fountain at Colorno. Beyond the terrace, to the west of the house, the gardens are laid out as a circuit for visitors to stroll round, or to be driven in a pony trap, and their interest was maintained by carefully paced points of interest. First was the Aviary, in which Ferdinand took a special delight; he fed the birds himself, which learned to come in response to his whistle: according to the *Westminster Gazette*, 'they all knew him, and great was the commotion when his spare delicate figure was seen approaching, accompanied by his burly bailiff, and preceded by his French poodle "Poupon".' While visitors were at Waddesdon, the parrots were tethered to stands on the

lawn, where they could be individually admired—not a practice permissible today. The Aviary had its own garden, with another 18th-century Italian marble group, the *Infant Bacchus with a Ram* by the Florentine sculptor Vittorio Barbieri. Beyond this was the Tay Bridge miniature valley, overlooked by Laurent Delvaux's figure of *Hercules*. From here the path wound back towards the house by way of the miniature artificial cave and hill that housed the mountain goats, llamas and other exotic animals, referred to by Ferdinand as his 'zoo'. Its inhabitants were purchased from Charles Jamrach's Menagerie in London, which seems to have specialised in exotic animals for country-house collections, since it also supplied the Marquess of Bute's famous herd of wallabies for Mount Stuart on the Isle of Bute. 'Zoos' were a characteristic feature of Rothschild gardens: there were llamas at Gunnersbury; at Ferrières, James had kept geese, donkeys, and talking parrots; at Pregny, Ferdinand's eldest sister, Julie, had antelopes and kangaroos—the early signs, perhaps, of that passion for zoology which was to distinguish the Rothschilds in the 20th century.

After the goats, energetic visitors could carry on down the hill to see the stables, which, according to *The Jewish Chronicle*, 'are a miracle of order down to the gleaming brass tap, the name of every horse stands above his stall . . . the long coach-house holds an array of vehicles, barouches, pony carriages, broughams, wagonettes'. Ferdinand had no special enthusiasm for the turf, and did not own racehorses, so there was never anything like the parade of Derby winners that Hannah Rothschild and her husband, Lord Rosebery, liked to show their visitors at Mentmore. However, beyond the stables were the glasshouses, where Waddesdon came into its own. Here were collections, most notably of orchids, Malmaison carnations, and anthuriums, which in their day were far more famous than any of Waddesdon's works of art. Ferdinand's orchid collection was created for him by Frederick Sander, the author of the international register of orchid hybrids, who in the 1870s had opened a nursery in St Albans that developed into an international business, with branches in Belgium and the U.S.A. He provided plants for several Rothschild houses, and was proud of the fact that he was Ferdinand's exclusive supplier, the source of the prize-winning miltonias, odontoglossums, and cattleyas for which Waddesdon was best known: in 1884 he wrote to his chief orchid hunter, Benedict Roezel, that 'Baron Rothschild of Vienna and Nathaniel Rothschild order from me. He lives at Waddesdon Manor near Aylesbury, where he has spent over a mil-

The Pluto and Proserpina fountain, which incorporates early-eighteenth-century figures made for the Farnese palace in northern Italy by Giuliano Mozani.

OPPOSITE ABOVE: *Ferdinand feeding an ibis at the Aviary, about 1890.*

OPPOSITE BELOW: *Parrots on stands, about 1910. The abundant flower beds were abandoned during the Second World War, and the garden was remodelled to a simpler design by Lanning Roper in the 1960s.*

RIGHT: *Vittorio Barbieri's* Infant Bacchus with a Ram, *carved in Florence in the eighteenth century.*

LEFT: *An aerial view of the Aviary, a rococo trelliswork pavilion which exploits late-nineteenth-century technology by being made entirely of iron. It was restored, after falling into decline in the 1960s and is now decorated in blue and gold.*

ABOVE: *A detail of trelliswork on the central Aviary pavilion, derived from a French architectural treatise of 1771.*

BELOW: *The central pavilion, with the Fountain of Minerva (Italian, eighteenth century). Minerva, patroness of the arts and goddess of war, reclines on a gun barrel and raises a trumpet-shaped flower to her lips.*

FURNISHING THE HOUSE

lion pounds in recent years and built a most beautiful schloss. I am his only supplier. The sister of Baron Rothschild [presumably Alice] lives in Paris in the winter. She asked me to go there last week—she has given me an order for £100 and I must send a gardener to Germany in April.'

Beyond the glasshouses were rockwork and a Water Garden—home to a flock of ornamental fowl—which led down to the model Dairy, where visitors could admire Ferdinand's prize-winning Jersey and shorthorn cattle (each identified with a Meissen name-tag). According to the obituary of Ferdinand published in *The Farmer & Stock Keeper*, 'with regard to the achievement of his shorthorn herd alone, he had a position in the front rank of breeders'. The Dairy, like that at Schillersdorf, was decorated with German stoneware and Meissen animals. According to *The Jewish Chronicle*, 'the lower parts of the walls are panelled with rich carvings, whilst on the walls is a collection of quaint and fanciful china. None of the chairs are alike; two have for backs carvings in the form of a man's face . . . Curious are the plates filled with realistic China fruit, the old English and foreign jugs and plates.' Guests were invited to sample the cream with some strawberries from the glasshouses.

Once Waddesdon was fully functioning, Ferdinand was forced to admit that Destailleur had been right in predicting that the final design would prove too small for his needs. 'After I had lived in the house for a while, 'wrote Ferdinand in *The Red Book*, 'I was compelled to add first one wing and then another; and a greater outlay was eventually incurred than had the original work been carried out, not to speak of the discomfort and inconvenience caused by the presence of workmen in the house. Though more picturesque the building is less effective, and while spreading over as much ground it is less compact and commodious.' Ferdinand had been determined not to have a large central hall, like that at Mentmore (the first in an English country house designed to function as a living room), presumably because he found it uncomfortable: he tended to predict that every ambitious building project undertaken by his family would be subject to draughts. Yet the drawbacks, including lack of privacy and domestic intimacy as well as the difficulty of keeping them warm (which led to such rooms being condemned by contem-

LEFT: *Ferdinand's picturesque tiled Dairy, now restored and extended, overlooks the enchanting Water Garden, which has paths winding between pool and grottoes.*

OPPOSITE: Cattleya Dowiana Aurea, *one of Ferdinand's prize-winning orchids, illustrated in* Reichenbachia Orchids *by Frederick Sander, Volume I, 1888.*

J.L. Macfarlane Del. et Lith.   M & N. Hanhart Imp. London. W.

porary manuals of house design, most notably Robert Kerr's 1863 *The Gentleman's House*), were offset, as Ferdinand came to realise, by the great convenience of having a large room that was available to both family and guests of both sexes as a place to meet throughout the day. By the 1890s, top-lit and double-height rooms were out of fashion—partly because it was hard to find a suitably domestic style for such a room once the Gothic revival was over—so Ferdinand was not unusual in seeking to add a large new single-height room that might function in the same way.

It took some time, however, for the precise form and even the position of the new room to be decided upon. Destailleur's first suggestion, drawn up in 1884, only a year after Waddesdon's first big house party, was for an extension on the east end of the house's south façade, standing in front of the Bachelors' Wing. This involved replacing the Conservatory with a gallery of Renaissance form leading to a barrel-vaulted Winter Garden which would have risen higher than the first floor of the house itself. His next proposal, reduced in size, retained the gallery, but in the form of a 15th-century French Gothic cloister, which now led to a ballroom. Why Ferdinand should have wanted a ballroom is difficult to imagine, unless it was to double as a living room. Destailleur derived his design for the ballroom from the pavilion added to the Tuileries by Jean Bullant in the late 16th century, which led Bruno Pons to argue that Ferdinand may have been planning to incorporate into the new wing actual fragments of the palace, which were then available on the architectural salvage market (the Tuileries had been demolished in 1883, after having been gutted during the Commune of 1870). If that were the case, the idea was not pursued, and in 1888 Destailleur drew up further proposals in a Renaissance style before it was finally decided not to build on this site at all.

Instead, it was decided to add the new room onto the west side of the house. The presence of the big tower on the garden front meant that the new wing could not be aligned with that façade, and so it was designed as an extension to the entrance front. The addition of a single, massive room—originally it was to double as a library and a reception room before Ferdinand resolved simply to make it a morning room—was a challenge for Destailleur, who may have suggested a Gothic idiom because the style offered a greater variety of motifs for breaking up the extension's large façades than a Renaissance design

The Curio Room in the Dairy at the end of the nineteenth century. Rare white Meissen figures of a turkey and a goat, combined with humorous German stoneware, and antlers, create a quirky atmosphere, in contrast to the refined French taste of the Manor.

would have done. This was especially important on the north side of the wing, which had no windows at ground-floor level, and the difficulty Destailleur had articulating this façade is evident in the finished result. He was no more successful in devising the link with the main house, which involves a clumsy subdivision of the West Hall. He was probably not helped by Ferdinand's insistence that he retain the West Hall's external door onto the entrance courtyard, presumably because, when there were no guests staying, it was his principal access to the house and his private apartment, which was moved to the first floor of the new wing.

The choice of Gothic may have been intended to suggest that Waddesdon is a building that has grown over time, the main house appearing as a great Renaissance block added to the late-medieval west wing. By the 1890s Destailleur was well practised in Gothic architecture, since his success at Waddesdon had led to his other great English commission, the monastery and church at Farnborough in Hampshire, built for the exiled Empress Eugénie in 1879–88 as the setting for the tombs of Napoleon III, the Empress, and their son, the Prince Imperial. That was Destailleur's first major Gothic work, and he put his experience of the style to good use at Waddesdon. Great care was taken over the ornamental details, and full-scale plaster models of the carving for the dormer windows, the bay window, the doorways and the gargoyles were made in Paris under his supervision and then sent to Waddesdon for the carvers to follow. In execution, however, much of the Gothic detail in Destailleur's drawings was replaced with Renaissance motifs, presumably in the interests of harmony with the main house: on the bay window, for example, crocketed pinnacles have been replaced by Classical vases, and the chimney stack was given a 16th-century form.

The Morning Room was completed by May 1891, when the clerk-of-works wrote to the builder, Edward Conder, that 'I saw the Baron about midday on Saturday, and told him I had finished up everything. He seemed very pleased with the new large room.' Some of Ferdinand's friends were critical: when Edward Hamilton saw the completed shell of the new wing in May 25, 1890 he wrote in his diary: 'I don't much like it. It is not quite in character with the rest of the house, and the roof is too pointed. He is not quite happy about it himself; and it does not much matter for he can have it all down again if he likes.' In Ferdinand's accounts he lists payments for building work at Waddesdon in 1889–91 of £15,150, which must largely have been accounted

for by the costs associated with the new wing. However, there was an additional unwanted expense in April 1890, as a result of a fire being lit in the West Hall grate by some 'French decorators' employed to fit out the extension, almost certainly workmen sent by Decour. Presumably a fire had never been lit there before, since the flue had a hole in it and the flames penetrated the Baron's Room behind it, in which works of art were being stored during the building work. Fortunately, the fire was discovered quickly, for it caused the bell wires to melt and the bells to sound, but not before a full-length Gainsborough, *The Sisters*, had been destroyed. This portrait of the Ramus sisters had been bought for Ferdinand by Agnew's in 1887 for 9,251 guineas (then the second highest price paid at auction for a Gainsborough).

While work on the Morning Room wing was being completed, Ferdinand embarked on the extension of the Bachelors' Wing, largely to provide more bedroom accommodation for single male guests—perhaps necessitated in part by the visits of fellow MPs after his election to parliament in 1885. The wing was almost doubled in size with a range being added to the east. At the same time, the opportunity

ABOVE: *The Ramus Sisters, by Thomas Gainsborough, destroyed by fire at Waddesdon in 1890: A watercolour copy of the original painting.*

OPPOSITE: *A detail of the French nineteenth-century stamped and gilded leather which lines the corridor of the Bachelors' Wing.*

the works of art previously displayed in the Tower Draw-ing Room. Photographs of the collection in this setting give only a dim idea of its glamour, as they cannot convey the way richly coloured historic textiles were used to set off the glitter of gold and silver, enamel and glass. The room was not completed until the spring of 1896, when Edward Hamilton commented in his diary that 'Ferdie R. has . . . finished his room upstairs of *objets d'art*. The ceiling is very successful and every object arranged with the great-est care and the greatest success.' The relative contribu-tions made by d'Estailleur and André to the Bachelors' Wing are not easy to disentangle, especially as further alterations were made to these rooms after Ferdinand's death by d'Estailleur and possibly by André as well. Once the collection had been installed in the Smoking Room, Ferdinand remodelled the Tower Drawing Room by the installation of panelling which, as he accurately recorded in *The Red Book*, came from a house at Issy 'which was for some time the residence of the famous Fermier Général Beaujon to whom the Elysée also belonged'; it had been designed for Beaujon by the celebrated neoclassical archi-tect Etienne-Louis Boullée in about 1771 and demon-strates that Ferdinand's tastes in interior decoration were by no means limited to the Rococo.

By 1896, with the installation of the works of art in the new Smoking Room and the remodelling of the Tower Drawing Room, Waddesdon was complete, and by 1897, with the purchase of the paintings from the Six collection for the Morning Room, there was little room left for major acquisitions. Not surprisingly, the completion of Waddesdon prompted Ferdinand to think hard about its future. He concluded *The Red Book* with a much-quoted peroration: 'A future generation may reap the chief benefit of a work which to me has been a labour of love, though I fear that Waddesdon will share the fate of most properties whose owners have no descendants, and fall into decay. May the day be yet distant when weeds will spread over the gardens, the terraces crumble into dust, the pictures and cabi-nets cross the Channel or the Atlantic, and the melancholy cry of the night-jar sound from the deserted towers.'

Poignantly, Ferdinand would be dead only a year after writ-ing those words. What changes would he have made at Waddesdon if he had lived longer? It seems likely that his library would have become

was taken to remodel the suite of rooms set aside for the entertain-ment of male guests. Although Destailleur was nominally in charge, by the early 1890s he had retired, and in 1893 he died. The alterations to the Bachelors' Wing were largely designed by his son, Walter-André d'Estailleur, then only in his mid twenties. He collaborated with Alfred André, a professional interior designer and furniture restorer from Paris, over the design of the new Smoking Room, which was to house

LEFT: *The Smoking Room, from* The Red Book, *1897. Created to display Ferdinand's collection of Renaissance works of art, most of which are now in the British Museum.*

BELOW: *The Smoking Room, re-created in the 1990s by Lord Rothschild from Miss Alice's and other family collections. In the niche are a portrait of Robert Dudley, 1st Earl of Leicester painted about 1564, and a Brussels hunting tapestry of about 1600.*

OPPOSITE: *The Tower Drawing Room. This was the original home of Ferdinand's Renaissance works of art. It was fitted out with Neoclassical panelling by E.-L. Boullée after its contents had been moved to the Smoking Room in 1896.*

By the end of his life, Ferdinand's passion for collecting had focused on books, and in particular on fine eighteenth-century French bindings, notably the complex coloured 'mosaic' designs favoured by Parisian bookbinders. This is the one aspect of his collecting that is well documented, thanks to the catalogue which he commisioned and to the survival of records of the principal dealer who supplied him, Morgand et Fatout in Paris.

LEFT: *A mosaic-bound book:* Fête donné a Chilly Le XIII Septembre, M.DCC.LXX à Monseigneur le Dauphin, Madame la Dauphine et Mesdames de France, *1770.*

BELOW: *Frontispiece from* Fête Publique donné par la ville de Paris à l'occasion du mariage de Monseigneur le Dauphin le 13 février 1747, *1751.*

OPPOSITE: La prima [seconda] parte de le novella de Bandello *by Matteo Bandello, 1740, in mosaic bindings by Louis-François Le Monnier after 1742.*

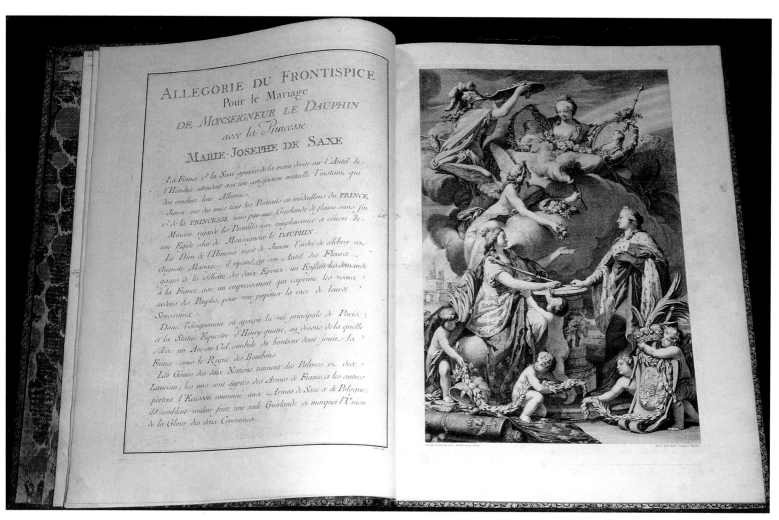

an increasing enthusiasm. When Mary Gladstone, the prime minister's youngest daughter, visited Waddesdon in 1885, she commented that 'the pictures in his sitting-room are too beautiful, but there is not a book in the house save 20 improper French novels'. For most English people, anything in French was imagined to be improper, and by Gladstone standards few houses had many books, but it is true that Waddesdon had as yet no notable library. Ferdinand owned a small group of fine medieval manuscripts, which he considered part of the Smoking Room collection, for they were bequeathed together with those treasures to the British Museum. The best-known of them, the early-16th-century *London Hours* from the workshop of Gerard Horenbout, is one of a group of manuscripts by the same artists of which his brother Nathaniel and cousin Edmond also owned examples. According to the *Times*, by the time Ferdinand died, book buying had become 'one of his latest hobbies; he used to say that while pictures of the kind he liked had become unattainable, there were still fine French bindings to be had'. Yet he was interested in more than his books' covers (magnificent although they are), for he was developing an absorbing literary career as a contributor to *The Nineteenth Century*, the popular Liberal monthly edited by James Knowles. He was also the author of two books: a privately printed account of a tour of South Africa in 1894–95, which appeared in 1895, the year before his *Personal Characteristics from French History*. When he attended a dinner given by Knowles in February 1890, at which Gladstone was present, conversation turned to the question of the number of books needed to make a really good library. As one of the guests, Sir Henry Ponsonby, recalled, 'It was generally agreed about twenty thousand, of which Rothschild immediately made a note.' As so often in descriptions of Ferdinand in company, there is some suspicion that he was being teased, but his devotion to literature was never in doubt, nor were his intellectual abilities. As he contemplated the completed Waddesdon, he formulated, on the basis of his reading, a prescient understanding of his house's place in history, as well as its role in contemporary society.

Like most of the English branch of his family, Ferdinand was a Liberal by political instinct: the Rothschilds' participation in the struggle for Jewish emancipation could hardly make them otherwise. Although his allegiance to the Liberals was severely compromised by the split in the party over home rule for Ireland in 1886, he remained philosophically a Whig, with a Whig's vision of history as essentially progressive. This is often underestimated, perhaps because Waddesdon is frequently interpreted as a rich man's nostalgic recreation of

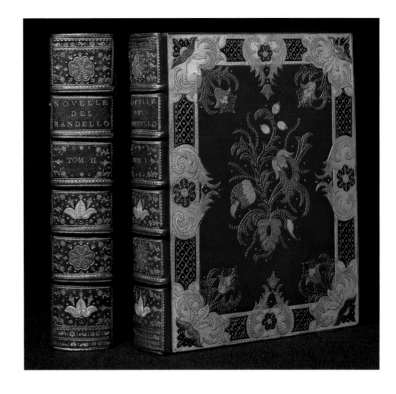

the certainties of the *ancien régime*. That was not how Ferdinand saw it at all. 'When . . . we throw off the spell exercised by the superficial attractions of the French eighteenth century', he wrote in an article in *The Nineteenth Century* in April 1888, 'Century for Century', which unfavourably compared French achievements in the 18th century with British, 'then we perceive beneath the brilliant veneer of art, wit and refinement, those vices of character and constitution which could only be eradicated by a supreme convulsion'. For him, the French Revolution had not merely been inevitable, it had also been a necessary preliminary to the achievements of the 19th century. It had swept away 'the rottenness and effeteness of the old order', which, as he put it in the conclusion of *Personal Characteristics from French History*, 'fell to pieces like a house of cards at the first gust of the popular whirlwind . . . Soon all Frenchmen would be united in a common bond, animated by the same spirit, and working for the same cause, welded into one people, and developing the vast and unexplored resources of the land, not for the advantage of a limited and selfish class, but for that of the whole people.'

Ferdinand's beliefs about what he was doing at Waddesdon become clearer if he is compared to members of an earlier generation who collected the French furniture or porcelain brought onto the market by that 'popular whirlwind'. In the 1820s English royal and aristocratic collectors used their acquisitions to emphasise that they were the inheritors of the *ancien régime*. Once the threat posed by

A selection of books from Ferdinand's magnificent
collection housed in the Morning Room:
Spaccio de la bestia triofante, *Giordano Bruno,
1584;* bound with La cena de le ceneri, 1584
Chaos del tri per uno, *Teofilo Folengo, 1527;*
De gl' heroic furore, *Giordano Bruno, 1585;*
and Liber psalmorum, 1541.
*All but the middle volume were either bound by or
attributed to Antoine-Michel Padeloup le jeune in Paris.*

Napoleon had passed, a vogue for French decorative arts and interior decoration could flourish once more without any suggestion of lack of patriotism. It was a fashion with distinct Tory undertones: the Duke and Duchess of Rutland installed their Louis XV *boiseries* at Belvoir in a castle remodelled in a style they called 'Anglo-Saxon', just as George IV and Wyatville's restoration of Windsor blended new Francophile interiors with a reassertion of the castle's Gothic identity. It was the continuity of the English landed classes with the past that was being emphasised, as well as their role as inheritors of a tradition irretrievably severed in France by the Revolution. That use of French decorative traditions in the service of aristocratic identity lingered surprisingly long in some families: at Clumber in Nottinghamshire, for example, the 5th Duke of Newcastle commissioned opulent new Rococo interiors from Charles Barry in the 1850s to provide a setting for the French furniture and porcelain his father had collected. The 4th Duke was so notoriously opposed to political reform that a mob burned down his principal seat, Nottingham Castle, during the upheavals accompanying the passing of the 1832 Reform Bill. That bill was the climax of a political movement which signalled the beginning of the long Liberal ascendancy. It marked a change of temper that helped precipitate a change in architectural fashions: taste for the art of pre-revolutionary France gave way to the Gothic Revival, appreciated by its aristocratic patrons for the way it suggested a national, historic and Christian justification for their authority.

Ferdinand's choice of 18th-century styles for the interiors at Waddesdon had little to do with nostalgia for the *ancien régime*. His family had, after all, risen to greatness on the back of the struggle for a new European order during the Napoleonic wars. In a sense he aestheticised a style that had been politicised in 1820s England, a process that was to be taken a stage further by the American plutocrats who enthusiastically adopted the *goût Rothschild* but drained it of any suggestion of political sympathy for monarchy or aristocracy. Ferdinand saw himself as part of a self-made generation that took the art of the past and created something new out of it, as collectors had done throughout history. As Ferdinand wrote in 'Bric-à-Brac', 'Art is a small factor in history, perhaps only an incident in it, yet it follows history in all its stages. So long as the Church and the Throne were the primary forces of civilisation it was the aim and ambition of the artist to devote his genius to the adornment of Churches and Palaces, which he filled with all that was noblest and richest in art; but when the growth of the democracy destroyed the spell of the old influences it sent the artist adrift and carried away, scattering broadcast, the old

artistic accumulations of centuries. A new centre of attraction has been formed on the ruins of the old, produced by the very action of the democracy. If the artist no longer gravitates towards the Prelate and the Prince, he now does homage to "the people", whom he idealised into an entity, competing for their patronage in academies and exhibitions, while the artistic productions of the past turn to the same magnet and pass into the hands of the People in museums.' One of Ferdinand's early memories was of being taken to the Great Exhibition of 1851, and he shared with the generation that had created the Crystal Palace and the museums that had sprung up in its wake a belief that public art collections could stimulate contemporary designers (shortly before his death he was appointed to the committee of the 1900 Paris Exposition). 'To architects, skilled workmen, cabinet makers, even to dressmakers and hairdressers,' he wrote, 'a museum affords a source of new ideas which never fails.'

So just as Ferdinand's career as a collector came at a mid point between the fashion for buying second-hand 18th-century decorative arts simply as furnishings and the appreciation and pursuit of such works as collectors' items, so his role as a creator of interiors came midway between the aristocratic traditions for which the works of art had been created and the democratic tide that would sweep them into museums. He recognised that the English aristocracy had been more resilient than its French counterpart, but he doubted whether in the long run it would be any more successful in hanging on to its treasures. After all, he had been able to buy his estate thanks to the financial difficulties of the Duke of Marlborough and many of his most valued possessions had once been in English aristocratic collections—for example, the Morning Room secretaire came from the Fitzwilliams, the Beaumarchais desk from the Buccleuchs and the Cellini vase from the Devonshires. Many of the lesser items had similarly distinguished provenances: a glance through the catalogues of the Waddesdon collections reveals what he bought from Knole and Althorp, Cassiobury and Ham, Belvoir and Aske, to say nothing of the great treasures from Hamilton Palace. Ferdinand argued that this was part of an inevitable historic change that in England had been prompted not by revolution but by the agricultural depression which had set in from the mid 1870s and by one of its consequences, the Settled Land Act of 1882, which allowed land owners, short of liquid cash as their rents declined, to sever entails, and so release land, houses and works of art for sale.

Further encouragement for them to do so came with the 1894 budget, during the premiership of Ferdinand's close friend Lord Rosebery, although Rosebery had no responsibility for its most celebrated initiative, prepared by the Chancellor of the Exchequer, Sir William Harcourt. As a deliberate strike against what Gladstone had called 'class-preference', it introduced an aggressive new system of death duties, whereby estates were to be valued on their actual capital value and taxed on a graduated scale, so treating land in the same way as unsettled personal property. Ferdinand feared that this measure would encourage owners to sell works to foreign buyers, notably Americans, who were now a major force in the market, encouraged by the abolition of the steep import tax imposed by the U.S. government on works of art in 1883. 'At the time Sir William Harcourt's Bill was being debated in Parliament', recalled Ferdinand, 'I ventured to observe to him that if passed unamended its results would be the loss to England of some of her finest works of art.' The arguments that Ferdinand put to Harcourt were to echo throughout the following century: old wealth was being drained of its resources and would be forced to sell its possessions; since British museums were less well subsidised than those abroad, the result would be the loss to the British public of the art accumulated by collectors in the past. Harcourt would not be persuaded. 'Some few weeks later', continued Ferdinand, 'when Sir William happened to be staying with me in the country, we again broached the topic . . . A member of the party . . . whose professional experience enabled him to speak with more authority than I could, stated that during the last decade or two upwards of fifty Rembrandts alone had been exported—and Sir William had to give in.' The concession that was eventually granted, in the budget of 1896 (by Sir Michael Hicks Beach rather than Harcourt, since the Liberals were then out of office) allowed owners of works of art deemed worthy of a national collection to defer paying capital taxes on them until they were sold. Ferdinand believed he had played a significant part in the lobbying that led to this. At the back of his mind, there must have been concern for the fate of Waddesdon, or at least of its collections. Ferdinand's understanding of history suggested that one day the house and its works of art would have a public role, but it was not immediately clear what that would be. But there was no need for anxiety, as yet. In May 1880, when he had his first house party at Waddesdon, Ferdinand was only 40, and could contemplate a long future for the house as the setting for the entertainment of his guests: in that sense, it had a part to play in public life from the beginning.

FURNISHING THE HOUSE

5

LIFE AT WADDESDON
1880–1898

WHEN FERDINAND CELEBRATED his first house party in May 1880 with 'a grand display of fireworks, frequently illuminating the whole of the mansion and the grounds', in the words of the *Buckinghamshire Herald*, he was on the brink of a new stage in his life. His successful creation of Waddesdon Manor, its gardens and estate had given new confidence to the shy, nervy man who had arrived in England 20 years earlier. Yet no sooner had his first guests departed than he suffered a set-back, for during his summer travels he contracted a serious illness, thought to have been malaria, that compelled him to leave England for a period of convalescence. In September, the *Buckinghamshire Herald* reported that he was 'breaking up his hunting establishment at Leighton Buzzard owing to continuing ill-health. His two favourite hunters have been shot; other horses of the stud have been taken by Mr Leopold de Rothschild and transferred to his stables at Ascott... It is also reported that the works at the mansion on Lodge Hill have been suspended owing to the Baron's critical condition ... [which] causes grave anxiety to his friends.' However, by December he was back, and work had resumed on the house. For the rest of his life, his health seems to have been poor, and his surviving letters frequently complain of 'seediness', ranging from regular bronchial attacks to chronically bad digestion. While his guests enjoyed the magnificent meals prepared by his chef Auguste Chalanger, and confectioner, Arthur Chategner (who had worked for the Tsar), Ferdinand dined on cold toast and water: as Lillie Langtry recalled, 'whenever he ate a meal a tray of medicine bottles appeared as an antidote'.

The Dining Room with the table laid as for an 1890s house party with a hedge of blooms down the table.
A maximum of forty-two diners could sit and admire the Beauvais tapestries, La Noble Pastorale *and* La Leçon de Flageolet,
designed by François Boucher, 1755 to 1778, and the elaborately carved mirror frames from the hôtel de Villars, Paris, France.

Ferdinand was now a figure of some public celebrity, described by the *Manchester Evening News* as ' a slightly-built man, a little above the middle height with narrow features, thinly-bearded, his hands habitually housed in his trousers pockets. He walks with a quick jerky stride, and his head is in continuous motion, as if in search of some one.' The apparent loneliness of this solitary widower in his hilltop palace appealed to journalists eager to show that money could not buy happiness: according to the *London Morning News* 'he would shut himself up in his country home, dining off a grilled cutlet, playing patience by himself, and going to bed when the world was going to the theatres'. This was a picture that Ferdinand would have recognised: 'I am a lonely, suffering and occasionally a very miserable individual despite the gilded and marble rooms in which I live', he wrote to Lord Rosebery in September 1878. There was an element of self-dramatisation in this attempt to win Rosebery's fickle affections, but it is possible that he had what would now be called a manic-depressive streak, perhaps exacerbated by recurrences of malaria, in which bouts of intense activity alternated with periods of melancholia.

Assuming that he did not choose his solitary life, newspapers occasionally speculated that he was about to remarry, and in May 1895 there was a strong rumour that he had become engaged to Julia Peel, daughter of the Speaker of the House of Commons, the Hon. Arthur Peel; in fact, she had become attached to his close friend the MP Rochfort Maguire, and they spent their honeymoon at Waddesdon. In some ways, it is surprising that he did not remarry, especially as his family's tradition of endogamy was fading. Yet although the marriage of female Rothschilds to Christian husbands was increasingly tolerated, as was shown by the marriage in 1878 of Meyer's only daughter and heir, Hannah, to Lord Rosebery, it remained much more difficult for

ABOVE: 'Ferdy' Rothschild in the House of Commons. *A cartoon by Hay in* Vanity Fair, *June 15, 1889. Ferdinand was a Liberal and subsequently Liberal Unionist Member of Parliament for Aylesbury from 1885 until his death in 1898.*

BELOW: Archibald Philip Primrose, 5th Earl of Rosebery (1847–1929) in about 1890. Ferdinand's cousin and closest friend, he was the first guest to sign the Visitors' Book, on May 18, 1880.

male members of the family to find appropriate partners. Although, in the absence of his private papers, it is impossible to be sure, Ferdinand does not seem to have contemplated marrying again. Nor is there any evidence that he kept a mistress. Perhaps to temper their tradition of what were virtually arranged marriages, the Rothschilds were relatively relaxed about the male members of the family conducting affairs. For example, Ferdinand's cousin Alfred let it be known that he had a daughter, Almina (a future Countess of Carnarvon), by his mistress, Marie Wombwell. Although Ferdinand dropped hints in a letter to Rosebery in 1884 about 'a little pall' in Paris, one Madame de Jouy, a 'regular enfant du boulevard', he may possibly have had some homosexual tendencies as well. Certainly, the occasionally anguished tones of his correspondence with Rosebery, 'my best and darling friend', suggest a relationship that in its early days passed through a phase of what can only be called unfulfilled love: 'You are endowed with such powers of fascination that I have given myself up to your affection—you honoured me last year', he wrote to Rosebery in 1884. 'This year your heart seems to be toward me like a barren desert. Do not forsake me. You have the whole world before you, I but an empty future. Be warmer towards me, kinder, be as you were. . . . I love you. Do not spurn me.'

In the words of his friend Edward Hamilton, Ferdinand was 'rather selfishly disposed, which is not to be wondered at. The spoilt child became rather the spoilt man.' Many of the stories told about him allude to his self-centredness. For example, Lillie Langtry recalled an experience at a house he had rented for entertaining during the racing at Goodwood: 'One evening my maid's dress caught fire when I was

dressing for dinner and our united screams were disregarded. When I got down the baron was raging because he thought the owners had left children in the house. So, had I not put out the flames, we might have burned to death.' In consequence, although regarded with undoubted affection, he was, as Hamilton said, 'a subject of chaff and merriment among his friends which he seldom resented'. But he was more easily wounded than that suggests: although he could brush off as merely irritating the perpetual teasing of his cousin Natty, he was occasionally reduced to tears by Rosebery, whose sense of humour was rather feline. In November 1888 he was forced to write to Rosebery to make up after losing his temper: 'I am the incessant butt of your chaff which no doubt you think very amusing but is not always equally gratifying to myself. I was doubly wrong to lose my temper before the servants but I may add that I did not think it very pleasant to be made an object of fun before my servants.'

Such outbursts of temper suggest the emotional drives that found their outlet in an energy which belied his reputation for effeteness. 'His leading characteristic was perhaps his impulsive and impatient nature,' recalled Hamilton. 'He was always in a hurry. He did not eat, but devoured. He did not walk but ran through galleries and places to be seen. He could not wait for anybody or anything. He played 3 games of patience when most people would be playing one.' The determination and organisational skill he brought to the building and furnishing of Waddesdon were combined with great attention to the responsibilities of wealth. Like all Rothschilds, he took his support for charities very seriously. In his accounts for 1887, for example, he listed payments to unnamed charities amounting to £1,570, but this did not include his annual £2,000 to the Evelina Hospital, nor expenditure on his estate or in the county that could loosely be called charitable, ranging from the annual and soon celebrated 'Baron's Treat' for nearly 1,500 local schoolchildren to the building and endowment of a working men's institute in Aylesbury, opened in 1883. Much charitable help went unnoticed. Among the numerous letters written to Dorothy de Rothschild to congratulate her on the publication of her book *The Rothschilds at Waddesdon Manor* in 1979 was one from a Mr Ladyman, born in 1897, whose father had been one of Ferdinand's gardeners and whose mother had been in service with Mr Sims, the estate bailiff: '[I] can recollect my mother saying when we were children being 6 of us that we should never have managed to bring up all you kids if she hadn't had the doctor's bills paid by the Baron's good and kind nature.'

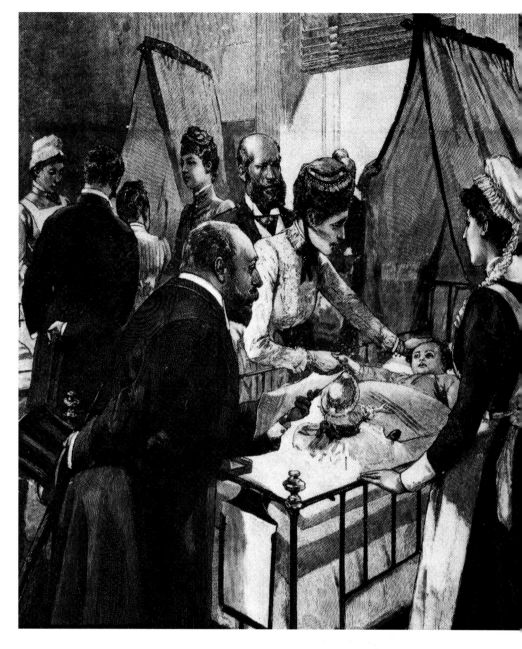

The Prince and Princess of Wales visiting the Evelina Hospital, Illustrated London News, *August 1890. The most up-to-date children's hospital of its day, it was built in Southwark, south London, in the late 1860s in memory of Ferdinand's much-loved young wife.*

Little evidence survives about Ferdinand's religious life. He made light of it in a letter to Rosebery of September 29 1884 which refers to 'my coreligionists . . . making to the dinner table after a fast of 24 hours. I have fasted today from 10–2 and again from 3. Unlike my brethren I shall not eat until this evening.' New Year was certainly celebrated at Schillersdorf, since Evelina wrote to her mother that the family preferred to say their prayers at home rather than endure the

151

'entire absence of cleanliness' of the congregation at the local synagogue. However, there are no descriptions of Ferdinand keeping such ritual obligations as lighting candles on Friday evenings or fasting and praying on the Day of Atonement, as his cousin Hannah did at Mentmore. He presumably attended the synagogue in London, for in 1868, accompanied by Alice, he laid the foundation stone of the North London Synagogue, and between 1868 and 1875 was treasurer of the Jewish Board of Guardians. He became a warden of the Central Synagogue in 1870, the year it became part of the newly constituted United Synagogue. This was combined with an active career as a Freemason. In 1892 he was one of the founders of the Ferdinand de Rothschild Lodge (No 2420), which originally met in a Lodge Room in the Five Arrows Hotel in Waddesdon, but later moved to Aylesbury, and in 1893 he became the lodge's master. He was also an adherent of the temperance movement, on which he occasionally spoke in public. A lifelong teetotaller, who once claimed that 'I never want a cure, because I never drink wine; wine to me is poison', he did not attempt to impose his views on either his guests or his tenants, for whom he rebuilt the Five Arrows inn—just one of eight public houses in the village in his day. However, the reading room he had given to the village served only non-alcoholic drinks: the *Daily Chronicle* recalled that 'it was a common experience to see the wealthy MP and landlord sipping a cup of cocoa at the coffee tavern'.

Outside Waddesdon, Ferdinand was best known as a member of parliament, and it seems that the campaigning and entertaining he had to undertake in this role helped remove any lingering hostility to him in the county following his imperious remodelling of his estate. Since the Rothschilds had bought land in Buckinghamshire largely to secure a political power base, there must have been pressure from his family on Ferdinand to take up a parliamentary career once the house was complete. He laid the foundations in the usual way with county offices, and was elected High Sheriff of Buckinghamshire in 1883; he also served as Deputy Lord Lieutenant, a justice of the peace and a member of the county council. At the beginning of 1885 he put his name forward for a London seat, St George in the East, but then withdrew it when a far more attractive proposition emerged. In 1865 his cousin Natty had secured election to parliament unopposed as the member for Aylesbury. Natty's political career was marked by the family's slow drift away from support for Gladstone, alienated by the prime minister's lukewarm support for the empire and by the radicalism of many of his followers, which was increasingly discomforting the party's landed supporters: by 1880 Ferdinand was able to write to Rosebery, a rising Liberal star, that 'I wish your Mr G. at the

bottom of the sea.' Gladstone was conscious that Natty was becoming a critic of the government, and this may have encouraged the prime minister to replace him as member of parliament with somebody he assumed would be more biddable. The long-standing idea of a Rothschild peerage was revived, and—a mark of the increasing acceptability of Jews at the highest level of society—Queen Victoria dropped her opposition, which had scotched Gladstone's attempts to ennoble Lionel in 1869 and 1873. On July 9, 1885, Natty was elevated to the House of Lords as Lord Rothschild of Tring.

Ferdinand took up the offer of the newly vacated seat and stood as the Liberal candidate in a by-election. Given his political beliefs, this surprised some observers: the radical MP Sir Charles Dilke commented that 'F. Rothschild wants to get into Parliament and I told him that he is a Tory and ought to stand as a Tory . . . He will never get in as a Liberal nowadays, I'm sure'. Such an opinion is understandable, given the way Ferdinand balanced loyalty to Gladstone's party with more than an echo of the imperial expansiveness of the Rothschilds' old friend Disraeli. 'I am not as you think by nature a conservative', he wrote to Dilke. 'Conservatism has been the ruin of several foreign countries and liberal politics have been the making of England. . . . On the other hand . . . I deplore for the sake of the country which I have adopted and I love truly the restricted policy of the present Govt. who have sacrificed if not the interests yet the magic powers of the English flag and name to the narrow issues of Parliamentary reforms . . . I would cheer the Union Jack planted on every island of the Polynees, on every crag of the Himalayas, on every minaret of the east (this is a metaphor).' Such ambivalence did him no harm in the polls, and he was elected with a comfortable majority of 1,582. However, Dilke was to prove right, and Ferdinand did not remain a Gladstonian for much longer.

In the House of Commons, Ferdinand made an impression more for his mild eccentricities of dress than anything else: according to the *Birmingham Gazette*, 'he was one of the few Parliamentarians who never appeared in a frock coat. On the other hand he never appeared in a jacket, as so many members do now-a-days, but always wore a tailed morning coat'. With some plausibility, the *Birmingham Mail* remarked that 'he shunned the House because of its draughts'. When he did attend, he was usually silent, and, according to the *Daily Chronicle*, 'even when he did speak, the foreign accent and the rapidity of his utterance made the Baron difficult to follow'; according to another parliamentary correspondent, 'for hours at a stretch he twisted his thumbs, turning them slowly once or twice and then rapidly half a dozen times'. Yet he pursued

one or two minor political campaigns, most notably to improve the poor conditions and pay of post-office clerks, and spoke up in favour of his local interests, such as the extension of the Metropolitan railway line; when it was suggested that the British ambassador in Paris ought not to attend the opening of an exhibition in Paris because it was assumed to be a covert celebration of the French Revolution, he lectured his fellow MPs about 18th-century French history. Perhaps encouraged by his participation in parliamentary debates, Ferdinand took up lecturing as a pastime, and, although Hamilton commented that 'he had no great natural turn for it', his talks, on literary and historical topics, were prepared with great care. Published as *Village Lectures*, they were delivered not only to the villagers of Waddesdon and the working men of Aylesbury but also to the Prince of Wales's guests at Sandringham.

Between the end of May and the middle of August and again in September, the main focus of Ferdinand's attention was the house parties he gave at Waddesdon. Although there were also smaller shoot-

ing parties in the winter, the house came fully to life for only five months of the year. For example, in 1891, an exceptionally busy year for entertaining, there were 11 house parties between May 20 and September 25, but outside that time only seven people came to stay. Fortunately, a good record of Ferdinand's guests survives in his visitors' book, which forms a revealing portrait of his social life. It demonstrates that the usual number for a 'Saturday to Monday' party (the term 'weekend' was not used until the following century) ranged between 14 and 20, although on occasions there could be substantially more. As Hamilton commented in May 1887 when he paid one of his many visits to the house (he signed the visitors' book no fewer than 52 times), 'we are a very large party—about 30, which is estimated means the housing of

BELOW: *A house party for Edward VII (then Prince of Wales) and members of the diplomatic corps, hosted by Ferdinand at Waddesdon in 1894. The Prince of Wales, in a white fedora, sits behind the women; Alfred de Rothschild stands behind him on the right. Ferdinand is seated second from the right and Lord Rosebery stands on the far right. Other guests included the Austrian and Russian ambassadors.* FAR RIGHT: *A group of photographs of the Prince of Wales at a more relaxed house party, enjoying tennis on the grounds.*

about 90 persons'. That was because every man brought a valet and every woman was accompanied by at least one maid, all of whom had to be given bedrooms. In addition, Ferdinand's indoor staff of 24 was accommodated in the house itself. In 1891, Waddesdon Manor was home to a steward (a post usually described as a butler), a housekeeper, a cook, a kitchen maid, two scullery maids, two still-room maids, an under butler, eight housemaids, two footmen, a porter, an attendant for the electric light, a needlewoman, an odd man, and a hall boy (for carrying luggage and other minor duties). In addition, there were 16 servants based in the stables (including the stud groom and his family), five in the laundry, and three in the Dairy. In the house, little now survives of the interiors they inhabited, since the service accommodation was largely emptied when the house was taken over by the National Trust in 1957, although the French kitchen range survives in what is now the Manor Restaurant, together with part of the original copper *batterie de cuisine*, inscribed FRW for Ferdinand Rothschild, Waddesdon.

In terms of numbers of staff, Waddesdon's establishment was not unusually large, given the size of Ferdinand's income: it has been calculated that in the 1870s, the average number of indoor servants was 22 in houses with an annual income of over £20,000, although in practice the numbers could range from 12 to 31. What differed at Waddesdon was that the staff served the needs only of two unmarried people, not a large family with numerous dependants. For example, in one comparable household, Hillington Hall in Norfolk, the bachelor Sir William Ffolkes and his unmarried sister managed in 1871 with a household staff of only five, despite an income of over £10,000 a year. Lord Haldane, a Liberal politician and the Rothschilds' legal adviser, loved to tease Ferdinand with the remark he was supposed to have made when he was elected to parliament that '143 of my gardeners almost threw themselves into each other's arms with joy at the result'. How large was the gardening staff in reality? Its scale can be deduced from Ferdinand's notes of his estate expenditure. In 1897, for example, the total annual wages of his permanent household staff amounted to £821, whereas garden labour cost him £2,256. Since the household staff numbered 24 that gives an average annual salary for them of £34; although no figures survive for Waddesdon, wages rang-

LEFT AND ABOVE: *The Head Groom and his staff in front of J. E. Boehm's bronze study of Gorse at the stables, about 1900. In the 1891 census, Charles Lane and George Lawson were the coachmen, with a staff of eight.*

OPPOSITE: *Copper fish kettle and straining spoon, braising pan and vegetable stewpan inscribed with Ferdinand's initials and W for Waddesdon.*

OVERLEAF: *The Head Cook, chef and kitchen staff, circa 1890. In the 1891 census, Susan Smith was cook, assisted by Susan Cole, kitchen maid, Emma Howitt, scullery maid, and two still-room maids. The pastry chef came down as required from Ferdinand's London house.*

ing from £15 per annum for an experienced housemaid to £100 for a steward or butler would be in line with other sizeable country houses in the 1890s. Assuming the gardeners were paid equivalent amounts—and they probably received less, since gardeners were usually paid agricultural rates—they must have numbered at least 66. The bedding out, which was such an important part of the garden, could hardly have been accomplished with fewer men: by the end of the century, some 50,000 annuals were planted out every year on the terrace alone. At a speech he gave at a dinner of the Gardeners' Benevolent Society in 1887, Ferdinand said that 'it was not right that those who derived gratification from their gardens should forget the gardeners, to whom they owed so much', and he was praised in the gardening press for the way his gardeners were looked after, most notably the provision in the village of a substantial and well-appointed dormitory house, 'The Bothy', for unmarried men. According to the 1891 census, it accommodated 13 gardeners—3 foremen and ten journeymen.

Waddesdon's numerous gardeners were recalled by the Countess of Warwick (who was later to open a school of gardening): she arrived for a house party after a violent storm had flattened all the flower beds. When she rose early the next morning 'I saw an army of gardeners at work, taking out the damaged plants and putting in new ones that had been brought from the glass-houses in pots . . . After breakfast that morning I went into the grounds. The gardens had been completely transformed! Not a damaged plant was to be seen anywhere. Also the small army of gardeners I had watched earlier in the morning had vanished, leaving behind them a new garden. Everything had been done so quietly that, save for the fact that by chance I had risen at dawn, I should never have realized the extent of Baron de Rothschild's consideration for his guests' pleasure.' Even better known is another story told by Haldane about the comforts of life at Waddesdon: 'I love luxury,' he remarked to a fellow guest, David Lindsay, the future 27th Earl of Crawford, when both were staying with Ferdinand in June 1898, 'notwithstanding my ardent radicalism . . . I admire my host, he does things so very well . . . When lying abed in the mornings it gives me satisfaction when a lacquey softly enters the room and asks whether I will take tea, coffee, chocolate or cocoa. This privilege is accorded to me in the houses of all my distinguished

friends: but it is only at Waddesdon that on saying I prefer tea, the valet further enquires whether I fancy Ceylon, Souchong or Assam.' This story (it is told about Halton as well) improved in the retelling, for it is also recorded that having made a choice of tea, the guest was offered milk, cream or lemon, and having opted for milk, received the reply, 'Jersey, Hereford or Shorthorn, Sir?'

Such a level of service was similar to that provided by new luxury hotels, such as the Savoy in London (opened in 1889) or the Waldorf in New York (opened in 1893). It was not something that appealed to everyone: after the novelist Henry James had stayed at Waddesdon in 1885 he wrote to Grace Norton that 'the gilded bondage of that gorgeous place will last me for a long time'. James was one of several literary and artistic figures Ferdinand occasionally entertained at Waddesdon—Maupassant, who visited in 1886, was another—but on the whole Ferdinand's intellectual and aesthetic interests were not notably reflected in his choice of guests. In part this was because of social restrictions—even a dealer as prominent as William Agnew, who was invited to look round Waddesdon, was never asked to stay, nor did the Wertheimers ever sign the visitors' book, and the fellow collector outside his own family whom Ferdinand knew best, Richard Wallace, refused invitations because his *demi-mondaine* wife was not received in society. David Lindsay sensed something of the gulf between his host's social life and artistic interests when he observed how at Waddesdon, 'Baron Ferdinand whose hands always itch with nervousness, walks about at times petulantly, while jealously caring for the pleasure of his guests. I failed to gather that his priceless pictures give him true pleasure. His clock for which he gave £25,000, his escritoire for which £30,000 was paid, his statuary, his china, and his superb collection of jewels, enamels and so forth ('gimcracks' he calls them)—all these things give him meagre satisfaction: and I felt that the only pleasure he derives from them is gained when showing them to his friends. Even then one sees how bitterly he resents comment which is ignorant or inept.'

Ferdinand's house parties were mixed, in the sense of drawing upon several sections of aristocratic and plutocratic society. A sense of their somewhat miscellaneous variety is conveyed by a letter from Maupassant to his friend Count Primoli in August 1886, shortly before Primoli himself went to stay there: 'I am here in an English mansion, surrounded by Englishmen—the Archbishop of Canterbury, the Prime Minister, etc., etc., plus the German Ambassador with whom I have spoken a lot because he does not know any more English than I do (at least that's what he says). Not many women here—a

ABOVE: *In a corner of the State Dressing Room is a wash-stand and Minton washing set, embellished with the Rothschild arrows, typical of those used by Ferdinand's guests.*

OPPOSITE: *Ferdinand with Poupon, who entertained the guests with tricks.*

young girl, Lady X (cannot possibly remember her name), and the wife of the Archbishop who does not give me any desire to make the eminent churchman a cuckold. My host, M.Ferdinand de Rothschild, is a charming man, I greatly prefer him to his guests.' Despite the implication that people were rather thrown together, Ferdinand clearly gave great thought to his guests, and expected similar consideration in return: as Lady de Grey wrote to a friend who had been invited to Waddesdon, 'You know Ferdy is rather a funny person about his parties, and does not like to be kept waiting long for an answer.' According to the *Standard*, 'He was eclectic in his social predilections . . . Having brought his guests together, Baron Ferdinand did not take any very active part in making them known to one another or in leading them in conversation or amusements. He provided them with every kind of delight to the eye, with every material luxury that the most fastidious could desire; and having done so, his idea seemed to be that they would entertain themselves'. Not all guests appreciated this *laissez-faire* diversity: 'Ferdie Rothschild has got a large party and rather an ill-assorted

one,' commented Hamilton on a visit in July 1894, 'Of course it is difficult to manage to get together always people who are friends. But he might ask people more in sets than he does.' Ferdinand's 'sets' were principally four, all of which overlapped considerably: Rothschilds, both from England and abroad; the circle around the Prince of Wales; his political acquaintances; and the group of aristocratic and aesthetic friends known as the Souls.

Of Ferdinand's own family, the chief member was his sister Alice, his companion and hostess at Waddesdon. A major gap in our knowledge of their lives is the lack of anything to document this central relationship. It was the custom for house parties at Waddesdon to visit Alice's 'pavilion' at Eythrope, as described by Mary Gladstone on her 1885 visit: 'After luncheon drove to Alice de Rothschild's place 4 miles off for tea. This quite small, but a model of comfort and everything in it a gem of its kind, the garden beautifully arranged, all the farm buildings and stables etc, perfect, but she never sleeps there and it felt a waste. In a steam launch, rather absurd, to see the tea house, up a wee stream widened by her to hold the boat.' Other visitors were more readily pleased: to Hamilton, Eythrope was 'a charming little place—a sort of magnified and very substantial tea house in a beautifully bright and beautifully kept garden'. Ferdinand and Alice's brothers and sisters do not seem to have been frequent visitors to Waddesdon, although Nathaniel, Albert, and Hannah signed the visitors' book on a couple of occasions, and Salomon's wife, Bettina, a Rothschild by birth, came several times by herself. By the time Waddesdon and Eythrope were completed, most of Alice and Ferdinand's English uncles and aunts had died, and so domestic social life revolved around the cousins who had inherited the Buckinghamshire estates. Their uncle Mayer, the builder of Mentmore, had died in 1874, bequeathing his wealth to his only child, Hannah, who married Rosebery four years later. Anthony had died in 1876, and Aston Clinton was now the home of his eldest daughter, Constance, and her husband, Cyril Flower, a Liberal MP who was raised to the peerage as Lord Battersea in 1892. Rosebery, Hannah and Constance were close friends of both Ferdinand and Alice, but Ferdinand's relationships with the sons of his uncle Lionel, who had died in 1879, were more ambivalent. He never really got on with Natty, who inherited his father's estate at Tring, although they saw more of each other after Ferdinand had entered parliament. Leopold, who lived at Ascott, was more congenial. He combined a mild interest in the arts—he bought sporting pictures by Stubbs and others—with a passion for the turf and was twice winner of the Derby.

Closest to Ferdinand in temperament and interests was Lionel's second son, Alfred, although his career as the builder of Halton and the greatest collector of his generation of English Rothschilds added an element of competitiveness to the relationship, exacerbated by his (not entirely deserved) reputation as an effete and rather dissipated bachelor, which at times made him seem almost a caricature of Ferdinand. Alfred had little of his cousin's shy and fastidious nature; he was a show-off who enjoyed entertaining his guests with a miniature circus, with himself dressed as the circus master. When the Countess of Warwick visited Halton in 1884 for its inaugural house party, she was amused by an acrobatic performance by 'a number of small Japanese dogs'. Ferdinand was not to be outdone, and Waddesdon's guests were in future treated to the sight of his beloved poodle Poupon performing jumps over a course set up in the East Gallery. However, he never tried to imitate the sort of sporting facilities—from a skittle alley and skating rink to an indoor swimming pool—that made Alfred's house comparable to a Long Island mansion. Lady Warwick remarked that it was at Halton that 'I saw Baron Ferdinand de Rothschild at a disadvantage for the only time in my life. He was really jealous of his cousin, because he feared that Halton would rob him of his house-parties. He was critical, and even found fault. Mr. Alfred was the more accomplished host, but Waddesdon was the more attractive home, and I do not think there was any real danger that the one cousin would deprive the other of his friends.'

Lady Warwick was a popular guest at Waddesdon for she made life more agreeable for the house's most distinguished regular visitor, the Prince of Wales, whose mistress she was. Rather surprisingly, Ferdinand was an inner member of the Prince of Wales's fashionable and fast-living circle, although superficially the two had nothing in common: Ferdinand had little interest in racing or gambling, was not known to pursue pretty women and was a teetotaller with a poor digestion, whereas the Prince—nicknamed 'Tum Tum'—was a celebrated trencherman. Their friendship was a tribute to the prince's broad-minded social outlook: as the Prince's biographer Philip Magnus explains it, 'As social phenomena, the Rothschilds' quizzical detachment from the familiar European class pattern fascinated the Prince, who relished their cosmopolitan

ABOVE: *Henry Taylor, Ferdinand's valet from 1887 until his dismissal by Alice the day after her brother's death in 1898. Ferdinand depended absolutely upon Taylor, who accompanied him on all his travels, including voyages on the steam yacht,* Rona.

OPPOSITE: *The south front of Halton House, designed by William Rogers for Alfred de Rothschild, 1881.*

outlook, public spirit, geniality and panache, as well as their generosity and the invaluable advice and help which they gave.' The family had known the Prince since 1861, when he was introduced to Natty while both were at Cambridge. He shared the younger Rothschilds' passion for the turf and joined them at the Derby in 1864; within a few years he was hunting with the Rothschild staghounds at Mentmore. Ferdinand and Alice had known him since at least 1872, when he invited them to a royal garden party and in March 1875 he stayed with them at Leighton Buzzard for a day's hunting. He thoroughly enjoyed the luxurious comforts of the Rothschilds' country houses, and soon made himself at home at Waddesdon, which he visited for the first time in July 1881, causing immense excitement in the neighbourhood. The affectionate friendship that developed between the Prince and Ferdinand suggests that the common perception of Ferdinand as fussy and self-centred cannot have been the entire truth, for the Prince would not have become fond of somebody he considered a bore or a prig. Although there is no evidence that the Prince shared his friend's artistic and intellectual interests, it was at his suggestion that Ferdinand was made a trustee of the British Museum. One mark of their intimacy was that when Ferdinand needed a new valet in 1887, the Prince offered him one of his own, Henry Taylor, who remained in Ferdinand's service until his master's death.

Although the Prince was not entertained at Waddesdon with the actresses and chorus girls whom Alfred invited to Halton, there were always attractive young women to occupy his attention: when Hamilton attended a party at Waddesdon for the Prince in July 1894 he noted that the Prince was 'in good humour . . . The lady to whom most attention is shown is Mrs Lancelot Lowther—the change of Queens is rapid.' Photographs survive to show how the Prince enjoyed himself at Waddesdon, with the intervals between meals being taken up in summer by the newly fashionable game of lawn tennis on the avenue leading up to the entrance front. Here Ferdinand erected a tent, which, according to *The Daily Telegraph* 'serves as a smoking-room or summer lounge for the Baron's bachelor guests . . . charmingly decorated in a semi-Eastern fashion with shawls, tapestry and Persian rugs, and . . . covered with azaleas and bright flowers'. Yet there were more serious reasons for the pleasure

ABOVE: *The Prince of Wales falling down the West Staircase at Waddesdon, as imagined by Max Beerbohm. The final scene shows the injured Prince listening to divine service by theatrophone, while perusing* Sporting Life.

OPPOSITE: *The West Staircase. Its dramatic sweep gives visitors unexpected views down into the West Hall.*

the Prince took in Waddesdon and Ferdinand's friends, for it was an opportunity to make the sort of political contacts that compensated for his mother's obstinate refusal to give him access to state papers. In May 1885 Ferdinand provided the social setting in which Hamilton, Gladstone's principal private secretary, raised with Sir Henry Ponsonby, the Queen's private secretary, a proposal that the Prince should be sent minutes of cabinet meetings. Although Gladstone was happy to oblige, the Queen was not: 'she is very jealous of anything tending to derogate her Sovereign powers', wrote Hamilton in his diary.

The Prince's last visit to the house, in July 1898, was the first occasion when Waddesdon made headlines in the newspapers, for on his way down to breakfast, the Prince slipped on the west stairs and broke his knee. Even today, villagers in Waddesdon will tell visitors to the house that he fell while pursuing a housemaid along the corridor, a story that may go back to the 1890s, but since the accident happened at 10 o'clock in the morning, it can probably be discounted. Lord Warwick, a fellow guest at the time, recalled in his memoirs how he was summoned from the garden by the butler: 'I hurried into the house, and found the Prince where the butler had left him, sitting on a step of the main circular staircase. He smiled re-assuringly at me, although I could see at a glance that he must be in great pain, and said: "I fear I have broken something in my leg; my foot slipped, and as I fell I heard a bone crack". . . . The Prince was ever the kindliest of men, and his great anxiety was to reassure Baron Ferdinand, who was so grieved to think that he should have met with a serious accident under his roof.' The Prince's patience was further tried by the inexpert attentions of the local doctor and then by another accident when the invalid chair in which he was being carried through Aylesbury station to catch the London train broke under his weight.

Ferdinand made several important friendships through the Prince, most notably with his private secretary, Francis Knollys, and with the worldly and witty Harry Chaplin, later Viscount Chaplin, the Conservative president of the Board of Agriculture (and later of Local Government), whose name appears in the visitors' book 26 times. Most important of all, to judge by their frequent visits, were two of the Prince's most intimate companions, Christopher Sykes and Laurence Oliphant. They made a curious contrast. A Yorkshire landowner, Sykes was a fashionable man about town, whose generous devotion to the Prince and indulgence of his whims eventually brought him close to bankruptcy, leaving him reliant on the generosity of wealthy friends such as Ferdinand. Oliphant, a friend of the Prince's since 1862, was an adventurer who had travelled with Speke

in Africa and had been war correspondent for the *Times* during the Franco-Prussian war. He had the sort of forceful, raffish personality to which Ferdinand always responded, but they may also have had serious interests in common. Oliphant was an ardent campaigner for Jewish liberties, who had personally raised some £100,000 for the relief of Jews in Russia, after the Rothschilds had passed to the *Times* reliable information about the 1881 pogroms there. Oliphant was one of the first to propose Jewish settlement in Palestine, and he personally sounded out the Sultan on the idea. It seems likely that he would have discussed the proposal with Ferdinand, who must surely have contributed to the relief fund. It is possible, therefore, that the thread of Zionist politics so important in Waddesdon's 20th-century history can be traced back as far as Ferdinand's house parties of the 1880s.

In political terms those parties were unusually broad, demonstrated by the fact that although Ferdinand entertained two Liberal prime ministers at Waddesdon—Gladstone and Rosebery—as well as a future Liberal leader, H. H. Asquith, he was on equally good terms with Disraeli and with such Conservative grandees as Lord Randolph Churchill, George Curzon, the future viceroy of India, and Arthur Balfour, nephew of the Conservative leader Lord Salisbury and a future Conservative prime minister himself. The path that was to lead Ferdinand out of the Liberal party was already clear when Gladstone paid his visit in August 1885, two months after his resignation as prime minister. His daughter Mary recalled how 'a deputation came from Aylesbury and the ex-P.M. stood, bowed and looked unutterable things as they poured out upon him every most fervent compliment . . . Baron Ferdinand shaking with nervousness got through all right.' Gladstone noted in his diary that Waddesdon was 'a remarkable construction; no commonplace host'. The house was to play another role in Gladstone's career, although possibly he did not know it, when the Liberal party was returned in 1891 with a slim majority. The Queen loathed Gladstone and talked of persuading Rosebery to form a government in his place. At a house party at Waddesdon on July 17–18, Hamilton was able to exploit Ferdinand's connections with the royal family by discussing the situation with two of his fellow guests, the secretaries of the Prince of Wales and the Queen, Knollys and Ponsonby. He was more successful than he had been with the issue of allowing the Prince of Wales access to cabinet minutes, and the Queen gave way.

By then the whole political landscape had been changed by Gladstone's adoption of a policy of home rule for Ireland. Although, like many Liberals on the right wing of the party, the Rothschilds disliked the policy's threat to the integrity of the United Kingdom, and the implied decentralisation of Westminster's imperial authority, it was Gladstone's attempts to strengthen the position of the Irish tenantry that really alarmed them, since, like many landowners, they feared the extension of this socialist programme to England. 'If I do not call myself a radical', wrote Ferdinand to Sir Charles Dilke in 1885, 'it is that I consider it unworthy . . . to court popularity with the masses by advocating such trivial measures as the abolition of the game laws for instance and stimulating an unhealthy desire for social and pecuniary equality the disastrous results of which have been only too well illustrated in France, instead of governing the people on broad principles and leading them into wider issues'. As a result, he joined forces with Natty and Joseph Chamberlain when the opponents of home rule for Ireland, the Liberal Unionists, made their break from the party in April 1885, a month before the Home Rule Bill was defeated and Gladstone resigned. In the general election that followed, Ferdinand stood as a Liberal Unionist and gained an increased majority. Although it had been at a Waddesdon house party that the possibility of the Liberal Unionists joining forces with the Conservatives had first been mooted, the Rothschilds were rapidly disillusioned with the new coalition government, disliking the way it imposed coercive measures on Ireland. They hoped for a Liberal leader to succeed Gladstone who would abandon home rule and restore party unity, but when he emerged in the form of their cousin-by-marriage Lord Rosebery, who became prime minister in 1894, they were disappointed. Rosebery's lack of sympathy with the increasingly radical tone of his party prompted his retirement from the leadership after only two years and the Rothschilds were left with no alternative but an ever-closer alliance with the Conservatives, to which Ferdinand would surely have gravitated had he lived longer.

Natty's famously close friendship with Arthur Balfour, who succeeded Lord Salisbury as Conservative prime minister in 1902, can in part be traced back to Balfour's pre-eminence among the Souls. The fourth of Ferdinand's 'sets', the Souls may have been a coterie, but they were as broad in their political sympathies as the house parties at Waddesdon in which they participated so fully, for they ranged from Balfour and Curzon to the daughters of the Liberal MP Sir Charles Tennant, all celebrated beauties, one of whom, Margot, married Asquith. The Souls coalesced as a group in the late 1880s, and received their name in 1888 after a teasing remark by Lord Charles

Beresford about their soulful highmindedness. Their character has been memorably described by Algernon Cecil: 'Free from any disastrous exclusiveness either social or conversational, interested in really interesting things, alive to the claims of art and not dead to those of morals, blending politics with fashion and fashion with philanthropy, they contrived to sacrifice to Beauty, Truth, and Goodness against a background of West-end dinner parties and great English country houses.' That lack of exclusiveness helps to explain the friendship of so many Souls with Ferdinand. Although, on the whole, they disliked racing and favoured abstemiousness, some, most notably Lord and Lady Desborough, were also companions of the Prince of Wales; some members of the Prince's set, notably Lady Warwick and Harry Chaplin, both good friends of Ferdinand, were close to the Souls' circle, if not quite part of it.

Ferdinand would have appreciated the contrast between the Souls' artistic milieu and the philistine heartiness of so much late-19th-century aristocratic society, which he regretted: 'the taste for old art which for so long prevailed among most members of the great houses of this country has now almost vanished. Not a few who might have preserved their heirlooms, parted with them to purchase race-horses or yachts, or to indulge in the fashionable amusements of the day. Prevalent as it at present is, the mania for old art has shifted from the descendants of the old to the founders of the new families'. Despite their artistic interests, the Souls bore out this analysis, for almost none was a serious collector in the way the Rothschilds understood the term; the major exception was Viscount Windsor, but his tastes tended towards early Italian pictures, which were not an interest of Ferdinand's. Although Sir Charles Tennant, founder of a 'new family', was a significant collector of 18th-century English pictures, none of his children followed his example. The Souls favoured contemporary English painting and sculpture: they were patrons of Edward Burne-Jones and G.F. Watts and friends of Alfred Gilbert, whereas Ferdinand had no interest in modern art, even though one of his cousins, Blanche FitzRoy, a frequent guest at Waddesdon, had married Sir Coutts Lindsay, founder of the Grosvenor Gallery, a celebrated home of avant-garde English art, and of Burne-Jones in particular. It was only in the more general appreciation of harmonious and artistic interiors that Ferdinand's aesthetic interests compared with those of the Souls.

It was through Waddesdon's international links, not through Ferdinand's friendships among the British aristocracy, that the house was to be an influence in artistic terms. Ferdinand was a good friend of the secretary to the American legation in London, Henry White, a frequent visitor to Waddesdon in the 1880s and early 1890. He may have provided introductions for the American plutocrats and their families who stayed with Ferdinand, including Winthrop Rutherford and William Waldorf Astor, whose families were to develop the Rothschild taste into the next century. In 1883, Waddesdon was visited by Alva Vanderbilt and her daughter Consuelo, who knew Ferdinand's friend Lady Paget, a New York heiress who had been born Minnie Stevens. Alva was the wife of W. K. Vanderbilt, whose Fifth Avenue mansion by Richard Morris Hunt so closely paralleled Waddesdon in taste; Consuelo was in due course married off to the 9th Duke of Marlborough, and it was her influence that brought French interior decorators and a French landscape designer to remodel Blenheim Palace and its gardens. Tantalisingly, there is no evidence in the Waddesdon guest book for the often-repeated story that the house was visited by W. K. Vanderbilt's brother George, who is said to have been taken there by Hunt to look for models for the country house he was planning to build in North Carolina. Yet Biltmore, begun in 1889, seems in so many ways a great architect's homage to Waddesdon, in its French 16th-century idiom and overpowering luxury. After a mid-winter visit to Biltmore's 'polar rigour' in 1905 Henry James described the house as 'a thing of the high Rothschild manner, but of a size to contain two or three Mentmores and Waddesdons'. Moreover, Vanderbilt's employment of Frederick Lee Olmsted to transform the bleak fields around the house into an English landscape park, complete with village and parish church, closely parallels Ferdinand's carving of a model estate out of the bare Buckinghamshire landscape.

The international flavour in Waddesdon's guest lists was enhanced by visits from Continental royalty, so assiduously cultivated by the Rothschilds. While still based at Leighton, Ferdinand entertained the former King and Queen of Naples, and in 1876 he was visited there by the Empress Elisabeth of Austria, who was a good friend of his family—his brother Salbert broke the news to her of the suicide of her son, Crown Prince Rudolph, at Mayerling, and it was while she was leaving Geneva after a visit to Ferdinand's sister Julie at Pregny that the empress was assassinated by an Italian anarchist in 1898. No doubt at her request, Ferdinand entertained Rudolph with a dance at his house in Piccadilly, to which every fashionable beauty of the day was summoned. To set off his white Louis XVI ballroom, Ferdinand offered a dozen of his female guests new dresses from Doucet. One of them, Lillie Langtry, made such an impression on Rudolph that he insisted on dancing with her as much as possible: her embarrassment was compounded by the sweaty handmarks he unapologetically left all over her dress of clinging pink crepe-de-chine. 'Months after', recalled Mrs Langtry, whose memories of Ferdinand were rather waspish, 'the famous couturier sent me the bill for the petticoat (an insignificant one), saying the baron refused to pay it, holding himself responsible for our dresses only. Certainly, at this particular entertainment, credit was done to his white room, all the beauties being present, and looking perfectly gowned.'

Ferdinand's ability to stage-manage social occasions in this way was given its ultimate test in royal visits to Waddesdon. The two that made the greatest impression on his contemporaries could hardly have differed more, for one was designed to entertain the Shah of Persia and the other Queen Victoria herself. Shah Nasru'd-Din Mirza visited England in 1889, largely to purchase armaments in Birmingham. A social programme was devised for him by the Prince of Wales, who summoned Rothschild hospitality to his aid, and so it was that after lunch at Halton, the Shah travelled over to Waddesdon for dinner. The newspapers were full of stories about the problems posed to his hosts by his entourage, rumoured to include a favourite Circassian slave girl who dressed as a man, escorted by two eunuchs. At Hatfield, the difficulty of accommodating the Shah's servants, who expected to sleep in the corridors outside their master's room, drove the Marchioness of Salisbury to distraction, and she no doubt tipped the Rothschilds off about the problems they would encounter. Ferdinand took the precaution of assembling an entirely male house party. They included General Sir Garnet Wolseley, hero of the Ashanti wars, who wrote gloomily to his wife that even 'the gentle Alice' had thought it wise to stay away: 'The housemaids, Ferdinand R. tells me, are ugly on purpose to put

temptation away from these horrid-looking Persians'. According to the *Buckinghamshire Herald*, 'All the guests met [the Shah] at the gate when he arrived from Halton late on Tuesday evening, and it was a quarter to nine before the superb dinner of 42 covers was served. The table was covered with pink and crimson roses, and every menu was

ABOVE: *Empress Elisabeth of Austria. Ferdinand's attachment to his Viennese origins remained warm, and he entertained members of the Imperial family at Waddesdon, in London and on his yacht.*

OPPOSITE: *This is the 1774 elephant automaton and music box by Martinet whose rotating trunk and tail, as well as oscillating trees and flowers, so entranced the Shah of Persia in July 1889.*

headed by an excellent vignette of the house. The Shah sat in the centre, with Baron Ferdinand on his left and Prince Albert Victor on his right. The Blue Hungarians played during the dinner.' The newspaper report does not reveal the real reason for the delay in serving dinner, which was the Shah's sulking retreat to his bedroom when he discovered that the Prince of Wales would not be present, although he had sent his two sons, Albert (later the Duke of Clarence) and George (later George V) in his place. He was drawn out only by the promise of an entertainment after dinner by a conjurer, Charles Bertram. This performance was a great success, and was followed by tricks by Poupon, who obediently jumped over hurdles and flags. The Shah's tour of the house and grounds the next morning was hampered by bad weather, but he was especially delighted with the performance of Waddesdon's celebrated 18th-century automaton in the form of a jewelled elephant, which had to be wound and rewound so many times that eventually, in the tactful words of *The Buckinghamshire Herald*, 'it became necessary to distract his Majesty's attention from a curiosity of considerable historical interest.'

In 1888, at an audience at Windsor with the Empress Frederick of Germany, Queen Victoria's eldest daughter, Ferdinand was considerably taken aback when she casually announced that her mother would like to pay a visit to Waddesdon. The Queen, by then aged 69 and very set in her ways, did not make frequent visits, and the newspapers could think of no other occasion when she had been entertained by an unmarried man in this way. She was also usually wary of her eldest son's choice of friends, but the fame of Waddesdon and Ferdinand's

charm were enough to arouse her ever-alert curiosity, especially as he had entertained the Emperor and Empress Frederick there in 1887 while they were in England for the Queen's golden jubilee. 'For some considerable time', recalled Ferdinand in an account he wrote of the royal visit, which eventually took place on May 14, 1890, 'the best part of my day was employed in exchanging notes and telegrams with Sir Henry Ponsonby; settling the hour of Her Majesty's departure from and arrival at Windsor and Waddesdon respectively; the list of guests, the number of carriages and the servants, and last but not least, the etiquette that was to be observed on the occasion.' It was an encounter full of potential pitfalls, but everything proceeded smoothly, marred only by a *faux-pas* by one of Ferdinand's guests, the Marquess of Hartington, who instead of kissing the Queen's hand when they were introduced, absent-mindedly shook it warmly, so offending the Queen that she kept her hand to herself for the rest of the day. Having arrived with her daughter Princess Beatrice in time for lunch, she was received by Alice and another daughter, Princess Louise, who was staying at Waddesdon, while, as Ferdinand put it, 'the other guests were, by command, locked up in the adjacent drawing rooms'. The Small Library had been converted into a dressing room for the Queen, and once she had finished there, she went into the Dining Room for lunch, where she was accompanied solely by members of her own family, while Ferdinand and his guests ate in the Breakfast Room. 'That she lunched alone with members of her family, instead of lunching with us, has been commented on in society—but without reason', wrote Ferdinand. 'The proposal that she should do so emanated from me, as I was well aware, not only of her disinclination to take her midday meal in the company of strangers, but of the invariable rule, which she never breaks, of so doing .' After her customary hearty meal—the Queen was served consommé, followed by trout, pullet and quail, beef (of which she had two helpings), duckling with ortolans and asparagus, and finally 'Beignets a la Viennoise' and 'Petites Souffles a la Royale'—Ferdinand introduced her to the other guests and showed her some of his treasures in the Tower Drawing Room: 'I showed her a large miniature picture, representing my Grandfather and Grandmother with their seven children, with whose intricate relationship and marriages she was thoroughly conversant. She told me that she particularly remembered my Grandfather, and on my expressing some surprise, seeing that he died in 1836, she said, with one of those charming smiles of which no one has the secret better than Her Majesty and her children, 'Why not? I was then eighteen years of age'. The Queen was also struck by the newly installed electric

light, and the specially made lights for the chandeliers which were designed to look like candles: according to *The Buckinghamshire Herald*, she 'had the room especially darkened so that she might better witness the effect'.

After that, the Queen retired upstairs for a nap in the State Bedroom—she used the stairs, although Ferdinand had had an elevator installed for the occasion—while her host smoked a cigar on the terrace, throwing it away unfinished when his family protested it would make him smell of tobacco. He was then summoned up to the Green Boudoir so that he could present the Queen with a memento of her visit in the form of an 18th-century fan set with diamonds which he had bought the day before from a visiting German dealer: 'I delivered a harangue worthy of an Elizabethan courtier, and having received the Queen's acceptance of the present, I knelt on one knee and handed it to her.' After that, Ferdinand escorted the Queen on a tour of the grounds in her own pony-carriage, brought down to Waddesdon for the occasion. She planted a pine tree in the garden, and Ferdinand was amused to note behind the bushes an artist from the *Illustrated London News* making sketches of the occasion. This had been arranged in advance, and the fully illustrated account of the royal visit which subsequently appeared suggests that Ferdinand was well aware of the power of what we now call public relations in establishing his position in society. During a tour of the stables and glasshouses, which was followed by tea in the oriental tent on the tennis lawn in front of the house (with music from a military band), he took the opportunity for private conversation with the Queen about international politics and their mutual acquaintances among the royal families of Europe.

The visit was clearly a great success: the Queen reported in a letter to the Empress Frederick that she thought 'the position, view, approach are all beautiful and I think the style of the house— a real French chateau—so fine', perceptively adding that 'the interior reminds one of Eu and St Cloud etc, and again bits of Cliveden'. Waddesdon does indeed combine the romantic profile of Napoleon III's Eu with the 17th-century classicism of St- Cloud and the modern luxury of Cliveden in Buckinghamshire, which then belonged to the Duke of Sutherland. But the Queen was probably paying a greater tribute to Ferdinand when she commented that her visit 'was all very well and quietly managed'. However, although requests came from Windsor for more information about the dishes served at lunch and the royal librarian asked permission to examine the works of art, Ferdinand was expecting something more: 'Beyond a formal letter of thanks through Ponsonby he had no recognition of it; but he hears today that a bust of H.M. is on its way', wrote Hamilton in his diary. 'I think he is somewhat disappointed; though an autograph letter, which she certainly might have written, is about the only form which the recognition could have taken.' The miniature bust of the Queen, by J. E. Boehm, eventually arrived, and was placed in Ferdinand's sitting room, where it sits amidst the Sèvres and gold boxes like a slice of plum pudding in a French confectioner's shop window. In his account books, Ferdinand added to the record of his spending in 1890, "Queen's visit, £564'.

Not all the entertaining at Waddesdon was private: indeed, the house and grounds were visited by a remarkably large number of people during Ferdinand's lifetime, thanks to his habit of making it available for charitable events and for the annual 'Baron's Treat' for the village and some 1,300 local schoolchildren. Originally a modest picnic in the garden of the Wilderness, by the 1880s it had become a great festival in Waddesdon's grounds, for which the girls were dressed in scarlet cloaks and hats presented to them every year by Alice. It seems to have been closely based on a similar annual event at Schillersdorf, for in September 1865 Ferdinand's wife Evelina reported to her mother that they had spent the day at a great party for all the local schoolchildren in the park, when all the estate staff had been served a dinner of sausages and beer. At Waddesdon's treats, the children met at the entrance gates and formed a procession which walked up to the house, preceded by a band from the local militia, until, as *The Buckinghamshire Herald* recorded, 'reaching the grassy plateau where the

Queen Victoria planting a fir tree in the Waddesdon tradition for distinguished visitors, from the London Illustrated News, *May 14, 1890. Presentation spades made for these occasions now hang in the Kitchen Corridor. The grove of trees includes some planted by recent prime ministers, as well as royalty.*

LIFE AT WADDESDON 1880–1898

ABOVE: *Preparations for the Baron's Treat, an annual summer party that Ferdinand and Alice hosted for local children and their families.*

OPPOSITE ABOVE: *The Earl of Carmarthen, Ferdinand and Poupon at Miramar, Palma, while enjoying a cruise on the* Rona, *1897–98.*

OPPOSITE BELOW: *The deck saloon on the* Rona *, 1897.*

6th Earl Spencer, who accompanied Ferdinand on his Mediterranean trip. On New's Year Eve, they were in Marseilles: 'Played patience after Ferdy had read to me his story which I liked as it is original in its development . . . Squalls every minute—after luncheon Ferdy went to take flowers to the Empress of Austria . . . I landed and walked . . . through slums after climbing many steps to the new cathedral overlooking the other harbour Cathedral enormous Byzantine style, rather fine from its size . . . Four officers from the Empress of Austria's yacht came to tea. Only 2 spoke English at all fluently, so conversation was restricted. They were much struck by the engines aboard this yacht.'

marquees were erected, and which commands a magnificent view of the surrounding scenery, they were disbanded and in the twinkling of an eye the swingboats, roundabout, and Punch & Judy show were literally besieged with eager customers'. Ferdinand made a welcoming speech from the grandstand roof of the cricket pavilion and 'in the cool of the evening dancing was indulged in, the Baron himself participating in the enjoyable pastime. Several prizes were given during the afternoon for running, jumping and other competitions among the schoolchildren, and the party broke up with hearty cheers for the Baron'. The casual dress adopted by Ferdinand deceived some of his visitors on these occasions, and he enjoyed telling the story of how he was accosted by one man who told him to 'get off the grass, and don't smoke your pipe, it ain't allowed'.

Ferdinand's social life was not confined to Waddesdon, for in 1897 he acquired a steam yacht, the 1025-ton *Rona*, which he used to entertain friends on cruises. The early months of 1898 were spent in the Mediterranean, stopping off to look for antiquities to buy, and in the summer he took a party to Holland, to attend the ceremony in Amsterdam to proclaim the new queen, Wilhelmina. A flavour of life on board the *Rona* is given by the diary of Charles Spencer, the future

Although Ferdinand's friends no doubt took for granted the wealth that provided their entertainment at Waddesdon and on the *Rona*, and would have thought it vulgar and impolite to ask how much it all cost, historians are not so bound. The survival of Ferdinand's private account books for the years after 1882 makes it possible to estimate his spending on entertaining and on the running of Waddesdon and its estate. His summary accounts for his household expenditure give only the chef's bills as a separate item, so it is not always possible to explain monthly fluctuations in the amounts, but over the years a clear pattern emerges. Running the household, including servants' wages and the stables, cost on average £10,000 a year. When he was not entertaining, the monthly expenditure was usually in the range of £400–£500. There was always a large payment in April, before the beginning of the season: £1,185 in 1892 and £1,399 in 1893, for example, and this was presumably to get the house ready for guests. Between May and September, expenditure was at its height. In July 1893, for example, after he had entertained an unprecedented 67 guests in the preceding month, the bills amounted to £2,303. Expenditure tails off for the rest of the year, apart from December, when annual salaries were paid. There is evidence that some guests were more costly to entertain than others: in October 1892, for example, there is a puzzlingly high payment of £1,085, although only 16 guests were entertained: a glance at the visitor's book reveals that the Prince of Wales had come for the shooting.

Ferdinand's records of his estate expenditure are more detailed, and included payments for building, furnishing and decorating work. The accounts open while the construction of the house and

grounds was being completed: in 1882 he spent £118,000 on Waddesdon, and in 1883 the highest sum of all, £120,000. Once work was over, the total amount then decreases steadily to £30,990 in 1895 and £33,161 in 1896, although there were three years of exceptional expense—1887, when he paid for the building of the village club and bought more land (£63,000); 1890, when the Morning Room wing was added (£68,000) and 1894, when the Smoking Room suite was remodelled (£47,300). So had Ferdinand lived longer, it seems likely that his expenditure on Waddesdon would have settled down to an average of between £30,000 and £35,000, well under half of his annual income of £80,000–£100,000, and so leaving plenty of spare cash for works of art, the *Rona* and his house in Piccadilly.

Since he kept these accounts in note form, it is not always possible to work out what individual payments were for, but certain facts emerge clearly. The first is what seems to us the extraordinarily low cost of labour, especially in relation to the high expense of technology, a complete inversion of twenty-first century economics. Maintaining a household staff of 24 cost Ferdinand comfortably less than £1,000 a year in salaries, although they received the additional benefits that made employment in a household such as Waddesdon so eagerly sought after: as well as free food, accommodation, and (where appropriate) livery, they received money for their board when he was not in residence and traditional perquisites such as cast-off clothes and partly used candles. In contrast, the cost of electrifying the house was substantial: between 1888 and 1890 Ferdinand spent over £4,000 in having it installed. Even though the largest single payment was always for estate labour—£7,426 in 1894, for example—taking an average salary of £35, which is almost certainly an overestimate for this sort of largely unskilled labour, Ferdinand could have commanded an estate workforce of 212. The real figure is likely to have been closer to 300.

It is clear that the garden was scarcely less expensive to maintain than the house. The glasshouses alone demanded a constant large annual outlay: in 1896, for example, new glass, repairs to old glass and repainting cost £4,408. The menagerie and Aviary were not cheap either: in 1897 Ferdinand spent £567 on them, more than half of what he spent on new trees and plants (£947). Payments for orchids are, however, listed separately, and usually range between £350 and £450. There are plenty of intriguing details: the tea tent on the front lawn cost £415 in 1887, the Aviary an astonishing £7,726 in 1889—unfortunately, there is no clue about its provenance, only that its construction was overseen by the groundsman, Mr Sherwin. Carriage and horse hire were an additional large expense—£1,273 in 1897, for example.

No less striking than the amount Ferdinand paid out to run the estate is the amount he made from it. When he bought Waddesdon it was estimated that its rental value was some £6,000. That was before the agricultural depression set in, yet even so it is a shock to learn that after his enormous expenditure on improving the estate, Ferdinand's income from Waddesdon had declined to £4,450 in 1896, the first year for which a figure is available. In 1897, this income had risen to £6,042, which consisted of £2,642 from the sale of cattle and the prizes he won at agricultural shows, £600 for 'sundries'—probably the sale of surplus produce—and only £2,860 from rents. In other words, after 25 years and an expenditure of well over £1 million, Waddesdon was producing a rental of less than half of what it had done when Ferdinand bought the estate. By 1897, the estate's revenue was barely a fifth of what it cost to run it. This emphasises how different Waddesdon was from the traditional country house, which relied on agricultural income for its maintenance. It remains a central fact of Waddesdon's existence that it has never paid for itself. In 1898, although we know that Ferdinand's thoughts often turned to the future of his creation, that cannot have seemed too pressing a problem. The visitors would keep on coming and the Rothschilds would foot the bill and the only possible criticism could be the one noted by Gladstone's secretary, Algernon West, in his diary after a visit in 1897, that Waddesdon and Eythrope were 'too perfect—if that is possible'. But how long would it last? That was a question which had to be faced with tragic suddenness. On Saturday December 17, 1898, Hamilton wrote in grief in his diary: 'A horrible rumour reached me today between one and two o'clock—that poor Ferdie Rothschild has died.'

OPPOSITE: *The Dairy Garden, Rock Walk and Rose Garden were praised by* Country Life *in 1898 for their 'glorious ironwork' and beds 'filled with the most effective and glorious of summer plants.' The gardens at Waddesdon were considered 'a precious adornment to be itself adorned' and 'ranking among the most splendid in England.'*

ABOVE: *Ferdinand Rothschild in his London house, seated in a Louis XVI chair of the 1780s. The eighteenth-century French panelling, probably from the Hôtel Thiroux de Lailly, Paris, is now at Waddesdon.*

6

ALICE

FERDINAND'S DEATH CAME AS A SEVERE SHOCK to his family and friends, although it had been preceded by a period of worse than usual ill health. 'It appears that on Thursday he was seized with sudden pains in the chest and the left arm', wrote Edward Hamilton in his diary on December 17. 'He … was easier yesterday and after a good night felt so much better this morning that he was able to read his letters and newspapers and to despatch telegrams. A little before 11 o'clock, he ordered a hot bath to be got ready for him, and though his servant demurred he insisted on having it. Finding the bath did not suit him, he did not remain in it and no sooner had he got out than he fainted. There was no sigh or moan and by the time he had been put back to bed life was extinct. There is something rather sublime as well as truly sad about his dying in solitude as he had lived in solitude at Waddesdon within the walls of his magnificent abode.' The death certificate gives the cause of death as 'syncope', a sudden rise in blood pressure; that, and the symptoms Ferdinand had experienced, suggest a heart attack. 'It is astounding how the doctors failed to notice anything wrong with his heart', mused Hamilton, 'or how its action could have been so suddenly stopped without there being something more than mere exhaustion.' However, since Ferdinand was notorious for ignoring medical advice, despite seeking it after the merest twinge, it seems unlikely that his doctors could have helped even if his heart condition had been detected. The only witness to Ferdinand's death was his devoted steward and manservant, Henry Taylor, who was immediately dismissed, much

Alice Charlotte de Rothschild (1847–1922), Ferdinand's youngest sister, who inherited Waddesdon upon Ferdinand's death.

to his distress, leaving him feeling that he was being held to blame. Taylor's sons never forgot their father's employer and after Waddesdon opened to the public the eldest, Walter, made an annual pilgrimage there until he died in the late 1960s.

Preparations for the funeral were delayed until Salbert's arrival from Vienna. It was to be a major Rothschild conclave, attended by Ferdinand's relatives from France and Germany, as well as England and Austria. Although the Jewish cemetery at West Ham had been closed for some years, it was opened so that Ferdinand could be buried in Evelina's mausoleum, which he had visited only a week before to lay flowers there on the anniversary of her death. 'The family gave out that they wished no-one to attend the actual interment', wrote Hamilton, 'but I felt so strongly that he would have liked some of his real friends to be present that last night I wrote to Leo R[othschild] and begged to be allowed to find my own way there in company with Francis Knollys and R[ochfort] Maguire, who were as anxious to go as I was. . . . Only the family and servants followed the body; but Bobby Spencer and Algy Lennox also found their way down there, of their own account . . . At 4 o'clock I went to the Memorial Service held at the Synagogue in Great Portland Street . . . there was not a spare seat in the building . . . The Prince of Wales and the chief mourners sat on a sort of dais underneath the raised platform where the Rabbis conducted the service . . . the Chief Rabbi delivered an address at the end in remarkably good taste. Poor Ferdie R. would I am sure have been highly gratified, had he been able to witness the striking ceremony in his honour.' The Prince of Wales's presence at a Jewish service, although not unprecedented, drew a great deal of comment contrasting the position of Jews in England with the hostility they faced in France, then convulsed by the Dreyfus affair: 'What strikes me more than anything else', wrote Henry James to the French novelist Paul Bourget, who had once accompanied him to a house party at Waddesdon, 'is the difference between English and French nerves by the fact that the Crown Prince (by whom I mean of course the Prince of Wales) assisted yesterday, with every demonstration of sympathy, at [Ferdinand's] severely simple Jewish obsequies.' That afternoon, London's hansom-cab drivers tied black crepe to their whips with ribbons in the Rothschild blue and yellow.

No sooner was the funeral over than speculation began in public about Waddesdon's future. The newspapers canvassed a wide range of candidates as Ferdinand's heir, from his dashingly good-looking nephew Georg, Salbert's eldest son, who was then an undergraduate at Cambridge, to one of Rosebery's sons or even the

Duke of York, the future George V. But Henry James was sounder in his prediction when he wondered 'what is to become of [Ferdinand's] great cold impossible palace—but of course the Rothschild abyss is big enough to absorb it to the very last racoon.' Ferdinand's heir was his sister Alice. She inherited not only Waddesdon, but also the Leighton estate and his house in Piccadilly, although its contents were largely bequeathed to other members of the family. In addition, she was left the money in his accounts with the English and French branches of the bank and an annuity of £24,000 a year. His other brothers and sisters and some of his cousins were left works of art, and his cousin Alfred received £150,000, a rather puzzling legacy which may suggest that Ferdinand's jealousy of his cousin's social successes concealed real affection. The servants were all left a year's wages, as was customary. There was also a private letter attached to the will with further instructions for Alice: this may have included a request that she destroy his private papers, bequeathed to her, for almost nothing of them has ever come to light.

Although Ferdinand had made various small legacies to his close friends, he left nothing to the Prince of Wales, which seems to have been the cause of some hurt feelings. It was hinted to Alice that she might like to make the Prince a gift of one of the treasures at Waddesdon, such as a Romney, but, commented Hamilton, she 'turned a deaf ear entirely and proposed to make over a Leighton to HRH. She ought never to have been put in the position of having to refuse. Though occasionally she makes handsome presents, she is by nature very close and hates spending money.' The Prince, not one to take offence, pressed her in addition to erect a memorial to Ferdinand, but this too met with a rebuff. As Hamilton recorded, 'I heard yesterday from Rosebery to whom I write (by desire) about the idea of a Ferdie Rothschild memorial. He is strongly against it. Wren's famous epitaph "si monumentum requiris circumspice" was, he thought, so applicable to Ferdie that nothing more was needed. He says one might as well put up a little tablet to connect the Escurial with Philip II as to erect something to connect Waddesdon with its founder.'

It might have been added that Ferdinand had in any case created his own monument by his most unexpected legacy, the gift to the British Museum of 'the principal works of art in the new Smoking Room at Waddesdon'. He requested that they should be kept together in the museum in a room set aside for their display as 'The Waddes-

OPPOSITE: Evelina's mausoleum, designed by Sir Matthew Digby Wyatt in 1866. Ferdinand's body was interred here in 1898.

don Bequest'. Exactly as he had predicted in his memoirs, Waddesdon's collection had proved to be the intermediate stage between the princely courts for which so many of the works had been created, and the democratic world of the museum. The gift also enabled the estate to meet some of the tax liability created by the recent changes to the law governing death duties. Inspiration for this generous gesture probably owes something to two events in the year preceding Ferdinand's will, drawn up in October 1897. The first was the announcement of Lady Wallace's bequest to the nation of the contents of Hertford House, which were to form the Wallace Collection, and the second was the duc d'Aumale's gift to the Institut de France of his estate and château at Chantilly. The collecting careers of the Marquess of Hertford, Sir Richard Wallace, and the duc d'Aumale had developed so closely in parallel to Ferdinand's that it would have been surprising if he had not been influenced by the fate of their creations. If he had lived longer, and seen a future in which country houses opened to the public as a matter of course, it is possible that one day he might have contemplated Waddesdon itself becoming a museum, like Hertford House and Chantilly. 'Collectors may deplore the fact but it should be a source of gratification to the public', he wrote, 'that most fine works of art drift slowly but surely into museums and public galleries. In private hands they can afford delight only to a small number of persons.'

Waddesdon was a formidable inheritance, but its heir, as Ferdinand surely realised, was more than capable of taking it on. It was very rare for a woman to have independent control of an estate on this scale, unless she were a widow or, like Hannah at Mentmore, an only child. Even with a widow or an heiress, there would almost always be an entail governing the estate's future, so their control over it would not be absolute. The closest contemporary comparison with Alice's situation was probably Emily Meynell Ingram's inheritance in 1871 of her husband's estates at Temple Newsam in Yorkshire and elsewhere, which were unentailed, since there was no male heir. Mrs Meynell Ingram had an unfettered income equal to Ferdinand's; as with Alice, her success in administering her inheritance was achieved at the expense of a reputation as a hard and masculine personality. Alice's character had been tempered by her mother's early death, when she was only 12, and her father's emotional detachment from his children. She was brought up by one of her older sisters, Hannah, who had married their cousin Wilhelm. Once Alice was old enough to travel independently, she left their affectionate but austere

Snuff boxes and rings decorated with miniatures painted by the Van Blarenberghes. Two-thirds of those shown were collected by Alice or inherited from her father.

and religious household for England, to join Ferdinand, accompanied by her constant companion and former governess, Cecile Hofer. Her English relatives contemplated her with pity: 'the poor girl is a real shuttle-cock', wrote her aunt Charlotte, Lionel's wife, 'flung from the home of one compassionate relative, under the roof of some other commiserating friends—and all this flying, travelling, rushing, hurrying work from the south of Germany to the north, from the country to the sea-side, from Imperial Austria to royal Prussia, from Switzerland to Italy, from Silesia to England, because she has no mother to love her—because she has an ugly face, and no husband to fall in love with her'.

The frequent references to Alice's ugliness are not borne out by photographs, at least not to 21st-century eyes, which can appreciate her strong and rather sensual features. Although her sharp intelligence was also probably a disadvantage in the marriage market of the 1860s—Matthew Arnold was impressed by her powers of argument—it was surely not a complete disqualification. It is possible that there was an unspoken reason for her remaining single: she may have been advised that her history of rheumatic fever made it unwise to try to have children. Nonetheless, an independently wealthy, unmarried young woman naturally attracted gossip, and Alice's close acquaintanceship with one of Ferdinand's friends, the radical Liberal politician Sir Charles Dilke, led in the late 1870s to such persistent rumours that they had become engaged that they were forced to end their acquaintance, much to Dilke's regret, for he found her 'a clever and agreeable lady'. In any case, the friendship would probably not have survived the scandal in 1885 that ensued when Dilke was named as a co-respondent in a divorce suit, for after that date his name no longer appears in Waddesdon's visitors' book.

With delight, Alice joined in with her brother's life in the countryside at Leighton and then Waddesdon; she was a fine horsewoman and hunted regularly. She also participated in his social life in London, acting as hostess at his balls, enduring for example the uncouthness of Crown Prince Rudolph, who refused to sit next to her at dinner because he wanted to talk to the far more attractive Lillie Langtry. Gradually she adopted a uniform of spinsterhood: as her cousin Constance recalled,

Mᵉˡˡᵉ C. Fʰ. — vue par derrière prenant une autre vue.

Aoūt 1863.
Chat: de Guill: le Conqué:t.

'she never changed her style of dress summer or winter, that of a tailor-made suit in soft grey cloth, with old-fashioned collars and cuffs, and her head covered by a panama hat'. Her force of personality hardened into a sternness which intimidated even her brother on occasion, for all her undoubted devotion to him, and his letters to Lord Rosebery record at least one major falling out between them. By the time of his death, she was described to Hamilton as 'a regular virago'.

Almost all of the published accounts of Alice's personality record her towards the end of her life, and describe, often with some relish, her intimidating behaviour. Her insistence on complete visual perfection in her surroundings undoubtedly had an inhuman streak. Constance wrote to her mother Louise during a visit to Alice's villa at Grasse in the south of France, 'I was warned by Alice never to put my foot upon the *grass* anywhere in her domain. Fancy, in a fit of abstraction, I did so, right under Alice's eyes, which sent her into a violent passion.' Not surprisingly, Constance found it hard to repress a desire to dance all over the lawn. It was rumoured that Alice had even ordered Queen Victoria off the flowerbeds at Grasse, but although the Queen did indeed privately call her 'the All-Powerful', the story has its origins in Alice widening the garden paths to accommodate the Queen's pony trap. Victor, the 3rd Lord Rothschild, recalled how he had been told what had happened when Edward VII paid a nostalgic visit to Waddesdon: Alice 'being asked by him whether the sunblinds could be raised so that he could see the pictures, replied NO; and . . . a few minutes later, on seeing the monarch touching a fine *bonheur du jour* rapped out: PLEASE KEEP YOUR HANDS OFF THE FURNITURE.' However, there was another side to her, captured for example by Lord Wolseley, the celebrated soldier and reformer of the army, to whom she was always 'the gentle Alice'. He appreciated the company of clever women, and thoroughly enjoyed his visits to her house in France. Like many highly intelligent but undervalued women of her time, she may have flourished more readily in the company of men. 'Her hair is now as white as mine', wrote Wolseley to his wife from Grasse in 1904, 'and she possesses everything this world can provide to make man or woman happy and contented. She is, moreover, clever and highly cultured, and only wants what money cannot provide, namely, good health, and, perhaps, the average allowance of good looks accorded to men and women.'

Dorothy de Rothschild, who married Alice's great-nephew James in 1913, described how an undeniably alarming personality was combined with a good deal of charm: 'she was a sparkling conversationalist and most entertaining, but she had one idiosyncracy which was rather unnerving. Whenever she said something amusing, as often happened, and one laughed, she would round on one, and ask with machine-gun speed "Why do you laugh?"' However, as Dorothy pointed out, Alice's contemporaries were aware of a softer side of her personality, for she was a regular guest at Edward VII and Queen Alexandra's annual children's parties. She was also a loyal and affectionate friend. The celebrated American beauty Mary Sands, a popular member of the Prince of Wales's set, turned to Alice for comfort when her husband, Mahlon Sands, was killed by a fall from his horse in Hyde Park in

1888; Alice gave her a string of pearls as a symbol of their mutual tears. After Mary Sands's equally sudden death in 1896, from heart failure, Alice assumed parental responsibility for the Sands's daughter Ethel, to whom she was a beloved 'Aunt Alice'. Ethel Sands later became a painter and a prominent member of London's artistic bohemia, making her an unlikely charge for Alice, who intervened more than once when Ethel's lesbian relationships seemed likely to cause public scandal.

While Ferdinand was creating Waddesdon, Alice had her own projects, which she pursued with an energy and perfectionism to match her brother's. The death of her father in 1874 left her independently wealthy. Anselm bequeathed her the family's estate at Grüneburg, which she promptly sold to Hannah and Wilhelm, retaining only a sculpture of a rhinoceros which had been in the garden there (and today is at Waddesdon). Having acquired Eythrope, and built the pavilion there and created a model estate, she rapidly laid out a garden which soon became celebrated in horticultural circles. Its 60 acres, overseen by her head gardener, Mr Gibbs, included a lawn extending over 20 acres, which ran down from the pavilion to the River Thame and was studded with flower beds, shrubberies and specimen trees. Around this was an artful juxtaposition of 'wild' gardens—shrubs, ivies and spring bulbs—with formal areas, includ-

OPPOSITE: *Cecile Hofer, Alice's governess and companion, drawn by Alice, August 1863. Miss Hofer was herself an accomplished artist, who painted watercolours of the Rothschild houses she visited with Alice.*

BELOW: *A rhinoceros made from a single piece of white Italian marble, brought by Alice to Waddesdon from her childhood home near Frankfurt.*

ing an Italian and a Dutch garden, a Mexican garden of succulents and a rose garden containing some 300 specimens. There was also a large range of glass houses, built by Halliday's, like those at Waddesdon. She laid out another garden of equally high standard around her house in Grasse, built on land acquired in 1888 and named Villa Victoria after the Queen, whom she entertained there in 1891. Stories of her life at Grasse impressed the novelist Henry James, who wrote in 1894 to Ethel Sands, who had recently stayed at the Villa Victoria, that 'Miss de Rothschild surely is a direct descendant of the Pharaohs, and her work will be the stupefaction of posterity. Very delightful it must be to have a hand in them—or to have at least a foot *on* them, as they seem mainly to be mountain roads and causeways.'

Since she did not sleep at Eythrope, fearing the effect of its riverside setting on her health, Alice had a suite of rooms at Waddesdon on the first floor, above the dining room. It appears that she did not take over Ferdinand's private rooms after his death. Instead she had a work room fitted out next to her bedroom (now the Fountain Bedroom), where she transacted her business with the heads of departments. Another room was set aside to receive tradesmen from outside the estate; Dorothy recalled that before the First World War 'every sort and kind of person used to call to offer her anything from works of art to garden plants'. Although Alice's rooms were dismantled after her death, they are recorded in a remarkable series of colour diascope photographs taken of Waddesdon and Eythrope in about 1910. They show that her taste was very close to Ferdinand's—or, rather, that both were loyal to family traditions. Some of her purchases were of an importance to match his. At the Hamilton Palace sale in 1882 Samuel Wertheimer bought on her behalf (for £2,310)

RIGHT: *The colourful garden and picturesque house of the Head Gardener at Eythrope, Miss Alice's daytime retreat, around 1910. Her visitors strolled around the extensive grounds and took tea at the Tea Pavilion beside the River Thames.*

BELOW: *The Tea Pavilion at Grasse, built in 1893, with its vibrant blue and yellow tiled roof, is all that remains standing on the 135 hectare estate.*

ABOVE: *Dutch silver toys, including a flat iron, rat trap, linen press, chair, cradle, and a boy on a swing. Bought by Alice from the Massey-Mainwaring Sale, March 1907. A contemporary fashion for displaying silver miniatures was shared by many women collectors.*

BELOW: *Louis-Philippe-Joseph, duc d'Orléans, as a child, by François Boucher, 1749. A rare image of eighteenth-century royal babyhood, it was bequeathed to Alice by a cousin..*

OPPOSITE: *A mid-eighteenth-century chest of drawers in blue and white with an entre-lacque frieze and ormolu mounts. Attributed to René Dubois,it is a fine example of Alice's individual taste for painted furniture. It originally stood in her Sitting Room at Waddesdon.*

a commode made by J. H. Riesener for the comtesse de Provence; she also owned two other pieces by Riesener with a royal provenance, a commode and a writing table, both made for Louis XVI's sister Madame Elisabeth. One of Waddesdon's three Savonnerie carpets made for the Grande Galerie of the Louvre was acquired by her. She also bought porcelain with an enthusiasm that matched Ferdinand's. Much of the Meissen in the house was hers, but so too was the Sèvres: her father had bequeathed her a *famille rose* service, and no fewer than 43 of the decorative pieces described by Svend Eriksen in his catalogue of the Waddesdon collection were acquired by Alice, compared with Ferdinand's 31.

It is possible, however, to discern an individual, feminine taste in Alice's collecting, evident for example in Christie's catalogue of the contents of her London house, which were sold after her death. In furniture, her eye was drawn to delicate marquetry (of flowers and musical trophies, in particular) on relatively modest, middle-class Louis XVI pieces. She also had a greater interest than Ferdinand in painted furniture. Like him, she was attracted to 18th-century toys and automata—both bought Swiss birdcage clocks with Meissen figures—but he had no equivalent of the Dutch miniature silver furniture which she arranged in the Green Boudoir. Although her paintings did not match Ferdinand's in quality, they exceeded them in range. Her English pictures were by no means, like his, limited to Reynolds, Gainsborough and Romney, but included a conversation piece by Francis Hayman and portraits by (or attributed to) Sir Peter Lely, Thomas Hudson and Richard Cosway. She had a taste for pastels of pretty women and children, buying works by Daniel Gardner—as did Ferdinand—and John Russell, a taste which the Wertheimers did much to pioneeer. Since we know from his correspondence with Agnew that Ferdinand did not seek portraits of children, he is unlikely to have been attracted by Boucher's enchanting depiction of Philippe, duc d'Orléans at the age of two, which Alice hung in the West Hall after inheriting it from a French cousin, Arthur de Rothschild, in 1903; both Ferdinand and Alice would probably have been surprised to be told that it is now the most popular painting in the house. Alice's tastes were not always predictable. For example, she bought north European paintings with more enthusiasm than Ferdinand. In 1882 she acquired a painting of the *Judgement of Paris,* then attributed to Bartholomeus Spranger but now known to be by the Dutch Mannerist artist Joachim Antonisz Wtewael. Although its jewel-like quality and attribution to a celebrated painter who had worked for Rudolf II make it a characteristic Rothschild trophy, it

possesses a relaxed eroticism that to 19th-century eyes would have confined it to a smoking-room, and so was a surprising acquisition for an unmarried woman. More conventionally feminine, although it was a taste shared by Ferdinand, was her collecting of historic textiles, both European and Middle Eastern. The inventories of her collections at Eythrope reveal her discriminating collecting of Renaissance and baroque embroidery; such treasures as the panels of 14th-century French embroidery now in the Smoking Room at Waddesdon once belonged to her.

Alice's best-known contribution to Waddesdon's collections probably does not reflect an innate enthusiasm, for it was made to fill the gaps in the house left by the departure of the Waddesdon Bequest. She rapidly acquired sufficient Limoges, Venetian glass, and other appropriate pieces to furnish the Smoking Room, although it was not of course possible to assemble anything equivalent to the col-

lection which had left. More challenging was the need to fill the walls of the corridor outside the Smoking Room, where Ferdinand had displayed the armour which was also bequeathed to the British Museum. This was a specialist and expensive field dominated by wealthy collectors such as Sir Richard Wallace, who had made spectacular *en bloc* acquisitions of the collections of the comte de Nieuwerkerke and Sir Samuel Rush Meyrick, paying 400,000 francs for the former alone. With the unveiling of the Wallace Collection in 1900, this was now all on view to the public and may have prompted Alice to seek advice from its Inspector of the Armoury, Sir Francis Laking. Although then only 25, he was the foremost connoisseur of arms and armour, and in 1902 was appointed Keeper of the King's Armoury at Windsor Castle, a post created specially for him. The provenance of much of the armour that Alice bought with his advice has proved difficult to trace, suggesting that it was acquired privately rather than at auction.

Laking, who was not well-off, dealt on his own account and in at least one case it is known that he sold a piece directly to Alice. This is a burgonet, or helmet (attributed to Caremolo Modrone), from the armoury of the Emperor Charles V in Milan, which had been stolen by its custodian and sold at Christie's in 1839. Laking had acquired it after it had come to light, covered in paint, in a kitchen cupboard during the sale of the Magniac collection in 1892. He also directed Alice to leading armour dealers and private collectors, such as Sir Duncan Hay, from whom Alice bought (for £2,000) an embossed parade shield made for Henri II. This was acquired in 1911, 13 years after Ferdinand's death, so the collection was not built up especially quickly. Yet it is of uneven quality

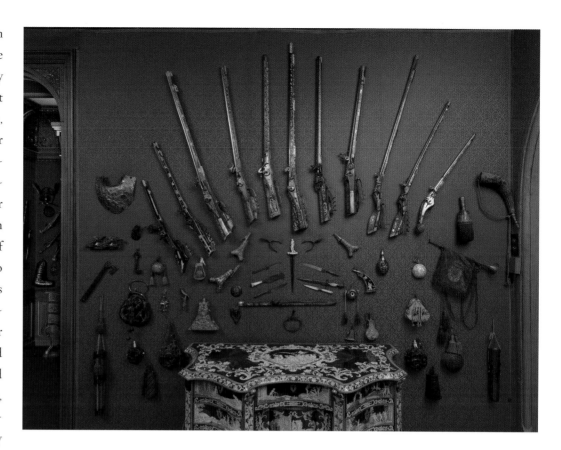

and includes a surprisingly large number of fakes, which is hard to reconcile with Laking's high reputation in this field. Alice, however, believed he had served her well, for she bequeathed him not only the burgonet but also a pair of elbow pieces by Filippo Negroli, which had similarly come from Charles V's armoury. However, since Laking died in 1919, before Alice, they have remained at Waddesdon.

Few visitors to the house seem to have been aware of Alice's contribution to its contents, for she presented herself as the guardian of her brother's creation. The atmosphere that resulted was memorably recorded by the French painter Jacques-Emile Blanche, a friend of Ethel Sands, who had arranged for him to be invited to Waddesdon to see the works of art. Blanche had met Alice at Grasse, where he had enjoyed her company, but he had heard that at Waddesdon she was 'a different Aunt Alice, forbidding and with a dislike for company, entirely absorbed with gardening and ordering about troops of workmen'. His fears were well-founded. Upon his arrival for lunch, he was led up to a guest bedroom by the house steward so that he could wash. When he asked for a glass of soda-water, he was informed by a footman,'I fear, sir, we are not allowed to bring in here fizzy water'. After being warned that he was not permitted to smoke in the house, except in the Bachelors' Wing, he was taken downstairs to 'a drawing room furnished in the Rothschild manner, i.e. a museum of Sèvres porcelain, furniture on

OPPOSITE: The Judgement of Paris, by Joachim Antonisz Wtewael. Painted on copper and only eight inches across, this masterpiece of Mannerist art was bought by Alice in 1882.

ABOVE RIGHT: A selection of eighteenth-century arms collected after 1898 by Alice to adorn the Bachelors' Wing corridor. They include knives, power flasks, horn flasks and wheel-locks, inlaid with ivory, bone and mother-of-pearl.

BELOW RIGHT: Parade helmet of the Emperor Charles V, 1534 or 1536. Made from a single piece of steel, it is the centrepiece of the armoury display in the Bachelors' Wing.

which one dared not sit, Beauvais tapestries with Boucher or Fragonard designs. There were carnations, all of the same shade, which, when the weather was hot, were renewed morning and evening, so I was told.' Lunch, however, was a delight, not least because of the magnificence of the food. Alice was in a good mood: 'Our hostess has intelligence of a high order, and her conversation was serious and full of originality and as masculine as her build. I had the impression that I was with the Iron Chancellor—even her accent was German and not unlike Edward VII's.' While being shown round the house by a footman, who had to warn him not to touch anything, Blanche visited the lavatory, while the footman stood on guard outside. 'I lighted a cigarette. He smelt the smoke of the tobacco, opened the door and informed me that smoking was forbidden. If they found out that anyone had smoked he would be *dismissed*. I put out the cigarette and threw the stump out of the window. The man again took me to task—some gardener, in raking the path under the window, might find the cigarette-end and tell his mistress; the servants would then be suspected of breaking the laws of the house.' Like so many visitors, Blanche speculated about the house's future: 'To whom was Miss Alice going to leave the place which had been built to take a hundred guests—according to me a fortress for prisoners on parole. The heir, I understand, will not have the right of varying a single article of the code.'

Another visitor introduced by Ethel Sands was even less sympathetic. In May 1909 Lady Ottoline Morrell drove over to Waddesdon with a small party of friends, including Henry James. It was not likely that Lady Ottoline, a patron of the Bloomsbury circle, would find Waddesdon attractive, and so it proved: 'The Terrible hard Museum like darkness of the House—with Jewish splendour & pomposity Added on—was crushing', she wrote in her diary. 'Lionel H[olland] was told Not to touch—Anyway we were sent—with relief by the lonely old oddity that ruled it—ruled it from a selfish Nervous irritable Centre—without one thought or care than that it was *hers*—& bought by her brother's money. Therefore to be kept like A Clock Ticking—in an empty room—L.H. talked to the Chauffeur on the way to & fro, & heard All manner of Tyrannies and eccentricities—I wish I could remember more of H[enry][J[ames]'s remarks. He sat next me at Miss Rothschild's & said Looking up at the enormously

tall footmen & the enormous white strawberrys "Murder and Rapine would be preferable to this"—He & the other men couldn't find a Lavatory & said there was a gt. want of "Physiological Necessities".'

Cruelly funny though these descriptions are, they touch on the aspect of Alice's regime that is best remembered now—her determination to preserve the house in as perfect a condition as possible, even if meant ordering the King to keep his fingers off. This went beyond those high standards of housekeeping that were recognised as normal in country houses until at least the 1920s, when changing attitudes led to windows and curtains being flung open to admit light and air into interiors that were thought stuffy and old-fashioned, with highly destructive results for their contents. It seems likely that Alice's exacting attitudes—which she referred to as 'Waddesdon standard'—derived from a feeling that the house had been entrusted to her by her brother so that it would be preserved, as well as from her innate visual perfectionism. It was part of a philosophy that led the grounds to look as though nobody had ever trodden in them, for a gardener was permanently on hand to rake the gravel and sweep the grass. Victor Rothschild's story that Alice had the leaves of shrubs visible from the house wiped free of dust every day is unlikely to be true, but it is not entirely unbelievable. What went for the garden went equally for the house. It seems probable that Alice imposed higher standards on its care than Ferdinand had ever thought necessary—he would not have appreciated being told to keep his cigars out of the house, not to touch the furniture, and never to raise the sunblinds. Yet to 21st-century eyes, educated by the requirements of modern conservation practice, Alice's rules seem eminently sensible—for example, porcelain was always to be handled with two hands, not one, and when it was being washed total silence had to be observed. She also refused to believe that a woman was capable of safely dusting the Sèvres, a task she entrusted to a footman rather than a housemaid.

Alice continued the tradition of estate philanthropy, and in 1910, for example, she converted a former school building into an 'institute', a clubroom for senior estate staff and prominent local tradesmen. Less expectedly, she also laid out a nine-hole golf course. She took an interest in local historic buildings. Despite their religion, the Rothschilds had contributed to the upkeep of the parish church—a major restoration in 1877 had largely been paid for by Ferdinand—and Alice arranged for a medieval tomb of a crusader to be moved into the church from the ruined chapel at Eythrope. It was in the garden, however, that Alice made her greatest impression on Waddesdon. Ferdinand's standards were high, and he often surprised his guests by his enthusi-

OPPOSITE: *An armchair covered with Beauvais tapestry, of about 1780. Although this eighteenth-century French chair is in outstandingly good condition, the brilliant colours of the upholstery, which has escaped exposure to light, explains why Alice instituted such rigorous housekeeping rules.*

asm for gardening: 'it is in the gardens and shrubberies that he is happy', wrote David Lindsay in 1898. 'He is responsible for the design of the flower beds; for the arrangement of colour, for the transplanting of trees: all these things are under his personal control and I was astonished at the knowledge he displayed: I don't mean about botanical lore, but about the history of the place. . . . Point to an oak or a maple and he will tell you precisely when it was planted, whence it was transplanted or whither it shall be moved in the autumn. It is only when among his shrubs and orchids that the nervous hands of Baron Ferdinand are at

rest.' As this suggests, Ferdinand's main interest was the overall look of the gardens; horticulture as such he left to his head gardeners, Arthur Bradshaw and, from 1887, John Jaques. That was not Alice's approach: Eythrope, wrote Edward Hamilton, 'is the most magnificent horticultural toy that can be seen anywhere. She has consummate good taste and great knowledge of flowers and plants.' Under her care, Waddesdon's gardens were soon more than a match for those at Eythrope.

Her right-hand man in their management was her headgardener, George Frederick Johnson, who first came to work at Waddesdon in 1892 at the age of 17. The son of an under-gardener at Swakeleys, an estate in Middlesex, he was ambitious as well as talented. Having completed five years' service, working in all the departments of the garden and learning German in his spare time, he was provided with an introduction to Ferdinand's brother Nathaniel. After four

In some of Waddesdon's most outstanding decorative furniture, the rich effects were achieved through Japanese lacquer, painting, marquetry with ormolu and inlays of ivory. Their colours have been preserved by Alice's exacting housekeeping standards. ABOVE: *A cabinet created around Japanese lacquered panels by René Dubois, about 1770.* RIGHT: *A detail of an eighteenth-century Vernis Martin chest of drawers decorated with Bacchic putti, by Pierre Macret.* OVERLEAF: *A detail of a drop-front desk with drawers ornamented with alternating ribbons of green-stained sycamore and unstained sycamore, by Roger Vandercruse, about 1775; and a detail of the Italian ivory-inlaid commode with scenes of boys at play, by Pietro Piffetti, 1735—40.*

years at Nathaniel's garden at Hohe Warte in Vienna, he moved in 1901 to Alice's garden at Grasse. Four years later, he received this summons from Waddesdon: 'Johnson, My head gardener here has given me notice that he does not wish to stay on; he is a very good man and the place and plants are in excellent order—I do not like changes and I know you well, I offer you the place of head gardener here.—a *furnished* house, coals, milk, potatoes and vegetables,—a horse and cart at your disposal; the doctor and medicine gratis for yourself and for your household—At first, you will have to depend on the advice of Sims, the bailiff, for many things; until you thoroughly understand the place. To begin with, I shall give you £100 a year. If you stay with me and give entire satisfaction, you will gradually be augmented up to 130 pounds a year. The park and trees [are] not under you. You must remember Waddesdon well and your department has been much improved since you last saw it.'

Johnson took the offer and returned to Waddesdon, to preside over the gardens for almost half a century, for he did not retire until 1952, two years before his death at the age of 79. During Alice's annual absences in France, she kept in touch with him by post, and most fortunately he preserved a number of her letters, which provide a

ABOVE AND RIGHT: *Autochrome images of 1910 showing the abundance and opulence of the gardens at Waddesdon. There were luxuriant beddings on the entrance front, and most spectacularly on the south-facing Parterre on the south front, planted twice a year with 50,000 plants, as well as in front of the Aviary and on the north front.*

OVERLEAF: *Autochrome images of 1910, showing the gardens at Waddesdon (left, above and below) and Alice's garden at Eythrope (right).*

valuable glimpse of her personality (her private papers have, like Ferdinand's, been destroyed) as well as a depiction of the daily workings of a great garden at its zenith. Pithy to the point of brusqueness, they reveal Alice's sharp curiosity about the people who worked for her and suggest an unspoken affection for her protégé, advising him for example how to improve his handwriting, or his French. Her insistence on the highest standards is a frequent refrain: '*Quality* is the one thing you must study in all your work at Waddesdon,' she wrote to him in November 1906, '*economy* too as long as you can effect it by a good organisation, but not by lowering the quality of the fruit, vegetables and flowers.' She expected him to take advice from Jaques, who still lived close by, and from Gibbs, Eythrope's head gardener: 'I am glad to hear from you that Gibbs and Jaques are satisfied with your efforts at cultivation,' she wrote a year later, 'but go on learning as much as you can, you have still a great deal to learn, you are very young to be at the head of the Waddesdon gardens.' If Johnson, then 31, found this discouraging, he soon proved himself, for by 1911, Alice was comparing his work favourably to the achievements of Jaques, who 'thoroughly understands the cultivation of certain green and stove house plants, such as orchids . . . but he never understood roses and his geraniums were not up to much—He must find a great difference in your Department during these last five years'.

The great success achieved by Ferdinand's gardeners with orchids and carnations was now matched by equal standards in other flowers, and in vegetables as well. Alice encouraged Johnson to grow for competition, and for the first time Waddesdon began to exhibit flowers other than orchids at Royal Horticultural shows. She recognised that the garden was not easy to work with, for the soil was poor, and at her insistence better soil was transported from nearby Brill, which was chosen probably because it was easily accessible on the tramway that Ferdinand had used to bring building materials to the site: 'All fruit, grown for *my table*, ought to be grown in the right soil, as the pure Waddesdon soil, even the best Waddesdon loam, gives an acid taste to fruit and makes vegetables hard', she wrote to Johnson in 1910. 'I suppose that you have been able to replace all the Waddesdon soil around the peach and nectarine roots with Brill soil.' More wor-

ried instructions came in the same year: 'I hope the Begonia beds in front of the aviaries will be all right again this season—they were so poor last year owing to your using *old* bulbs! Miss Hofer, Gibbs and Jaques all three told me, that *old* Begonia bulbs do not give a satisfactory bloom.' Alice's insistence on high standards for vegetables is a reminder that, unlike her brother, there was nothing wrong with her appetite or digestion: "The turnips here are delicious', she wrote to Johnson from Grasse in 1907, '*sweet* and neither strong, nor stringy and very white; they are of the long shaped variety and from 4 to 6 inches long. I believe that they are grown *very quickly*, in *very* light soil. Could we have that French variety for my table?' The only volume of gardening accounts to survive, for 1910–13, reveals the range of vegetables that were grown: ten varieties of beans, fifteen of peas, three of onions, five of cucumbers, six of cauliflowers, eight of cabbage and eleven of broccoli. Use of so many varieties was designed to ensure as long a season as possible for each vegetable; one of the stories told about Alfred de Rothschild is that when asked which month he liked least, he had replied 'February, because it is the end of the strawberry season'.

ABOVE: *George Frederick Johnson, Alice's much-trusted Head Gardener, who worked at Waddesdon from 1905 to 1954.*

OPPOSITE. *Alice in her sixties at Eythrope, about 1910.*

Insurance records prepared during Alice's ownership of the estate allow for the first time a precise calculation of the size of the gardening staff: over one year, wages were paid to 53 gardeners, of whom 14 were employed in the glasshouses. The gardeners were divided into different departments, each under its own foreman. There was one department for the kitchen garden, for example, one for growing fruit, one specialising in flowers for exhibition, one growing flowers for bedding out, and another for flowers grown for the house. Workers in each department did not communicate with each other, and methods were kept secret—Alice comments in one of her letters that Johnson will wish to remove the labels from a brand of fertiliser she has recommended, presumably so that the other gardeners could not identify it. A vivid record of the gardeners' lives is preserved in the memoirs of Aubrey Hicks. The son of one of the gardeners, he joined the staff at the age of 14, shortly before the First World War, as the 'bothy boy', helping out in the gardener's dormitory house in the village, an establishment praised in the gardening press of the time as an

ABOVE: *Horse-drawn mower outside the cricket pavilion at Waddesdon, about 1900.*

OPPOSITE: *The garden staff in the early 1900s. Several generations of local families have worked at the Manor, a tradition which continues today.*

embodiment of an enlightened employer's good practice, for as well as accommodation it provided a reading room, where the gardeners could study horticultural books and the latest journals. In Hicks's time, the men were looked after by a Mrs Speed, with her daughter Sally, who provided their breakfast at eight o'clock each morning. Work began at six-thirty and continued until five o'clock, or four o'clock on Saturdays, with half an hour's break for breakfast and an hour for lunch. The men were paid after work on Friday, when they collected their wages from the back door of the village hall. Hicks does not record what his wages were, but another boy, Ralph Saunders, who eventually became head gardener in succession to Johnson, was paid 10s a week when he started work in 1928.

After a year, Hicks was transferred to the main glasshouse, known as 'Top Glass', under the foreman, Fred Sawyer: 'a heavily moustached man . . . held in great respect by all under him . . . It is difficult to explain the authority men in charge of the departments had. Their word was law, one did one's best not to offend in any way.' Hicks fell foul of Sawyer, who discovered him playing darts in work hours, and he was banished to labour in the gardens around the house, referred to by the staff as 'Up Top'. There he tended the ponies that pulled the mowers: 'We put leather boots on their feet to save marking the turf . . . This job of mowing—a most tiring and foot wearing operation one

could imagine. In the Autumn, leaf sweeping was a back acher! We boys had to take it in turn to be in the cart when the leaves were loaded, trampling down the pitched up leaves, thus getting as large a load as possible . . . gangs of four or five including one boy, would be armed with a weeding iron to tackle the endless job of keeping the lawns free of plantains, daisies, dandelions etc, no chemical aids then-a-days. Strips of lawn were marked out and systematically weeded, I can think of no more miserable Winter job for anybody.' If they overlooked anything, Alice did not: 'she always carried a spud in her hand', recalled her cousin Constance, 'with which she removed any offending weed from the carefully kept paths.'

Hicks also described the hierarchical organisation of the estate staff, which at its peak in Alice's time numbered 346, although this included workers on the farms which were in hand. Like the gardeners, the labourers were divided into separate departments, under the agent George Sims, assisted by his son Eustace, 'a young man without his father's capabilities' according to Hicks. There was a team for the forestry, another for the grass verges and a third for the drives. The Aviary and menagerie, the gamekeeper's staff, the stables and coach house, the laundry and gas works, the electricity generator and the estate yard's painters and carpenters formed additional departments. There was also a large seasonal workforce for two important annual jobs, the repair and repainting of the glasshouses, under the supervision of Hicks's father, and the painting of the estate fences by a team of men nicknamed 'The Greenfinches'. In all, remembered Hicks, some seventy per cent of the inhabitants of the estate were employed by it; 'at meal times and knocking off it was like an army coming down the High Street'.

While Alice was absent from England, another small work force was employed in the house itself. As Hicks recalled, 'The Aylesbury firm Jenns & Sons [had] workmen all Winter through renovating curtains, carpets etc . . . Mackrill & sons the electricians were regulars . . . Another Aylesbury firm Randall Eaton & Son in conjunction with Jenns did delicate joinery, and window fittings, quite a wheel-within-wheels, much money to be made one way or another, in fact when the agent G.A.Sims passed away not very long after the war 1918, he left a considerable fortune over £80,000, it speaks for itself!' The household staff was maintained at the same level as it had been in Ferdinand's time, ruled 'with a rod of iron', according to Hicks, by the steward, Lawrence Richardson, and Mrs Boxall, the housekeeper. Again, it seems that Alice was determined to preserve her brother's legacy untouched: since she lived at Waddesdon far less than he had done, and did not entertain as frequently, she could have managed with a smaller establishment. One change she made was to introduce cars, among the first to be seen in the area. In September 1906 a journalist from *The Car* magazine paid a visit to inspect the garage: 'For traversing her own grounds Miss de Rothschild invariably uses either a chaise with her two dear little ponies, named Bella and Comet, or a small 9 h.p. De Dion; but when visiting other members of the family at Mentmore, Tring Park, etc., a luxuriously appointed 20-25 h.p. C.G.V., double landau is invariably employed. The body was built to her own design, and the car has a very long wheel base, ensuring the maximum of comfort.' The cars did not escape her meticulous attention to detail: 'Miss de Rothschild has invented and had fitted under each car a tray with a well and tap, which receives every drop of oil and water, so that when standing at the house entrance or elsewhere there is no dirty pool of oil observable on the ground when the cars move off.'

In July 1899 house parties were resumed, but on a smaller scale than in Ferdinand's time. Among the guests were the Prince and Princess of Wales—from 1901 Edward VII and Queen Alexandra—the Prince's sister Louise, and a handful of politicians, most notably Winston Churchill. Family members were a central element of each party, and in June 1913 Alice's great-nephew James brought his new wife, Dorothy, to Waddesdon for the first time. Lord Kitchener, a good friend of Alice, visited in 1911 and in 1913 helped settle a long dispute between Alice and the Royal Bucks Hussars, a local yeomanry regiment which had caused her intense displeasure by riding over growing crops on the Waddesdon estate during manoeuvres. On May 19, 1913 Alice gave a dinner for the regiment's officers, to celebrate the resumption of good relations. It was the last major party the house was to see for a decade. In the summer of 1914, 1,500 children attended the annual Baron's Treat, but there would never be another.

Upon the outbreak of war, Alice's immediate concern was for her far-flung European family. She wrote in grim mood to Johnson from London in September 1914: 'My Austrian nephews *so far* have

not been taken prisoners! . . . Baron Robert's château . . . was not pillaged by the Germans, who shot the pheasants and drank the wine there . . . the other Rothschild estates have not been in the German zone so far . . . Mrs James de Rothschild has so far good news of her husband. At Grasse *all* the hotels are full of wounded.' Now that the south of France was out of reach, Alice spent the winters in Bournemouth. Her letters to Johnson devote much space to comment about the international situation, and, increasingly, condolences to be passed to the families on the estate who lost men in the war. Although Waddesdon escaped requisition, at Alice's suggestion hay was grown on its lawns and its flower beds were turned over to vegetables: 'Yes, grow as much *food* as possible, do not let people imagine that we waste labour on useless luxuries! Grow your tomatoes well in sight! ' she wrote to Johnson in February 1918. 'I have been considering the potato question. It is advisable to grow as many as we can—so perhaps it will be best to grow them again on the terrace and in *all* the beds there; perhaps you could grow the beetroot and carrots by the aviaries, where the potatoes did not do as well as the terrace beds—but I leave that to you.' When in April it seemed possible that Johnson might be called up she wrote in distress, 'You must move heaven and earth to be left at Waddesdon in charge of the kitchen garden.—Everything looks very black indeed . . . Throw away as many of the plants and flowers you need not keep. You will be so short of labour!'

Peace dawned on a world that for a time felt very different. In December 1918, Gibbs, Alice's long-serving head gardener at Eythrope, died, and she took the opportunity to make changes: 'In the spring, if I am spared, we can go over Eythrope together and arrange the glass and gardens on a different footing', she wrote to Johnson. 'I shall not require it any longer as a show place. I shall empty the glass.' In 1919 she sold the Leighton estate she had inherited from Ferdi-

OPPOSITE: *Alice's specially-designed long-wheel-base automobile waiting by the North Porch in about 1910.*

ABOVE: *Alice at the north front, in about 1910, her strong and sometimes intimidating personality vividly apparent. During her last decade she entertained much less. From 1915 to 1922 there are no entries in the Waddesdon visitors' book.*

nand. In the same year, Alfred de Rothschild died, and Halton was sold by his heir, Lionel de Rothschild, to the Royal Air Force, which had established a camp on the estate during the war. Alfred's magnificent collections were dispersed. Some were bequeathed to other members of the family, but most were sent to the salerooms by his chief legatee, Almina, Countess of Carnarvon, demonstrating all too clearly what might have happened to Waddesdon if there had been no Alice to take care of it. Her thoughts now turned to its future, and she became increasingly unwilling to make decisions about the estate, telling her staff that she wanted to leave changes to her heir.

7

JAMES AND DOROTHY

As a European dynasty, linked through joint membership of an international bank, the Rothschilds felt the severing impact of the First World War more than most families. After 1918, the French, English, German and Austrian financial houses, which had found themselves on opposite sides of the battlefields, increasingly acted independently of each other. Yet their members remained a united family, as revealed by Alice's anxious reports in her wartime letters to Johnson on the welfare of her cousins, nephews and nieces. In November 1917 she received the tragic news of the death of Evelyn de Rothschild, Leopold's second son, as a result of wounds sustained when leading a cavalry charge against the Turks at El Mughar. The news came as a special blow: Evelyn was her heir.

In the remaining five years of her life, Alice hesitated long over choosing his replacement. Ferdinand's old friend Edward Hamilton recorded in his diary that during a visit to Alice in May 1899, 'she confirmed what I already knew she made no secret about: and that was, that Waddesdon was to be left to no-one who was not a British subject. This of course excludes the sons of her brother [Salbert], with whom moreover she is on bad terms. The choice would seem to lie between one of Rosebery's boys, whom Ferdie especially liked, and one of Leo's boys'. There was, therefore, a natural assumption amongst the English Rothschilds that Leopold's youngest son, Anthony, would take Evelyn's place. Alice's choice was unexpected. Ferdinand's will made generous bequests to his niece Baroness Edmond, who was clearly a favourite. She had two sons: James, born in 1878, and Maurice,

James Armand Edmond de Rothschild (1878–1957). Miss Alice chose her French cousin, Jimmy, to inherit Waddesdon.

three years his junior. Maurice, who had entered the bank and was following a political career, had been bequeathed a large fortune in 1909 by Alice's sister Julie, together with her estate at Pregny. James, however, although still working for the bank in Paris, had a house in London, was married to an Englishwoman, and in 1920 had been granted British nationality. He and his wife knew Alice well, had visited Waddesdon several times, and had no country house of their own. Nonetheless, when it was discovered after Alice's death in Paris in 1922 that she had left Waddesdon and Eythrope to James, Anthony was shocked, and, as his nephew Edmund recalled in his memoirs, the bequest caused considerable ill-feeling amongst his family.

It is likely, however, that Alice had recognised in James someone whose devotion to Waddesdon could equal hers. His upbringing had certainly fitted him for the task. His father, Edmond, born in 1845, was in academic terms the most intellectually gifted Rothschild of his generation, and having passed his baccalaureate with distinction was allowed by his father to visit Egypt as a reward, the beginning of a life-long involvement with the Middle East. Edmond was also perhaps the greatest of all Rothschild collectors, not in the sense that his collections were more distinguished than those of other members of his family, although they were of very high quality, but in the sense that they could not be understood as furnishings or investments. His greatest passion was prints, of which he owned some 40,000, matched by a scarcely less important collection of drawings. As his daughter-in-law Dorothy recalled, 'his knowledge of every detail of his thousands of engravings was astonishing. Even when almost blind, at the end of his life, he would show some portfolio to an interested visitor and point out unerringly the differences between the first as opposed to the subsequent states of the engraving concerned.' He was also a bibliophile, who assembled a major collection of medieval manuscripts. Like

other Rothschilds, he acquired 18th-century furniture and porcelain of the highest quality, and had, for example, bought alongside Ferdinand at the Hamilton Palace sale in 1882, using Samuel Wertheimer as his agent. By the 1890s he had become the most significant collector of 18th-century art in Paris and was paying legendarily high prices. Less usually for his family, he was an amateur archaeologist with a deep interest in Classical antiquity; he owned a major group of Roman silver, the 1st-century Boscoreale Treasure, now in the Louvre. Edmond's pre-eminence among the connoisseurs of his time was acknowledged even by such antisemites as the Goncourt brothers, who were delighted to accept his generous hospitality. Among the glimpses of his social life in Paris is a dinner given in April 1899 by Marcel Proust, a good friend of Edmond's cousin Robert, at which Edmond was joined by Gabriel Fauré, the marquis Boni de Castellane, Prince Giovanni Borghese, comte Robert de Montesquiou, and Charles Ephrussi, editor of the *Gazette des Beaux Arts*—a happy mixture of aristocracy, plutocracy, art, and intellect.

To these interests Edmond added another, which was to be of immense importance to his family in the following century: the establishment of Jewish colonies in Palestine. In 1882 he was approached by Shmuel Mohilewer, rabbi of Radom (then in Russia), who as a result of the Tsarist pogroms wanted to settle a group of Jewish farmers from Belorussia in Palestine, then part of the Ottoman empire. This was not an unprecedented scheme, for at the same time an already existing community at Rishon le Zion, south of Jaffa, applied to Edmond for financial aid. Edmond decided to give these groups not only money but also leadership, and within a few years it was evident that he had discovered a lifelong mission; by 1903, he was subsidising 19 of Palestine's 28 Jewish settlements in part or in whole.

In 1877, after having been rejected by Mayer Carl's daughter Margaretha de Rothschild, who subsequently married the duc de

Gramont, Edmond married his cousin Adelheid, known as Adelaïde after her move to France. She shared the strict religious beliefs of her parents, Baron and Baroness Wilhelm of Frankfurt, but not their austere way of life. A woman of great charm and modesty, she was a collector herself, with a particular interest in costume and textiles, and had acquired significant collections of lace and 18th-century buttons, both for their own sake and to wear. 'She was pretty, with an exquisitely fair complexion, which she kept all her life', recalled Dorothy. 'She attributed its perfection to her method of washing her face in strawberry juice whenever possible.' Every year she and her husband cruised the eastern Mediterranean in their yacht, both to visit Palestine and to look for antiquities and textiles. In France, their lives were divided between Paris, where they had a house at 41 rue du Faubourg-Saint-Honoré (reconstructed for them by the architect Felix Langlais after their marriage), a château at Boulogne-sur-Seine and another at Armainvilliers, near Ferrières, designed in a half-timbered Norman rustic style on an unusual S-plan by Langlais and Emile Ulmann. Begun in about 1880, the house shares some characteristics of Ferdinand's estate buildings at Waddesdon, notably the Dairy. Although they are known to have visited Waddesdon only once, in 1894, Edmond and Adelaïde's knowledge of her uncle's work is suggested by their choice in 1885 of Emile Lainé to landscape the grounds, no doubt on Ferdinand's recommendation.

Only one of their three children settled permanently in France. In 1910, in one of the last instances of Rothschild endogamy, their daughter, Miriam, married her cousin Albert von Goldschmidt, one of Minna's sons, and moved to Frankfurt. Although Edmond and Adelaïde's sons were both to follow political careers—Maurice achieved notoriety when his election to the Chamber of Deputies as a socialist member in 1924 was annulled after accusations of corrupt electioneering—they were otherwise different in interests and temperament. Maurice inherited his parents' enthusiasm for collecting, although he pursued an independent line as one of the first Rothschilds to acquire contemporary art on a significant scale, buying paintings by Picasso and Braque among others. James, however, was never a collector. Although his inheritance of Waddesdon is usually considered to be the explanation for this, on the grounds that he had no need for any more works of art, his brother's inheritance of Pregny seems to have been no disincentive to further acquisitions. In many ways, James exhibited all the classic signs of a son desperate to evade his family's expectations.

Languidly tall, with a long, aquiline profile that made him one of the most physically distinctive of all Rothschilds, James (always known as Jimmy to his family and friends) had a brilliant school career at the Lycée Louis-le-Grand in Paris, marred only by the extreme anti-semitism stirred up by the Dreyfus affair. That may have influenced his family's decision to send him to university in England. During his three years at Trinity College, Cambridge (when, with his father, he attended Ferdinand's funeral), James was able to indulge his passions for hunting, steeplechasing and racing. He was an enthusiastic gambler: his friend

OPPOSITE ABOVE: Edmond James de Rothschild (1845–1934), son of James Mayer, founder of the French branch of the bank, and James's father. This is a drawing made for The Sleeping Beauty panels by Leon Bakst, 1921.

OPPOSITE BELOW: Adelaïde de Rothschild (1853–1935), grand-daughter of Carl Mayer, founder of the Neapolitan branch of the bank, and James's mother, in another of Bakst's drawings for The Sleeping Beauty.

BELOW: James and his younger brother, Maurice Edmond Charles (1881–1957), about 1890.

Fred Cripps, an older brother of Stafford Cripps, recalled bumping into him in a restaurant during their undergraduate days: 'Jimmy said he thought I looked rather sad, and hoped I had not been silly enough to bet at Ascot. When pressed, I reluctantly admitted that I *had* betted and had lost about £700. I added that I was rather distressed, as my father then allowed me £400 a year, which did not leave any margin for losses on the turf. Instead of commiserating with me, he claimed I was a good winner, as I had lost only one and three-quarter years' income, while he had lost eleven years'. By a process of reasoning best known to himself he proposed that I should pay for the dinner.'

James enjoyed himself so much at Cambridge that he asked his father's permission to stay at the university for another year; when Edmond agreed only on the condition that James showed some evidence of academic endeavour, he proved his intellectual mettle by securing the Harkness Prize for an essay on Shakespeare. Then, after a miserable year in Hamburg to learn about banking, he vanished. It

was eighteen months before his anxious parents were able to track him down in Australia, where he was working as a cattle-hand under an assumed name. In relief, Edmond allowed him to make a round-the-world trip in 1902–03 with one of his Cambridge friends, Vere Ponsonby, a tour which took in the U.S.A, India—where he was a guest at the coronation Durbar organised by Lord Curzon—and China, where James dined with the dowager empress, and bought Chinese costumes that are still in the collection at Waddesdon.

This experience seems to have encouraged him to settle, and for the next decade he buckled down to work in the Paris bank, which he combined with owning racehorses. He had his first great success on the turf with his horse Bomba, which won the Ascot Gold Cup in 1909 as an outsider, beating the favourite, Santa Strato, which was owned by Leopold; in 1911 he won his only classic race, the 1000 Guineas, with Atmah. Then, in January 1913, his parents were horrified to receive a telegram from London to announce his engagement to a star of the musical comedy stage, Dorothy Minto. It took some time for the confusion to be sorted out: his fiancée was in fact the 17-year-old Dorothy Pinto, daughter of a stockbroker, Eugene Pinto, and a member of a prominent Sephardi family, who traced their ancestry back to Portugal.

It was a love match: Dorothy was a slim, dark-haired young woman, with the delicate, slightly apple-cheeked complexion she kept to the end of her long life. Barely out of the schoolroom (she had only just been promoted to dining with her parents), she stepped innocently but confidently into her husband's complex family life. Her recollections of meeting her in-laws convey something of the sense of ironic amusement that tempered her essential earnestness of purpose: 'Straight from the Gard du Nord Jimmy and I were conveyed in his family's electric motor to his paternal home in the Faubourg St Honoré, next door to the British Embassy. To Jimmy's embarrassment, the household took the view that our arrival was a momentous occasion; the lodge gates were flung open and we drove down into a brilliantly illuminated courtyard and entered the house by the imposing front door, instead of by the customary cosy little side door which I used ever afterwards . . . after dinner all members of the Rothschild family were invited to come and have a look at the prospective bride—an interesting ordeal for me.'

Dorothy was to form an exceptionally close relationship with her parents-in-law. In an unpublished memoir written after Edmond's death, she recorded her impressions of his personality and interests: 'Unlike his elder son, who at no time in his life was able to walk 200 yards without pausing, Edmond was an enthusiastic walker till the end

ABOVE: *James and Dorothy at their wedding in the Central Synagogue, Great Portland Street, London on February 25, 1913, as recorded by* The Graphic. *Dorothy's white satin and lace gown, later altered to make an evening dress, is still at Waddesdon.*

OPPOSITE: The Visit of the Good Fairy to the Christening, *the second panel of Leon Bakst's scheme for the drawing room at 34 Park Street, London, commissioned in 1913. The King and the Good Fairy are portrayed by the Marquess and Marchioness of Crewe, son-in-law and daughter of Lord Rosebery, and the three good fairies to the left of the crib are portrayed by Dorothy, her mother and mother-in-law.*

of his days. He was over forty when he suddenly decided to tackle the Matterhorn, without any specialist preparation . . . His memory was fantastic—he could quote accurately from books, recite poetry, sing (out of tune) songs from *La Belle Hélène* and the other musical comedies of the Offenbach of his youth. His appearance was striking; always beautifully dressed in spite of his insistence on all his clothes hanging loosely on him—and from time to time, he would use a Renaissance pin in his tie'. She recalled no less vividly the interiors he had created for the display of his collections in his Paris house: 'some of his rooms had appropriately 18th century panelling, but many of them were designed from the decorative drawings and engravings in his collection . . . His chosen period, for all his house, was an 18th century background, but his tastes were catholic and he mingled antiquities with ornaments of all ages and nationalities with very beautiful results.' The relationship with her father-in-law shaped Dorothy's appreciation of Rothschild history, taste, and values in a way that would, in due course, help her to understand Waddesdon; Edmond was only six years younger than Ferdinand, and had known him well.

Her marriage was the beginning of a new international life for Dorothy, for James continued his job at the bank, and so they divided their time between his family home in Paris and a house of their own in London, 34 Park Street, Mayfair. She continued to be introduced to his family, most notably (in view of what was to come) to two of his aunts, Ferdinand's surviving sisters. In 1913, she and James spent Passover with Baroness Wilhelm in Frankfurt; perhaps unexpectedly, it was the beginning of a warm friendship between the 18-year-old bride and the 81-year-old widow: 'she was not only brilliant intellectually', recalled Dorothy, 'but also endowed with that rare quality of understanding that made her the confidante of all the members of her family'. It took longer for Dorothy to feel quite so at home with Alice, especially as there was initially a *froideur* caused by the failure of the telegram announcing the engagement to reach Grasse. In a lecture she gave in 1959 to the guides at Waddesdon, Dorothy recalled her first impression of the house: 'It was—to put my more creditable reaction first—the Red Drawing Room with those four staggering full-length pictures. I have a fleeting impression of Miss Emily Pott; then, I am afraid, all else pales before the memory of the tea—a chocolate cake with gleaming icing and a hole in the middle and some black strawberries (really black—a variety which has now died out, I am sorry to say), and cream which sat stiff in a glass container.'

One of Dorothy's first tasks was to supervise the decoration of the Park Street house. Alterations were made by W. H. Romaine-Walker, who with his partners Francis Besant and Gilbert Jenkins had a busy and fashionable town-house practice, best known then for the 9th Duke of Marlborough's new Louis XV mansion (built with Vanderbilt money) in Curzon Street. The interiors were fitted out by Roberson's, a Knightsbridge firm, but unexpectedly James decided to contribute his one major venture into artistic patronage. Asking about for a Jewish artist he might commission, he was taken by his friend Philip Sassoon to an exhibition of watercolours by Leon Bakst at the Fine Art Society in Bond Street. Bakst had recently achieved fame for his stage designs for the Ballets Russes, which had taken London by storm the previous year and returned to Covent Garden for two seasons in 1913. In response to James's commission to decorate the drawing room at Park Street, Bakst proposed a series of seven paintings depicting the story of *Sleeping Beauty*.

It was the beginning of a long and tortuous job, which was not completed until shortly before Bakst's death in 1924. Its successful conclusion was thanks in large part to Dorothy, who kept up the gentle pressure. When Bakst complained about the difficulty of finding models for all the numerous characters in the story, she helped to realise James's inspired suggestion that his family and friends should

be the sitters. The result is a personal as well as an enchanting fantasy which conveys the gaiety and contentment of James and Dorothy's early married life. James appears as the Prince, Edmond and Eugene Pinto are courtiers and Adélaïde and Dorothy's mother are good fairies. Dorothy's brother, Richard, who won the Military Cross in the First World War, is a soldier, and among the other extras are Rothschilds, both English and French, including James's brother, Maurice, and his cousins Edouard and Robert. Perhaps surprisingly, the Princess is not Dorothy, who modestly gave herself a small part as a good fairy, but Maurice's wife, Noëmie Halphen (however, Dorothy's dog Muffin is yappingly present). Among their friends who are included are Fred Cripps, Vere Ponsonby (who became the Earl of Bessborough), and Lord Rosebery's children—Lord Dalmeny, Neil Primrose (who had been James's best man), and Peggy, Marchioness of Crewe. The jockey Fred Pratt, later to be James's trainer, was included as a courtier, and the old lady who guards the sleeping princess is Madame Marion, who for half a century was the housekeeper for Edmond and Adélaïde at 41 rue Faubourg-Saint-Honoré. Dorothy realised that the proposed design for their drawing room was unlikely to live up to the panels—and in any case Roberson's had proved unsatisfactory—so she suggested that the room should be redesigned by Bakst and installed by J.-E. Ruhlmann, the leading avant-garde furniture maker in Paris. The result would have been a room without parallel in England for its date, but Bakst's dilatoriness and James's decision to sell the house when its view of Hyde Park was lost to the new Grosvenor House Hotel meant that the scheme was abandoned. When James and Dorothy moved into their new house, in St James's Place, the panels were installed in the dining room, where it proved impossible to place them in narrative sequence.

By then, the young couple's carefree life had been transformed. Upon the outbreak of war, James signed up as a private in the French army, but was seconded to the British forces as a translator, work for which he was awarded the D.C.M. In 1915 he had a serious accident in France when a lorry in which he was travelling overturned, pinning him to the ground and crushing his pelvis. It was some time before he was dug out: while half-buried and presumed to be unconscious, he heard two English acquaintances talking: 'Do you know who it is?' 'Yes, Jimmy Rothschild.' 'Is he dead?' 'Not yet.' He had been so badly injured that it was three years before he was able to return to active service. From then on, James's fragile health was to be one of only two serious clouds in his life; the other, the absence of children, was never mentioned in public. In 1918 he was sent to Palestine to raise a Jewish battalion for service under General Allenby. This was his first opportunity to see for himself the work his father had been sponsoring. He had already begun to play a part in his father's mission, which by 1914, with the encouragement of Chaim Weizmann, had evolved into a belief that there was a future for an independent Jewish state in Palestine. In March 1914, James had been appointed as the Rothschild nominee on a committee for Weizmann's project to establish a Jewish university in Palestine; Weizmann found James, for all his occasional patrician hauteur, far more approachable than his autocratic and by now elderly father, and a close friendship grew up between them. When James was absent on military service, Weizmann turned to Dorothy for help, for he saw that she, like her husband, gave him a vital link to prominent English Jews and politicians. Initially, he approached her rather tentatively, assuming she was simply a society hostess, but within a year they had become close collaborators as well as friends; in 1916 she joined his family for Passover *Seder*. As a result, Dorothy, as the confidante of both Edmond and Weizmann, and by now well-acquainted with her husband's English cousins, played a part in the delicate negotiations that preceded the Balfour Declaration of November 2, 1917—the open letter from the foreign secretary, Arthur Balfour, to Lord Rothschild stating that the British government favoured 'the establishment in Palestine of a national home for the Jewish people'.

By the time of this moment of triumph, it was clear that Dorothy's commitment to the Zionist cause matched her husband's. It never flagged for the next 70 years. The couple's involvement in Jewish political activities in Europe was strengthened by personal acquaintance with the Palestinian communities, as a result of James's wartime activities. Among the battalion he raised in 1918 were David Ben-Gurion, Itzhak Ben-Zvi, and Joseph Sprinzak: as Dorothy commented, 'I don't know how useful they were as infantrymen but more than 30 years later the first became the Prime Minister, the second the President and the third the Speaker of the Parliament of the State of Israel'. Once the war was over, James and Dorothy began to travel to raise support for the Zionist cause, visiting Canada and the U.S.A as well as Palestine. Through the High Commissioner of Palestine, Sir Herbert Samuel, they met Winston Churchill, then the Colonial Secretary, who was to be a lifelong friend and—since he was an ardent philosemite—a supporter of their Zionist concerns.

In 1919, while playing golf at Deauville, James was struck in the face by a ball from a misdirected shot by the duc de Gramont and was so badly injured that he lost his left eye. It was a severe handi-

Three sketches by Leon Bakst for
The Sleeping Beauty *panels:*
Dorothy de Rothschild, Frederick Pratt
(who trained the majority of James's
racehorses), and Dorothy's dog, Muffin.

JAMES AND DOROTHY

cap, for his eyesight was not good, and by the end of his life he had become almost entirely blind. But for the moment, he carried off the disfigurement with stylish aplomb, sporting a monocle in his good eye; according to legend, when told after the accident that the eye was too damaged to save, he commented 'Well, this really is too bad, coming on top of £30,000 in the casino last night.' In the same year he applied for British nationality, the beginning of a severing of his formal links in France that led to him assigning his interest in the bank to his father. This may have been motivated by ambitions for a political career in England, which Dorothy believed had been in his mind since his undergraduate days, but he did not enter parliament immediately. He defied his family's drift into the Conservative party—and belied his friendships with prominent Conservatives such as Churchill—by a firm adherence to the Liberal party, although it had precipitously declined in political fortunes since Ferdinand's time. He continued his interest in racing, now enthusiastically accompanied by his wife, and won the Cambridgeshire with Brigand in 1919 and with Milenko in 1921; a year later he was elected to the Jockey Club.

In May 1922 Alice died. Dorothy never forgot the comment made by one of their friends, Lord d'Abernon, when he heard the terms of Alice's will: 'Waddesdon is not an inheritance, it is a career.' In her book *The Rothschilds at Waddesdon Manor* (1979), which forms the principal source for any account of life at Waddesdon between the wars, Dorothy has left a detailed picture of what she and James found when they took charge: an intact, immaculate, fully functioning Victorian country house, from which all trace of the changes made during the war had been expunged. Dorothy was greeted by the housekeeper, Mrs Boxall, with the remark: 'It's awful, if Miss Alice were alive today, I wouldn't be allowed to let you in.' It cannot have been an easy moment. Many of Ferdinand's old staff were still working. On the estate, George Sims still ruled supreme, and presented Dorothy with a list of the Christmas boxes expected by each member of staff, beginning 'Myself—A goose'. The household servants still received their wages once a fortnight from the Rothschilds' solicitor, who drove over from Aylesbury in a horse and fly with a Gladstone bag full of cash. The cook initiated Dorothy into the kitchen routines: 'In the Still-Room they prepared only breakfast, buns, English cakes . . . And in it was done the washing up of the best dessert china. In the Pastry Kitchen more elaborate cakes, puddings, chocolates and sweets were made; and in the Bakery, of course, only the bread—which was baked all night and the baker slept all day.' Most baffling of all to Dorothy was the Still Room Maid's account of her duties under Alice: 'we

OPPOSITE: *Visiting Palestine: Dorothy and James with Baron Edmond, about 1920. The couple shared Baron Edmond's passionate commitment to the Zionist cause.*

ABOVE: *The electric bell board, part of James and Dorothy's modernisation of the house.*

washed and prepared the parsley for the sandwiches—but naturally we did not make the sandwiches themselves; that was kitchen work.'

Most importantly for the future of the house, Mrs Boxall explained to Dorothy how the interiors were maintained, showing her the boxes in which the porcelain was packed up when the house was not in use and explaining the rules for handling it: 'white-haired, but with a young pink and white complexion, she had an encyclopaedic knowledge of all the arts of conservation on which Miss Alice had so much insisted . . . it was she who explained how textiles should be treated in a perfectly run house. I was let into the secrets of the great cupboards in the North and South Linen Rooms and was shown the enchantingly pretty patterned linen covers which Miss Alice had made for every chair in the house. In her philosophy, as in Mrs Boxall's, tapestry and silk uphol-

JAMES AND DOROTHY

stery should only be allowed to be visible when there were guests in the house.' Mrs Boxall was clearly a rather underrated link in the succession of Waddesdon's custodians, for she was responsible for passing on into the post-war world the rules for maintaining houses that were dropping out of usage elsewhere, partly because of a gradual disappearance of well-qualified household servants, but more significantly because domestic life in the 1920s no longer tolerated the lack of convenience that resulted from an insistence on this sort of scrupulous care. Owners increasingly wanted to use even the greatest houses all the year round, and, unlike previous generations, expected rooms to be brightly lit and open to the sunshine as much as possible.

Dorothy's resistance to changing fashions was perhaps, paradoxically, a result of her lack of a country-house background. As she

Putting the Manor to bed: Following Miss Alice's and Dorothy's rigorous household rules today, each winter the Sèvres porcelain is packed into its boxes and all the furniture is covered, as this view of the Small Library shows.

wrote: 'I never had any experience whatever of country life. All our holidays were spent in a small house in Brighton . . . nothing in my upbringing or experience had prepared me for life in the English countryside or, indeed, at Waddesdon.' As a result, she took Mrs Boxall's instruction in the standard rules of country-house housekeeping—which admittedly had been maintained with exceptional rigour—to be something unique, with which she was being entrusted. James undoubtedly confirmed this feeling: 'My husband . . . impressed on me that I should try to take the same care as had always been exercised in this house', she commented after his death. Perhaps she never realised how unusual her maintenance of this tradition was, for in her book she modestly gives the credit for Waddesdon's state of preservation to Alice. Yet Alice lived in the house for barely four months in the year, maintained a large staff, and entertained comparatively little. In contrast, Dorothy kept up the standards set by Alice in a house that was lived in all the year round, where there were guests almost every weekend, and fewer domestic servants. Hers was by far the more impressive achievement.

Nonetheless, changes were made for the sake of convenience. The house was rewired, bathrooms were added, and the drainage was given a thorough overhaul. Victorian parlour-palms were replaced by flower arrangements. Alice's first-floor sitting room was dismantled: 'its Savonnerie carpet, on which it would have been unthinkable to tread with muddy shoes . . . was hardly a surface on which one could chuck untidy books and newspapers' wrote Dorothy. 'But we needed somewhere in which we could tackle the affairs of daily life without being inhibited by the beauty or fragility of our surroundings. So this room was completely emptied; bookcases were put all round the walls; a plain carpet was laid on the floor and comfortable leather chairs and sofas installed. Emptied of its silks and drawings there was no need in this room to keep a constant and watchful eye on the position of the sun-blinds which were here, in fact, abolished. For us, it became a blissful snuggery.' Alice's pictures and furnishings were dispersed amongst the downstairs rooms, the first major embellishment of the principal rooms since Ferdinand's death.

While this was going on, Eythrope was prepared for being let, which necessitated the addition of a bedroom wing. One of its first tenants was Syrie Maugham, the fashionable decorator and estranged wife of the novelist Somerset Maugham. She popularised a taste for white, sparely furnished interiors—Eythrope was redone with white plasterwork palms designed by Serge Roche and Egyptian lamps by Giacometti—a reminder that Waddesdon was rapidly falling out of fashion. By the 1930s, it seemed to many visitors a period-piece, and,

since educated taste had swung violently against the 19th century, it was not much liked. In July 1939 Harold Nicolson came to stay, and wrote to his wife, Vita, to complain with characteristic housewifely acerbity that 'hardly a thing has been changed since the old Baron's time . . . Jimmy hates anything being altered, and the lavatories still have handles you pull up instead of chains you pull down. There is no running water in the bedrooms'. It was all very different from life at Sissinghurst, the Nicolsons' 16th-century home in Kent: 'There are marvellous pictures and Sèvres, but execrable taste . . . although it is very luxurious as regards food and drink and flowers, it is really less comfortable than our mud-pie in the weald.' If Dorothy ever noticed such attitudes she never mentioned them. We tend to take for granted her devotion to Waddesdon, but in England it was not typical of her generation. James would no doubt not have allowed any major changes to the house, but he might well have married someone like Vita Sackville-West, just three years older than Dorothy, who would have secretly longed to strip the panelling, thin out the furniture and then sell up in favour of a Tudor manor house. This was, after all, the era of Evelyn Waugh's *A Handful of Dust*, which describes the efforts of a young bride to introduce contemporary interiors into her husband's Victorian country house. But Dorothy was no Brenda Last—or Syrie Maugham: she had absorbed her tastes from her husband and parents-in-law and although not a Rothschild by birth, she had made their aesthetic outlook her own.

Other adaptations reflected James's enthusiasms: the small golf course laid out by Alice was extended and a stud was established. Although the subject of James's eager attention, it was not notably successful—he was fond of repeating a friend's remark that although many people backed outsiders, Jimmy Rothschild was the only person he knew who bred them. In the garden, Alice's standards were still maintained by Johnson. Here, James made more far-reaching changes, for he decided to convert the glasshouses into a commercial nursery, under Johnson's supervision. As Dorothy wrote, 'We came to the sad conclusion that the beautiful Alamandas, Bougainvillaea and Gloriosa Rothschildiana which ramped up the central sections of the "Top Glass" would have to be scrapped and that the exotic species in many of the other houses must also go . . . the huge fairyland of semi-tropical colour so enthusiastically created by our predecessors had ceased, in the 1920's, to be a viable project for any private garden to harbour.' In the place of fairyland came cyclamen, primulas, anthuriums, and other flowers grown in enormous quantities for sale. The anthuriums were the one major exception to the move towards commerce, and they continued to be exhibited at horticultural shows. In 1928, as Brent Elliott records, four of Johnson's anthurium varieties, including *Waddesdonense* and *Mrs J. de Rothschild* won awards of merit from the Royal Horticultural Society and in 1934 Johnson staged a display of anthuriums from Waddesdon that received a Gold Medal at the Chelsea Flower Show. Although the fruit ranges were initially maintained, a flood in 1924 damaged the glasshouse's grotto, and it was never restored; the water and rock gardens continued to be kept up until the late 1930s, when they too began to be neglected.

In commercial terms, the transformation of the gardens was successful: an account for 1939 reveals that the garden cost £8,864 to run—little less than in Alice's day—but that revenue from sales, at £4,138, covered almost half its costs. Johnson received a commission on sales—£343 in 1939, considerably more than his salary of £216, but did not record what he thought of the changes at Waddesdon. An account he prepared for the Inland Revenue in 1941 makes clear how little was left of the garden Alice had known: 'By 1931 the last ornamental bedding in the pleasure grounds was grassed over and thereafter the whole of the glass both at Waddesdon and Eythrope was devoted to flowers, fruit and vegetables suitable for commercial purposes . . . at first we sold direct to shops in Aylesbury but as our output increased we marketed the whole of the flowers through George Monro Ltd and as regards the vegetables and hardy fruit through a local wholesaler'.

A description of the glasshouses after this transformation has been left by Virginia Woolf, who paid a visit with her husband, Leonard, in April 1930. Leonard's family were relatives by marriage of the Pintos and, thanks to Dorothy's influence, his brother Philip, who had been invalided out of the army during the war, had been appointed the estate's agent in succession to Sims. After lunch with Philip and his wife, Barbara, at Upper Winchendon, they were shown round the glasshouses by Johnson, as Virginia recorded in her diary: 'Cyclamen by the hundred gross. Azaleas massed like military bands. Carnations at different stages. Vines being picked thin by sedulous men. Nothing older than 40 years, but now ready made in perfection. A figtree that had a thousand lean regular branches.

ABOVE: *James at the races: A cartoon by George Belcher, 1922.*

OVERLEAF LEFT: *The Wild Flower Valley with a glimpse of Waddesdon Manor.*
ABOVE RIGHT: *The Tropical Mound and the north front.* BELOW RIGHT: *The Parterre*

PAGES 228–229: *The Box View with a marble statue of Diana.*

The statues tied up, like dead horses, in sheets. The whole thing dead. Made, planted, put into position in the year 1880 or thereabouts. One flower wd. have given more pleasure than those dozens of grosses. And the heat, & the tidiness & the accuracy & the organisation. Mr Johnson like a nectarine, hard, red, ripe. He was taught all he knew by Miss Alice, & accepted admiration as his income. Sir he called us.'

A couple of days later she returned to her diary to record her impression of Johnson in more detail: 'There were rows of blue hydrangeas, mostly a deep blue. Yes, said Mr Johnson, Lord Kitchener came here & asked how we blued them . . . I said you put things in the earth. He said he did too. But sometimes with all one's care, they shot a bit pink. Miss Alice wouldn't have that. If there was a trace of pink there, it wouldnt do. And he showed us a metallic petalled hydrangea. No that wouldnt do for Miss Alice. It struck me, what madness, & how easy to pin one's mind down to the blueness of hydrangeas, & to hypnotise Mr Johnson into thinking only of the blueness of hydrangeas. He used to go every evening, for she scarcely saw anyone, & they would talk for two hours about the plants & politics. How easy to go mad over the hydrangeas & think of nothing else.'

Virginia Woolf had great sympathy for the rural constraints of her sister-in-law's life, writing in 1926 to Vita Sackville-West that 'she was worn to the bone with living. Seven miles from a village: no servant will stay; weekend parties at the Great House; Princess Mary playing cross word puzzles after lunch, my sister in law stripping her one pair of shoes and skirt to ribbons hunting rabbits in the bushes by way of amusing Princess Mary; two babies; and so on.' This glimpse of royal guests at Waddesdon is a reminder that, more than is often realised, social life in country houses revived vigorously after the First World War. In 1922, the old Rothschild Buckinghamshire network was still largely intact, despite the loss of Halton. Of all the English members of the family, Walter, the 2nd Lord Rothschild, was probably James and Dorothy's closest friend; the recipient of the Balfour Declaration, he was a major ally in the Zionist cause and they spent much time at Tring. His cousin Lionel also made them welcome at Ascott. Aston Clinton was then divided between Anthony's daughters, Constance Battersea and Annie Yorke, who still entertained there in the summer, but it was soon afterwards sold. In 1923 Lord Rosebery—whose combination of charm and banter fascinated and alarmed Dorothy almost as much as it had done Ferdinand—handed Mentmore over to his heir, Lord Dalmeny, an old friend of James, who shared his passion for horses and racing. Waddesdon also continued to be a centre for the international Rothschild cousinhood and their friends—James, like almost all his family, spoke French, German and English with interchangeable fluency, and could also make lively conversation in Spanish, Italian and Hebrew. His brother and sister and their families were frequent visitors, and at times, especially when such old friends of Ferdinand as Daisy Fellowes or Margot Asquith joined them, the conversation must have had many echoes of pre-war life.

Nonetheless, house parties were much less formal than they had been in Ferdinand's time. This is confirmed by the visitors' book, which records smaller parties than had been usual in the 19th century, but much more frequent ones. Dorothy recalled in an interview after the publication of her book that 'we were always having people to stay. We could put up 26 people comfortably . . . The Morning Room, curiously enough, was where everyone used to meet after dinner. There were two writing tables—Baron Ferdinand thought it important that two people should be able to write a letter simultaneously. And in my day there were two huge card tables—one under each chandelier.' When asked what the Tower Drawing Room was used for, she could only remember that 'we used to play the occasional game of bezique there', and that people used to congregate in the West Gallery. This rather low-key weekend social life, in which crossword puzzles and card games predominated, occasionally gave way to more elaborate parties, most notably when George V and Queen Mary were entertained in July 1926. James and Dorothy were expecting Queen Mary for tea on Sunday, when they received a telephone call from Buckingham Palace late on Friday asking if the King could come as well, and whether they could provide lunch. 'In a flash', wrote Dorothy, 'I realised the difficulty of dealing with this change of plan in the short time left to us and of securing guests and food for a luncheon party in the country at 24 hours' notice. I also became uneasily aware of my ignorance of the conventions which might rule the reception of a reigning monarch in one's own home—was it for him, for instance, to rise and thus signal the end of luncheon, or was this still the duty of the hostess?'

Once all this was sorted out, with advice on etiquette from Lady Crewe, a problem with the tree planting loomed: one cedar sapling had been provided for Queen Mary to plant, in the tradition established by Ferdinand, but now there would have to be two. Where could a second be obtained? 'I sped to the garden to consult Johnson. He was as resourceful as ever, and calmed my agitation by showing me, just next to the spot where it was planned the cedar should go, an old and fairly rare tree of a species which never exceed four feet in height, even when fully grown. This he thought could well be dug up and then after suitable titivation, could be returned with ceremony to the hole from whence it came, with no-one being any the wiser.' The stratagem worked, and despite the failure of the fountains to work on cue, the day was a great success. Over lunch, the King described to Dorothy in detail his recollections of visiting Waddesdon in 1889 to help entertain the Shah: 'he somewhat sadly remarked that he and Ralph Nevill were the only survivors of all those who had been at Waddesdon on that occasion'. As usual for important social occasions, the Razumovsky Sèvres service was used: Dorothy pointed out that it was 'convenient for this purpose because of its milk and cream jugs which were available for their Majesties' coffee, which . . . according to custom has to be served on a separate tray from that used for the other guests'.

The King and Queen were accompanied by their only daughter, Princess Mary, the Princess Royal, who with her husband, Lord Lascelles, later the Earl of Harewood, was a frequent visitor at Waddesdon (as Virginia Woolf had learned). The visitors' book records the sort of people who were invited with them: the Duke and Duchess of Westminster, the Earl of Carnarvon, the Earl of Wemyss and the Aga Khan, a mixture of old Rothschild acquaintances and members of James's racing fraternity. Dorothy was an anxious hostess: 'During the initial period of invitation one composed the perfect party which one learnt from experience would so rarely end up as planned. For excellent but varied reasons some guests would begin by accepting and then chucked; others refused for the date on which they were invited but wondered if they could not come on some other day or days invariably awkward for oneself. And when the party did assemble I understood all too well Baron Ferdinand's anxiety about his guests' plans and wishes. Presumably we knew in advance who preferred talk to bridge and the relative skills of players of card games, but the plans for the following day always depended so much on the weather—who wished to play golf? Who would be cajoled into visiting the garden or the Stud? Or who might be bent on some intellectual excursion to Oxford? Or who might have business at near-by Chequers [the prime minister's official country residence]? Preparations for all these possibilities were easier if made in advance.'

Dorothy remained prone to anxiety about social arrangements until the end of her life. That, combined with her thoughtful desire to keep all her guests entertained, led to her and James beginning to compartmentalise their guests according to their interests, a habit she never lost. Instead of Ferdinand's very mixed groups of guests, Waddesdon's house parties now tended to revolve round three groups, which were increasingly kept separate—racing, Palestine, and politics. Some overlap was inevitable, and when Harold Nicolson visited in 1939 he found himself amidst a racing party: Lord and Lady Hillingdon, the Earl and Countess of Bessborough, Lady Linlithgow, Richard Molyneux and, once again, the Princess Royal and Lord Lascelles. The daily routine was much as Ferdinand and Alice would have recognised—guests were left to themselves, to write and read, in the morning; ate a superb and soporific lunch; toured the glasshouses in the afternoon; and played poker after dinner (at which Nicolson won £2 from Princess Mary). As in the 19th century, artistic and intellectual society was not conspicuous, and as Dorothy explained: 'any interest in works of art seemed to be a rarity among our guests. Occasionally some of them conscientiously toured the pictures but more often it was the view out of the window which caught their eye: china, furniture and carpets were never objects of interest.' There were exceptions: when Isaiah Berlin achieved celebrity in 1932 by becoming the first Jewish fellow of All Souls' College, Oxford, he was at

Dorothy at her desk, photographed by Lafayette in 1935.

once invited to Waddesdon, the beginning of a life-long friendship with James and Dorothy.

In 1928, James agreed to stand for parliament as the Liberal candidate for the Isle of Ely. His success in the following year's general election was the beginning of a 16-year parliamentary career and brought a political dimension back to Waddesdon's house parties, although Dorothy was quick to dismiss any comparison with the 1880s and 1890s: ' Baron Ferdinand . . . had been an influential member of the governing Liberal party, whereas Jimmy, also a life-long Liberal, found himself an adherent of a party in opposition which, after a brief flicker of revival in 1929, steadily declined in numbers

OPPOSITE: *Dorothy and James at Wisbech on the Isle of Ely, campaigning for the 1929 election.*

BELOW: The Visitor, *a caricature of James in old age by Nagy, about 1950.*

and power from that date onwards. For this reason, if no other, I do not think that in our time the confabulations of leading politicians at Waddesdon can have led to spectacular results on the political life of the country. I like to think our friends, including even such dominant personalities as Mr. Asquith and Mr. Churchill, regarded Waddesdon as a place where they could relax from their labours and indulge in such pastimes as golf, bezique, bridge and Mah-jong'. However, this underestimates two important aspects of James's political career in which the social life at Waddesdon undoubtedly played a part. The first was Palestine, and James did not hesitate to use contacts made in Westminster to lobby for the Zionist cause. Successive prime ministers, first David Lloyd George and from 1922 Andrew Bonar Law, had looked to James to provide advice about Palestine, and he continued to be a source for authoritative information for the British government in the 1930s. In 1924 he became president of the Palestine Jewish Colonization Association (PICA); sponsored largely by his father, it was devoted to promoting Jewish settlement and self-defence in what was now a British protectorate. Almost from the beginning, he and other prominent Jews and Zionist sympathisers were struggling to keep Britain faithful to the commitment set out in the Balfour Declaration, a commitment sapped by Arab opposition. In 1930, Lord Passfield (Sidney Webb) put forward a White Paper proposing legislation that would impose stricter controls on settlement and immigration in Palestine. This prompted James to make one of his rare parliamentary speeches, and although the proposal was dropped by the prime minister, Ramsay Macdonald, the following year, James set up the Palestine Parliamentary Group to promote the beliefs that had led to the Balfour Declaration.

By the early 1930s, Jewish concerns were increasingly centred on Europe. Just as in the 1880s, when the Rothschilds were the first to publicise news of the Russian pogroms, the family's international links made it aware of the Nazi threat to German Jews well before it was a matter of widespread concern in England. James's sister, Miriam von Goldschmidt-Rothschild, lived in Frankfurt, where in 1933, in a sinister portent of what was to happen to the family, Rothschildallee was renamed Karolingerallee by the new National Socialist regime. Five years later, Rothschild property began to fall victim to the Nazi expropriation of Jewish assets, beginning with the family's charitable foundations, which were sequestrated or dissolved. Well before then, James's brothers-in-law, Albert, Rudolf and Erich von Goldschmidt-Rothschild, the sons of his aunt Minna, had sold the family estates at Grüneburg and Konigstein and had gone into exile; their father, Max,

loyalties. (He was a member of the Other Club, founded by Churchill and F. E. Smith in 1911 as a focus for Churchill's political supporters.) In the 1930s Churchill was still in the political wilderness, as the British ruling party refused to accept his message that war was inevitable. Many of Churchill's most prominent supporters can be found in Waddesdon's visitors' book at this time, including Duff and Diana Cooper, Lord Beaverbrook and his wife, and Brendan Bracken. At Cliveden, only a few miles from Waddesdon, a pro-appeasement political circle had crystallised around the Astors; it would perhaps be an exaggeration to see Waddesdon as a country-house counterbalance to Cliveden's influence, but the social and emotional support the Rothschilds gave to Churchill were never forgotten by him. The warmth of their friendship was noted by Churchill's private secretary, Jock Colville, who recorded in his diary that after a lunch party at Chequers on July 14, 1940, when Britain stood in the gravest peril it has ever faced, Churchill and James spent the afternoon admiring the paintings in the house.

In 1934 Edmond died at the age of 89, followed a year later by his wife. It was a symbolic break with the past—Edmond was the last surviving grandchild of Mayer Amschel Rothschild, the founder of the family's fortunes—and it prompted a major upheaval in the French branch of the family, as Maurice's inheritance of his father's share of the bank led to his cousins attempting to buy him out. That resulted in litigation that took five years to conclude, and made the settlement of Edmond's estate exceptionally long-drawn-out. Two major elements of his collection, the prints and the early Old Master drawings, were given to the Louvre, but otherwise his collections were largely divided among his three children. In 1936, the first crates began to arrive at Waddesdon, and James and Dorothy were faced with the problem of integrating Edmond's possessions into the interiors. They included some pieces as important as anything then in the house, most notably perhaps the commode by Charles Cressent that Edmond had bought at the Hamilton Palace sale. Also in the bequest was a third of his remaining collection of drawings, as well as paintings attributed to Rubens and Watteau, Gainsborough's *Pink Boy*, which Ferdinand had bequeathed to Adelaïde, and a writing table stamped by Martin Carlin which had once been owned by George IV. There was also a large group of Sèvres, including nine pieces that had been in Ferdinand's collection as well as the largest item ever made by the factory in soft paste, a potpourri vase with painted decoration attributed to C.-N. Dodin, which Ferdinand had greatly admired when he saw it in the collection of Edmond's father, James. Adelaïde also made bequests to her son and daughter-in-law, notably her lace

was too old to accompany them, and in the aftermath of *Kristallnacht* was forced to sell his remaining art collection and property to the city of Frankfurt for a derisory sum. Similar actions were taken against the Viennese Rothschilds after the *Anschluss* of March 1938. In part as a result of the fate that was overwhelming his family in Germany and Austria, James naturally allied himself with the anti-appeasement party that centred around Churchill, despite the fact that this cut across party

178

FROM LEFT: *Further examples of Baron Edmond's collections of drawings: a design by Pillement for a chinoiserie wall painting ; a drawing of a monstrance, by Meissonnier; and a drawing of a Salon for the Hôtel de Mailly-Nesle, by Cauvet.*

FROM LEFT: *Examples of Baroness Edmond's collections, now at Waddesdon:*
A parasol with lace race horses; a box containing her exceptional collection
of Brussels, Alençon, Chantilly and Burano lace; and one of her eighteenth-
century fans, depicting a Venetian carnival.

and button collections, together with further porcelain and *objets d'art*. Some of her pieces were still in Paris in 1940, when they fell victim to Goering, who confiscated them for his hunting lodge at Carinhall; recovered after the war and brought to Waddesdon, they still retain the inventory numbers inscribed on them by the Nazis.

'We hesitated quite a lot before changing the rooms at Waddesdon so that these extra objects could be included', recalled Dorothy in a lecture to the house guides in 1959, 'but we knew that Miss Alice had such a regard for my father-in-law's incomparable knowledge, taste and possessions, that she herself would not have hesitated to make room for them. It was a difficult jigsaw nonetheless. The 'Pink Boy' found his own place. He happened to be dumped in the Morning Room to await a permanent site. And it so happened that I walked into the Morning Room and from the West Hall saw it framed in the door, and realised that no more suitable place could be found for it. It meant a little shifting around . . . The other things more or less automatically placed themselves. If you look at the Red Drawing Room you will realise that only dark blue china would really blend there. As there happened to be a great deal of Royal Blue Sèvres available, it was only a question of arranging it symmetrically. The Grey Drawing Room seemed to scream for lighter colours. The turquoise ship was placed there already by Baron Ferdinand, and it seemed the obvious

haven for all my father-in-law's pink Sèvres. The *Commode Hamilton* was much more difficult to place. We tried it in the West Gallery, but it was too big and heavy. We finally chose the Grey Drawing Room where, anyhow, its proportions are in keeping.'

No sooner were Edmond's treasures in place than the war scare of September 1938 led to most of the contents of Waddesdon being packed up and put in the cellars. Although they did not remain there for long, James, convinced that war was imminent, suggested to the Ministry of Health that in case of conflict the house should be converted into a hospital. The idea met with no enthusiasm—'we came to understand that *boiserie*, even if covered up, would be a first-class harbourer of germs'—but the offer of refuge for evacuees was accepted. When war finally broke out, in September 1939, the house was adapted to shelter some 100 children from the outskirts of London, all under five, together with their nursemaids. James and Dorothy moved into the Bachelors' Wing (the Low White Drawing Room became their dining room) and all but three of the downstairs rooms were emptied, as were all the bedrooms. 'The average number of cots in each room was eight', Dorothy told the house guides in a lecture during the 1950s: 'the Red Drawing Room was used as their dining room and was full of diminutive tables and matching chairs—at Christmas time there was always a huge tree in the Breakfast Room—it looked lovely, all lit up . . . seen through the doorway of the East Gallery. The children used the big dining room as their daily rest room but at Christmas time they gave performances in it—I can hear their songs now—I must say these are very happy recollections.' These were the first—and last—children to live in the house.

Other evacuees were accommodated in the village: the gardeners' bothy became a home for expectant mothers, and for two

A selection of the treasures inherited by James from his parents:
BELOW: *An English étui, with two contemporary French designs for gold boxes.*
BELOW RIGHT: *A detail of the ormolu mounts on the magnificent commode by Charles Cressent, which Baron Edmond bought at the Hamilton Palace sale in 1883.*
OPPOSITE: *An illuminated manuscript depicting the Coronation Feast of Anne of Brittany (1505).* OVERLEAF: The Pink Boy *by Gainsborough and a late-fifteenth-century Book of Hours from Tours.*

Que parler
Vray du son
de la Korne
Le mel sut gra
sumptueux &
magnifficque

A lon sorcur achuenement
Et assauoir que en faisant
les preparatines de la Ville cestes
du palais ne demeurerent der
uere Car on osta tous les sieges
& bancs des aduocatz pracureurs
& aultres qui sont en ladicte
grant salle du palais Et les fit
on porter pour tenir le parlement
En la maison mons de paus
Et au lieu diceulx furent fetes
tables bancs sieges & assiectes
propices tout autour ladicte
salle Aussi a chun pillier buffetz

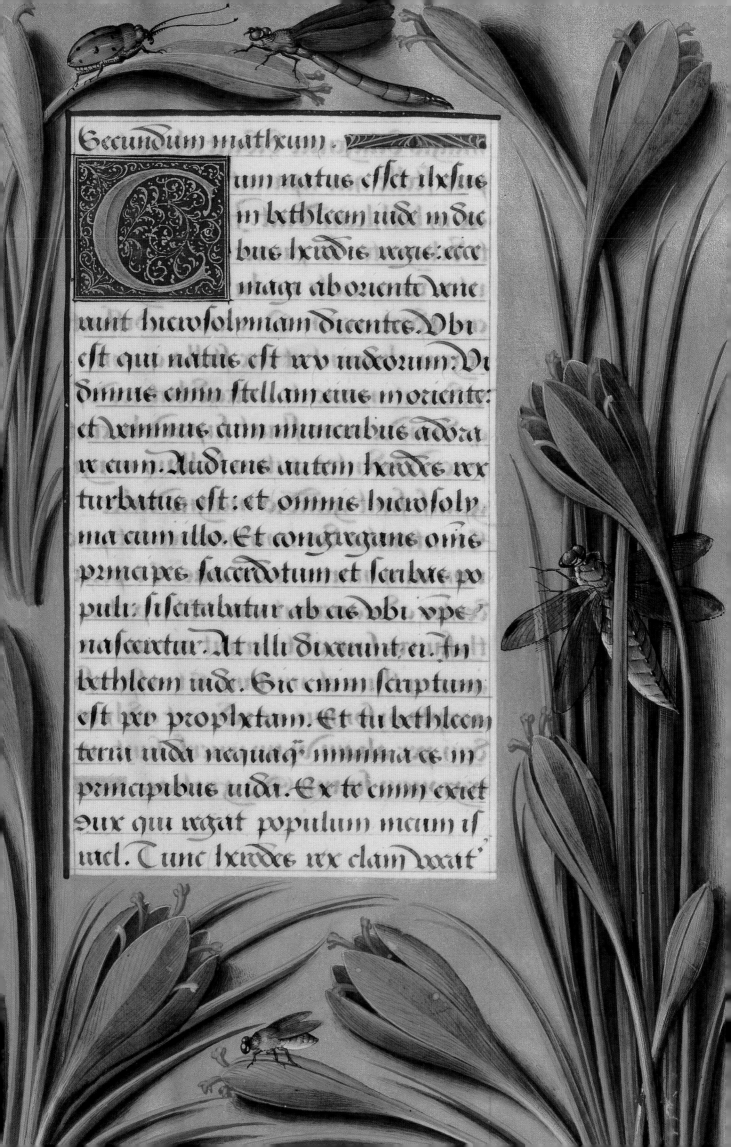

Secundum matheum .

um natus esset ihesus
in bethleem iude in die
bus herodis regis: ecce
magi ab oriente vene
runt hierosolymam dicentes. Ubi
est qui natus est rex iudeorum: Vi
dimus enim stellam eius in oriente:
et venimus cum muneribus adora
re eum. Audiens autem herodes rex
turbatus est: et omnis hierosoly
ma cum illo. Et congregans omes
principes sacerdotum et scribae po
puli: sciscitabatur ab eis ubi xpe
nasceretur. At illi dixerunt ei. In
bethleem iude. Sic enim scriptum
est per prophetam. Et tu bethleem
terra iuda nequaquam minima es in
principibus iuda. Ex te enim exiet
dux qui regat populum meum is
rael. Tunc herodes rex clam vocat'

CLOCKWISE FROM BELOW LEFT: *Wartime evacuee children putting on their boots in the Ante Room to the Dining Room; having their afternoon rest in the Dining Room; and helping to mow the North Lawn, 1939 to 1945.*

OPPOSITE: *Dorothy at a Women's Voluntary Service meeting, about 1940.*

years the village hall was a dormitory for nearly 200 people. In 1941, the park was taken as a petrol dump: 'there was not a sizeable tree within our boundaries which did not have a concrete platform and a Nissen hut full of petrol drums nestling beneath it', Dorothy recalled. Much of her time was taken up with the Women's Voluntary Service, for which she was the local organiser. This involved making camouflage nets, collecting salvage, and finding space at Waddesdon to house WVS central stores, away from the threat of bombs in London. The WVS member in charge of those stores was Maria Brassey, a descendant of Thomas Brassey, the celebrated Victorian railway contractor. She first signed the visitors' book in October 1944, and returned frequently thereafter. Described after her death as 'one of those rare people who combine brains and a sense of humour with an almost total commitment to the happiness of others', she became

Dorothy's closest friend, and an invaluable support to her, especially in the exceptionally difficult decade that lay ahead.

On top of their immediate concerns at home, James and Dorothy were bitterly aware of the ordeal of Europe's Jews. On December 17, 1942, a statement about the extermination camps was read out to Parliament. That night, the MP Chips Channon recorded in his diary how 'Jimmy de Rothschild rose, and with immense dignity, and his voice vibrating with emotion, spoke for five minutes in moving tones on the plight of these peoples. There were tears in his eyes, and I feared that he might break down; the House caught his spirit and was deeply moved. Somebody suggested that we stand in silence to pay our respects to these suffering peoples, and the House as a whole rose and stood for a few frozen seconds. It was a fine moment, and my back tingled.' James and Dorothy had also been able to offer some practical help. In 1939 they had been approached by Lt Col Julian Layton of the Jewish Refugees' Committee in London. Born Julian Loewenstein in 1904 to parents who had emigrated to London from Frankfurt in 1893, he had set up the organisation in 1933 with a fellow stockbroker, Otto Schiss. Thanks to them, homes were found for numerous Jewish refugees, notably in Australia. James agreed to house a group at Waddesdon, and in 1939 thirty orphans aged between six and 12—28 boys and 2 girls—from Frankfurt's Flersheim-Sichel Institute, which was a home for children attending the nearby Philanthropin school, were evacuated to England. James provided them with a house in Waddesdon, The Cedars, formerly a maternity home founded by Alice, where they lived under the care of their guardians, Hugo Steinhardt and his wife, who had been released from Buchenwald thanks to Layton's intervention. It was a last-minute escape: a second group from the same institute, destined for South America, was not allowed to leave. 'It says much for the understanding of the village, and for the tact of the newcomers, that this little orphanage was welcomed with open arms', remembered Dorothy. 'The children were all educated either in the village school or in the Grammar School in Aylesbury. They learnt English astonishingly quickly and were integrated into the life of the village almost immediately . . . one boy even represented Aylesbury in a boxing contest.' Although after the war the children scattered, some to Israel and others to North and South America, they would not forget Waddesdon, or the Rothschilds.

JAMES AND DOROTHY

ABOVE: *The Cedar Boys, German Jewish refugees, from Frankfurt, with one of their guardians, Mrs. Steinhart, in about 1940. In 2000 they were featured in a Warner Brothers film entitled:* Into the Arms of Strangers.

OPPOSITE: *James de Rothschild, photographed by Lafayette, about 1935.*

As a tribute to James's loyal support, and a token of friendship, in May 1945 Churchill made him Joint Parliamentary Secretary to the Ministry of Supply, but it was the briefest of ministerial careers, for in the general election in July, the Labour party was swept to power in a landslide, and James lost his seat in parliament. During the election campaign he had a serious fall, further weakening his already feeble health; for the rest of his life, he would be an invalid.

When the evacuees moved out of Waddesdon, he and Dorothy were able for the first time to contemplate the house's future. It cannot have been an optimistic moment. The furniture and paintings were all in storage, the silk hangings in the Red Drawing Room were in tatters, and on the very last day of the war, a tap was left running in an upstairs bathroom, causing a flood that cascaded into the Baron's Room on the floor below, drenching the delicate marquetry of the great Beaumarchais desk and soaking a pile of books. In retrospect, it seems an omen of the deluge that was shortly to sweep away so many of Britain's notable country houses. Waddesdon had survived two world wars, but few people in the autumn of 1945 would have predicted that it could last much longer.

8

THE NATIONAL TRUST

GRIM THOUGH THE FUTURE for Waddesdon may have seemed in 1945, in many ways it had escaped lightly in comparison with other country houses. Thanks to James's initiative in securing a benign use for it during the war, military requisition had been avoided. The presence of troops in a house almost always led to severe damage that was virtually impossible to repair quickly, since wartime restrictions on building work were maintained well into the 1950s. Apart from the water leak, and an outbreak of mould on some of the paintings (caused by their temporary storage in a damp cellar), the collections had survived unscathed. James and Dorothy also had the financial resources to resume their pre-war life in the house, should they have wished. However, there was little encouragement for them to do so. In 1922, as a young couple moving into Waddesdon, they had found that country-house life had revived with surprisingly few changes after the First World War. Circumstances were now very different. On a personal level, James was in his sixties and in very poor health, and the family network that had sustained the couple's social life between the wars had all but vanished. Halton and Aston Clinton had long gone, but now there were no Rothschilds living at Tring, which had been sold by Victor, the 3rd Lord Rothschild. In London, Gunnersbury was relinquished between 1925 and 1929 for use as a public park, and most of the family's great Piccadilly houses had been given up before the war. The Rothschilds' possessions in Germany and Austria had been sold or expropriated and most of their houses destroyed. Moreover, England in 1945 was in a

Dorothy de Rothschild at work in the Morning Room.

much worse state than it had been in 1918: virtually bankrupted by the war effort, with many cities badly damaged by air raids, it was not surprising that dramatic political change ensued. After its triumph in the general election, the Labour party embarked on the most determinedly socialist programme of legislation that the country had ever known. In its first budget, the new government increased the rate of death duties from 65% to 75%; by 1950, they stood at 80%. In 1945, there was no procedure for offering houses or works of art in lieu of tax; for most owners of historic houses or collections faced with massive capital tax bills, sale was the only option.

As a result, there seemed to be no future for country houses in private hands and the morale of the landowning class that had sustained them was in an apparently terminal decline. Everywhere that James and Dorothy looked, houses were being abandoned. To take only the very grandest, Chatsworth was no longer lived in by the Cavendishes, and after the death of the 10th Duke of Devonshire in 1950, the burden of death duties was so enormous that negotiations were opened for the house's transference to the nation as an outstation of the Victoria and Albert Museum. Castle Howard, which had been badly damaged by fire during the war, was no longer being lived in, nor was Woburn Abbey; and the Earl of Leicester's endeavours to sell Holkham were thwarted only by the entail on the estate. In 1948, James's old friend Princess Mary and her son, Lord Harewood, began negotiations for Harewood to be given to the nation. However, a lifeline was being offered by the National Trust. Set up in 1895 as a private charity (as it remains) to 'acquire land and buildings worthy of permanent preservation', the organisation had widened its remit in the late 1930s to help country houses. It proposed taking over the ownership of houses and their estates, so allowing families to continue to live in them free of the burdens of capital taxation. In order to make it possible for the Trust to do this, an act of parliament was passed in 1937, which permitted the organisation to hold land and funds for the endowment of houses.

This 'country-house scheme', as it became known, was not an immediate success, in the sense of traditional landowners rushing to avail themselves of the Trust's shelter; the very first house acquired under the scheme was not a Chatsworth or a Holkham, but Wightwick Manor, a Victorian house on the outskirts of Wolverhampton. The Trust's initiative met its warmest response from a particular sort of owner—those who had created houses or collections themselves and had no heirs. As a result, many of the houses acquired by the National Trust in the 1930s and 1940s were relatively modern creations, such as the Treasurer's House in York, which had been imaginatively restored and furnished by Edward Green, the bachelor son of an industrial family, or Packwood in Warwickshire, lovingly revived by a rather similar unmarried aesthete, Graham Baron Ash. It was a theme that was to be continued into the 1950s and 1960s, with such acquisitions as Anglesey Abbey in Cambridgeshire, created by another wealthy bachelor, Lord Fairhaven, with his family's American industrial fortune. There was no reason, therefore, why Waddesdon, a modern work of art without any heir to assume responsibility for it, should not also find a refuge with the National Trust, despite the popular assumption that developed during the 1950s, following the organisation's acquisition of several major historic houses of a more conventional nature, that its priority was help for the traditional landed classes.

In Buckinghamshire alone, the Dashwoods gave West Wycombe to the National Trust in 1943, and in 1956 James's near neighbours, the Verneys, handed over Claydon. Both families continued to live in the houses. In 1950, Anthony Rothschild—who had hoped to be Alice's heir—presented Ascott to the Trust. There was some hesitancy about this acquisition: although the Trust was entitled by Act of Parliament to declare its possessions inalienable, it decided not to do so in the case of Ascott, suggesting that it might in future allow the gift to be revoked. However, the house, which was opened to the public in 1951, continued to be the home of Anthony and his wife, Yvonne, utilising just the sort of arrangement that the country-house scheme had envisaged from the start. James may have been aware of the Trust's work since the early 1920s, because his cousin Charles, Natty's younger son, was then a member of its council. In addition, the decision to approach the organisation about Waddesdon may have been influenced by James's involvement in the negotiations that surrounded the Trust's acquisition of Chartwell, Winston Churchill's small country house in Kent. In 1946, Churchill had proposed selling the house, which he could no longer afford to run. At the prompting of Lord Camrose, a group of the former prime minister's friends bought it, with the intention that Churchill would be allowed to live there for the rest of his life, after which it would become a national memorial to him, in the hands of the National Trust. James contributed £5,000 to the £85,000 raised by Camrose for the house's purchase and endowment. Chartwell may have suggested to James the idea that a house could be preserved not only for its intrinsic merits, but also as a monument to its owners; it seems likely that he thought of Waddesdon's preservation in part as a means of commemorating his family.

More significant still were developments at a governmental level that promised to ameliorate the worst effects of punitively high capital taxation. The new chancellor of the exchequer, Hugh Dalton, was an admirer of the National Trust, which he described as 'a typically British example of Practical Socialism in action'. He wanted the Trust to help make the countryside more readily accessible to the public—he had no interest in country houses as such—and so in his 1946 budget he set up the Land Fund, which was empowered to acquire land and houses in lieu of death duty and pass them to the National Trust. The following year, Cothele in Cornwall became the first historic house to be transferred to the National Trust under this new legislation.

And so, on April 12, 1946, within a month of Dalton's budget and the announcement of the creation of the Land Fund, James's agent, Philip Woolf, wrote to the National Trust's Secretary, George Mallaby, to follow up an informal sounding-out of the Trust's reaction: 'I think I can safely say that Mr de Rothschild does contemplate making an offer of Waddesdon & the surrounding pleasure grounds to the National Trust with a substantial endowment. I think also that, subject to conditions as to its use, he would offer some of the contents with the house. He would certainly wish to retain the right for himself and his successors to live at Waddesdon Manor and, of course, he understood that the public would have access at specified times.' James left no record of his opinions about the National Trust, but there is every reason to believe that he accepted and even shared Dalton's view of its purposes, for British socialism in the 1940s and 1950s had to a large degree inherited its views about land and property from the Edwardian Liberalism with which James was politically identified. Many of the first country-house owners to offer their homes to the National Trust in the 1930s had been Liberals or socialists—Sir Geoffrey Mander at Wightwick, Sir Charles Trevelyan at Wallington, and the Marquess of Lothian at Blickling, for example.

Arrangements were made for the Trust's Historic Buildings Secretary, James Lees-Milne, to pay a visit to Waddesdon, accompanied at the Trust's suggestion by Sir Edward Salisbury, director of the Royal Botanical Gardens, who was to assess the importance of the gardens, and in particular James's orchid collection (although it turned out that Salisbury was too busy to go). Dorothy recorded the preparations for this inspection. The most serious wartime damage to the interior had been sustained by the silk wall hangings in the Red Drawing Room, and these were replaced with a replica woven by a British firm, Hammonds, who fielded an 81-year-old weaver for the task. 'It was curiously difficult to replace the furniture as it had been before the war,' wrote Dorothy. 'I kept on getting mixed up in my mind with the arrangement before and after my parents-in law's possessions had appeared from Paris. Moreover, although the exact angle and spacing of furniture can make or mar a room, much of the furniture at Waddesdon is heavy enough to prohibit many experiments to find out the best arrangement. I remember my joy when I suddenly realised that the carpets still bore the slight marks of flattened pile made by the legs of tables and cupboards which had stood on them before 1939. No longer was a replacement a question of "fish and find out"; one only had to search for those slight indentations on the carpet, retrieve the piece of furniture which corresponded to them and lower it gently into place.'

The reconstruction of the interiors was still in progress when Lees-Milne paid his visit in May 1946. His astonishment at seeing the house for the first time is a reminder of how little Waddesdon and its collections were then known, even to those with a serious interest in art. Like most people of cultivated tastes in his generation, Lees-Milne was not predisposed to like 19th-century art and design, but he was impressed nonetheless. 'What a house!', he wrote in his diary. 'An 1880s pastiche of a Francois Premier château. Yet it is impressive because it is on the grand scale. There is symmetry, and craftsmanship and finish. I suppose most people today would pronounce it hideous. I find it compelling. A nursery school, which was here throughout the war, has just left. It is being scrubbed and cleaned. The Rothschilds are moving back into the whole of it, which is huge. They have been living in the wing. Most of the rooms are panelled with gilded Louis XV *boiserie*. One drawing-room is lined with marble. Furniture French of the highest quality. One room stacked with pictures, taken out of their frames. Could not see them. A hundred acres of grounds offered too. Beautiful trees . . . I have written a report, by no means contemptuous, upon it.'

Nor was it: 'The [Historic Buildings] Committee will need to think very carefully whether or not to recommend the offer of this extraordinary property which, although of comparatively recent creation, is already a relic of a departed era', he wrote in his brief but acute summary. 'Mr Rothschild . . . realises that the endowment must be very heavy, probably in the neighbourhood of £200,000. He and Mrs Rothschild will live in the house until the death of the survivor. The Trust would have to consider what to do with the upstairs floors after Mr and Mrs Rothschild's time. The House, which is enormous, was built regardless of cost in 1880 by a French architect, for Baron Ferdinand Rothschild, in the style of a French château of the reign of Francis I. It is undeniably hideous, but there is an awful impressive-

ness about its symmetry, the high quality of the masonry, and the finish of every detail. It is built of Bath Stone. The interior is even more typical of the period and exhales the very quintessence of late 19th century cosmopolitan plutocracy . . . The Contents I could not see properly for they were all stacked in two or three rooms. Most of the furniture is French 18th century signed by the best known ebenistes, and probably some of it is up to Wallace Collection standards. . . . The Grounds are all concentrated upon the hill and are very beautiful . . . I was told that when the grounds are open to the public, thousands of visitors throng them. Indeed the property would be immensely popular. The glass houses cover a huge area and are in excellent condition. About 17 gardeners were employed before the war.'

Lees-Milne's report reveals that he had at once recognised the significance of Waddesdon as an ensemble, and does not unduly stress the importance of its collections—which admittedly he had not seen properly—at the expense of its architecture and setting. It was a point that he found difficult to convey to his colleagues who had not visited the house. In July, the National Trust's Historic Buildings Committee resolved to recommend acceptance 'on account of the great importance of the collections alone'. That narrow recommendation was accepted by the Trust's Executive Committee: 'In spite of their opinion that the house has no merits per se the Committee recognised the great importance of the contents and instructed the Secretary to accept the offer subject to satisfactory endowment.' Given the significance of the collection to the Trust's estimation of the house's value, Mallaby was instructed to write to Woolf to ask for precise details of the works of art being offered. He received a cool response: Woolf wrote in August that James wished to 're-consider the whole situation'.

There was then total silence from Waddesdon for a year, when in response to further enquiries from the Trust's new Secretary, Oliver Bevir, Woolf wrote that, 'I am afraid it is true, that the project cannot be pursued further for the present. Making an endowment under present conditions is out of the question, and I think we must resign ourselves to having "missed the bus".' Although the Trust assumed simply that James was not prepared to make an endowment of the size it required, it is possible that the issue of the contents was also a difficulty. The

Woodland walks are enlivened by white marble sculptures, including the Shepherd Boy with his Dog *after Bertel Thorvaldsen, 1817;* Winter Term, *eighteenth century;* Venus Arming Cupid *by François Girardon, 1668; and an* Apollo (OVERLEAF), *copied from the* Apollo Belvedere.

idea of making a gift of them may have become more attractive after 1951, when new legislation exempted the contents of historic houses bequeathed to the National Trust from death duties. In 1953, largely as a result of the prolonged negotiations over the fate of the contents of Petworth and Chatsworth, the principle of 'acceptance in lieu of tax' was extended to all chattels, so that for the first time a historic collection could be offered in satisfaction of death duties.

When James reopened negotiations with the National Trust in 1954, he was actively encouraged by his new agent, Duncan Mowat, who had served in the army during the war under the Trust's new Secretary, Jack Rathbone. Mowat informed Rathbone that James and Dorothy had decided to move out of Waddesdon into Eythrope, which was then being extended to accommodate them. Once they had moved, it was proposed that James would make a gift of Waddesdon to the National Trust together with an endowment of £250,000. Rathbone discussed this offer with Lees-Milne, who, although he had been replaced in 1951 as Historic Buildings Secretary by Robin Fedden, still advised the Trust on country houses and was moreover the only member of its executive—apart from the chairman, Lord Crawford—who had actually seen Waddesdon. 'It may be too difficult to go back on this,' Rathbone wrote to Lees-Milne, 'but I am all in favour of second thoughts. I am against accepting another indifferent but grand house just because of the contents, however wonderful, but I suppose if I saw them in their setting I might think otherwise.' Lees-Milne replied that 'I share your misgivings over another rich man's ugly house. But the contents are superb, far superior to Ascott's . . . I think you will find Crawford in favour.'

In that he was mistaken, for Crawford—ironically enough, given the strength of his subsequent support for Dorothy—was anything but enthusiastic about the house, which he had visited before the war. He wrote to Rathbone that he certainly did not think the house worth taking without its contents: 'I see little interest in anything that is so artificially planted on a pristine English landscape. All the same, in all its horror, it is something: & the contents should be a lot.' By then, Rathbone had visited Waddesdon, now fully recovered from its wartime depredations, and summed up his rather changed estimation of it in a long letter to the chairman of the Trust's finance committee, Lord Esher: 'I think, if we want to, there is no reason why we should not have second thoughts about accepting this place . . . we have taken a line (rather non-committally and indefinitely it is true), that our great thing is the holding of inhabited houses not museums—and I see little hope of Waddesdon ever being anything

but a museum.' However, he continued, 'the collection which is now beautifully arranged in the (uninhabited) show-rooms (the Rothschilds live in an adjoining wing) is of course superlative . . . There is not only a treasure-trove of superb French furniture, tapestries, books, china and objets d'art but some wonderful Dutch and English pictures. Lees-Milne and I thought the house of considerable architectural interest (style of Francois Ier built in 1880); although wildly ornate it does in a strange way reflect the character and splendour of the things inside it and is in a different category from Ascott.'

Rathbone had clearly been won over by the house (and perhaps by Lees-Milne's famous powers of persuasion) for his mind was already running on beyond the Trust's acquisition of Waddesdon to a future relationship with the Rothschilds. He added to Esher, 'I do not consider that Mr de Rothschild should be advised to give it away in his lifetime. He is a very shy man and would not take well to public access, but that we should seriously consider accepting a devise by will. The surrounding pleasure grounds are fine and so is the park and all the big agricultural estate. I think we should . . . get as much of the land as possible or, at least, covenants over everything possible within view of the house.' After a return visit to the house, Lord Crawford also revised his opinion, and, as he wrote to Rathbone, 'After he has seen Waddesdon Lord Esher may change his mind. He says this is another instance of the N.T. (or me!) worshipping the Golden Calf!' He wrote to Esher that 'I don't see how anyone who has seen it can fail to be quite overwhelmed by the beauty of the objects and the arrangement unless of Marxist principles he disapproved of luxury splendour and glitter'. Although no Marxist, Esher—memorably described by Lees-Milne as 'like a dormouse, small, hunched, quizzical, sharp and cynical'—was not so easily seduced by Rothschild glamour; Dorothy recalled being told that when he had learned Waddesdon was being offered to the Trust, he had said 'I hate French furniture'. But he submitted to the arguments put forward by Lees-Milne, as Rathbone explained in a letter to Crawford in July 1954: 'At the Finance Committee a vote was taken, almost for the first time I remember; 7 to 2 I think was in favour of accepting. The Executive took a similar view. Esher came round, having seen the place which he did not like at all, to the view that it should be preserved as an entity.'

Negotiations now proceeded in conditions of some secrecy, with all the Trust's correspondence being sent in plain envelopes to Mowat's private address, to avoid Waddesdon's staff having any suspicions about what was going on. Some decisions were made: the

Trust would not ask for the kitchen gardens or glasshouses, it would appoint a curator for the collections and it proposed converting the stables into accommodation for gardeners. Finally, in March 1955, the Trust was given a clear idea of exactly what was on offer when Mowat sent a list of works of art in the house which had been conditionally exempted from estate duty as being 'of national interest' when Alice died in 1922. These were to constitute the basis of the collection which would pass to the Trust. At the same time, he sent Rathbone a financial report that allowed an estimation of Waddesdon's running costs as being £24,170 a year. This enabled the Trust to determine the level of endowment necessary to maintain it: after a simple grossing-up calculation, based on the assumption that the capital would realise an income of 4%, it told Mowat in September 1955 that James would need to provide an endowment of £600,000. It was an enormous sum. To take just one comparison, in 1956 the Trust accepted Ickworth in Suffolk in lieu of death duties with an endowment of just £156,000, raised by the Marchioness of Bristol. James's response was worrying: total silence—not even an acknowledgement of the Trust's letter. For the next eighteen months, although Mowat almost certainly continued talking to Rathbone behind the scenes, official communication between Waddesdon and the Trust came to an end.

During this period, James's health had been failing rapidly, but he still kept up his close involvement with PICA's settlements in Israel, and in 1955 lobbied unsuccessfully for the country's admission to the Commonwealth. He had been deeply touched when in 1952 Churchill paid a warm public tribute to James and Dorothy's old friend Chaim Weizmann, Israel's first president, who had recently died: 'It will mean a lot to the many thousands & tens of thousands of Jews', James wrote to Churchill; 'it will mean a lot to those who are their friends, also perhaps to those who like them less.' It took a great effort of will for James at the age of 75 to find the strength to make his final visit to Israel, in April 1954, to attend the ceremonies that marked the burial of his parents in the country for which they had done so much. Edmond and Adelaïde's bodies were moved from France and interred in a plot set aside for them in 1936 at Um el Alaq, renamed Ramat Hanadiv ('hill of the benefactor') in their honour, where there

was a museum commemorating Edmond which overlooked the settlements of Zikhron Ya'aqov, named after him, and Binyamina, named after James. Both had been sponsored by Rothschild funds. In a moving farewell to his parents, James recited the mourners' *kaddish*. He modestly turned down the suggestion that he should be buried beside them, but on his death, on May 7, 1957, ensured that he would be remembered in Israel by the bequest of £1.6 million for the building of a new Knesset parliament building on the outskirts of Jerusalem.

James's estate was valued at £11.6 million—the largest probate valuation in the United Kingdom since the death of the shipping magnate Sir James Ellermann in 1933. Death duties amounted to £7.57 million: when the *Daily Mail* asked Miriam Rothschild, a daughter of James's cousin Charles, why he had left such a large tax liability, she replied that 'he did not believe in getting out of taxes—he told me that himself. He used to say that if you chose to live in a country and you were very rich, then you had to pay the taxes that country demanded, including death duties . . . He was a man of very strong principles.' The newspaper reports do not make explicit the understanding that this liability was to be met in part by James's principal

BELOW: *Sunblinds screen the rooms on the south, facing the garden front.*

PAGES *258*—*259: On the left is an aerial view of the house from the west; the Morning Room block is in the foreground. On the right is the inscription on the garden front recording the contribution made by the architect, Destailleur, and his chief sculptor, M Doumassy.* PAGES *260*—*261: On the left is the datestone recording the completion of work on the Bachelors' Wing. On the right is the north-east corner of the entrance front.*

THE NATIONAL TRUST

bequest. Waddesdon, its gardens and the contents of its downstairs rooms were left to the National Trust on the condition that they were accepted as an inalienable gift within three months. Under the original terms of his will, drawn up in August 1956, he left £600,000 as an endowment, precisely the sum the Trust had asked for, but in a codicil added just a month before his death, he bequeathed an additional £150,000.

This all seems to have come as a surprise to the National Trust, which had clearly not been consulted in detail about the terms of the will, for its solicitor at once pointed out a flaw in the proposal. James had stipulated that the endowment could be used to purchase works of art with a Rothschild provenance as additions to the collections at Waddesdon—in other words, the money was not solely for maintenance, which was understood to be the only purpose for which the Trust could use endowments. As a result, there was a threat that death duties would be charged on the bequest. This produced instant panic, and Lords Crawford and Esher at once made an appointment with the Chancellor of the Exchequer to put their case for leniency. Before the appointment was due, the Treasury Solicitor set their minds at rest on that issue, but then almost teasingly added that in the Treasury's view there was some question as to whether the £750,000 was not 'too large for its purposes', given that Waddesdon was not an old house, and therefore the endowment ought to be taxed, at least in part. It was not until April 1959 that the National Trust was able to persuade the Treasury that all the income from the endowment was required for maintenance.

In the interval, Dorothy busied herself with the probate inventory: 'If it be true that the best way of keeping grief under control is to be forced to be very busy', she recalled, 'the Estate Duty Office of the Inland Revenue must indeed be the widow's best friend . . . Most of the objects Jimmy had left to the National Trust were relatively easy to identify by comparing descriptions in the old inventories with what was now visible in the newly arranged ground floor rooms. But the arms collected by Miss Alice to replace some of the objects left by her brother to the British Museum presented far greater problems. At a guess I could distinguish a halberd from a rapier and, perhaps, an arquebus from a pistol, but my lack of knowledge was total when it came to identifying, say, "A pillow sword enriched with gold azzima" or "A main gauche with chased drooping quillions."' Meanwhile, there was the question of the future management of the house to be sorted out: 'Quite apart from my personal feelings, the sudden change for me

Waddesdon Manor from the south: a view that reveals
its height above the surrounding landscape.

from an existence which had been totally free from taking decisions of importance, was traumatic. My husband had indeed been the guiding light in all sections of my life, and now the struggle began to try to take the decisions which he would have taken and to act in accordance with what I thought would have been his wishes.'

As well as having the increasingly invaluable Maria Brassey at her side, Dorothy was fortunate to have the infinitely tactful and protective Lord Crawford to give advice and support. He was busy working out a proposed management structure for Waddesdon, which had to take into account a surprising aspect of James's will. The munificent endowment had not been left to the National Trust. Instead, James had vested it in independent trustees, who were to be constituted according to his instructions. They were to be Dorothy, Duncan Mowat, and a third 'family trustee' to be nominated by Dorothy; three other trustees were to be nominated by the National Trust and there was to be a seventh trustee appointed as chairman by the other six. That meant Dorothy would inevitably be a central figure in Waddesdon's future.

In July 1957 Lord Crawford proposed the scheme that was eventually put into operation: 'I suggest that Waddesdon should be managed by a Management Committee, appointed by and responsible to the National Trust, and that some of the Waddesdon trustees, or at any rate Mrs de Rothschild, should be appointed members of the Management Committee. This would in general coordinate the Waddesdon Trust and the Management Committee, and in practice have the advantage of securing Mrs de Rothschild's help, which is of the greatest importance. Her advice and her knowledge would be invaluable.' Although the arrangement which was agreed between Waddesdon's trustees and the National Trust was not paralleled in detail elsewhere, there was nothing new in the idea of letting families continue to have some autonomy in the running of houses they had transferred to the Trust. Partly to encourage more donors in the 1930s and 1940s, when the country house scheme was proving slow to establish itself, the National Trust ceded total control over a number of its major houses, notably Petworth and Knole, where the donor families continued in residence, and still owned most of the contents. At both West Wycombe and Cliveden, given to the Trust by the 2nd Viscount Astor in 1942, family management of the houses and their estates continued with remarkably few changes.

The three National Trust nominations to Waddesdon's trustees included Lord Crawford himself and Robin Fedden; the third 'family trustee' was Victor, the 3rd Lord Rothschild. Dorothy and Lord Crawford asked James's old friend Brendan Bracken, who had been Churchill's Minister of Information during the war, to be chairman. He was flattered: 'From 1926 until the war ended I must have stayed at Waddesdon four or five times a year', he wrote to Lord Crawford in August, 'and I always found the most pleasant company. Bob Crewe [the Marquess of Crewe] and Crinks [Harcourt] Johnstone were often there, and there was also a supply of agreeable French and Austrian Rothschild relations. It was indeed the most hospitable of houses and I should be lacking in gratitude were I not to try to fulfil any request made by Dolly.' A letter from Bracken to Dorothy in January of the following year suggests that James may have sought his advice about the bequest. Bracken's opinion of the National Trust was not high, because, as he explained to Dorothy, he had been dismayed by its behaviour after it had inherited Polesden Lacey in Sussex in 1942, together with a very substantial endowment, from Mrs Ronald Greville, a Scottish-born society hostess: 'after Wee Maggie died a high official of the National Trust created a flat in the most comfortable part of the house and dwelt there happily for many years without opening the house to the public . . . Very close to [Mrs Greville's] heart was that Polesden Lacey should be opened to an admiring public and having seen how this requirement was fulfilled by the N.T. I think Jimmy was very wise to limit the Trust's authority in dealing with Waddesdon'. Bracken wrote to Victor in December 1957 in similar terms: 'Jimmy knew what he was doing when he brought the National Trust in, but did not give them complete control. They are a bureaucratic organisation which have for the first time in a rather long life had a clear-headed and forceful chairman. A lot of the people in high places in the National Trust are inclined to be busybodies and to lay down rules for the management of their properties which Jimmy would have found quite unacceptable.' Bracken, who was then already stricken with cancer, died in August 1958; his place as chairman of the Waddesdon trustees was taken by the Marquess of Salisbury. Much responsibility for the smooth running of the trustees' committee devolved on its secretary, Maria Brassey.

In a memorandum of July 1957, drawn up after discussions with Crawford, Rathbone set out the National Trust's proposals for the way the house would be shown: 'I think the show rooms should look as lived in as possible and not like the Wallace Collection. There should be no guides and ropes should be reduced to a minimum. In each room, as at Petworth, we should have a custodian who in his or her spare time can help the curators clean and make the place look nice. Yawning and uninformed officials are to be avoided. There should be flowers everywhere. The carpets will be the main problem as druggets will look more hideous even than ropes. So I think we should now make enquiries through I.C.I. and other similar organisations about the possibility of providing some transparent, non-sticky, non-scratchy material which can be used to cover them. I cannot believe that the production of some such material is an impossibility.' In the event, the conservation of the interiors was largely left to Dorothy, whose approach to their care was probably more stringent than the Trust can have imagined. It was she, and not the National Trust, who found the first housekeeper, Gwyneth Morgan, who had been recommended by Dorothy's former boss in the WVS, Lady Reading. Miss Morgan was instructed in her new duties by Dorothy's old housekeeper, Mrs Green, who had succeeded Mrs Boxall. Then on the brink of retirement, Mrs Green and her close companion, the linen maid, Mabel Chatfield, introduced Miss Morgan to the rules laid down by Alice in Mrs Boxall's time: 'to their surprise', recorded Dorothy, 'she was so intelligently capable of absorbing their tuition that, when the day came, they left with lighter hearts and higher hopes for the future of Waddesdon than they had ever thought possible.' Further continuity was provided by the André family firm in Paris, which until the 1970s made an annual six-week visit to inspect and repair the furniture, continuing the involvement begun in Ferdinand's time.

Dorothy fully agreed with Rathbone's belief that the house should be shown as far as possible as though it were still being lived in, since that had been James's own wish. However, as she recorded, some compromises had to be made: 'All the sitting rooms had comfortable armchairs made by Howard, a fashionable upholsterer who, alas, vanished after the first world war. Now that we hoped each room would be filled with many visitors a choice had to be made; there would not be room for beautiful 18th century chairs, the modern armchairs and the public, and it was the comfortable chairs and sofas which had to be sacrificed. Old photographs taken before they were removed show how immensely liveable the house looked, even if a little more crowded.' Not surprisingly, she did not take up Rathbone's suggestions about plastic coverings for the carpets: 'We solved this problem by stretching in front of them thin coloured cord supported on slim stands only about one foot high. This is what Monsieur Pierre Verlet of the Louvre calls '*protection symbolique*' and so far it has worked admirably.' Fortunately, the discarded 19th-century furnishings were preserved, allowing some of them to be reinstated when problems about crowding proved less insuperable than had been feared; as Dorothy remarked, the stripped-down appearance of the rooms, which still lingers in parts of the house, gave a very misleading impression of how Waddesdon looked and functioned when it was lived in. A further compromise has proved less easy to undo. Since accommodation was needed for the staff taken on for the house's new role, the service accommodation and bedroom floors were emptied of their contents and partially remodelled by the architect R.J.Page to create flats and offices. At the same time, the kitchen was converted into a tea room. However, the Billiard Room, Smoking Room and Armoury Corridor were for the moment left untouched, since the armour had formed part of the bequest. The National Trust hoped to create rooms on the first floor of the house for museum displays: as Lord Crawford wrote as early as July 1957, this would afford 'the opportunity of keeping alive public interest by temporary exhibitions, and it is possible that Mrs de Rothschild would allow us to borrow some of her own collections for this purpose'. For the moment, that plan was put to one side while Waddesdon was prepared for opening to the public. In the summer of 1958 Dorothy moved into Eythrope; the last guests to sign Waddesdon's visitors' book were Lord and Lady Crawford on March 15.

Advice was sought about the running of the house from Francis Watson, director of the Wallace Collection, of which James had been a trustee. He sent a long letter full of very precise practical information, ranging from the duties of the night watchmen to the salaries of room wardens (they began at £8 2s a week at the Wallace) and the probable cost of maintenance of the clocks, based on the Royal Collection's annual payment of £300 a year for the upkeep of the 200 clocks at Buckingham Palace. He also emphasised the need for an academically trained curator with access to a good working library on the premises: 'you will need much more than the Wallace Collection started with, which was merely the 1840 edition of Encyclopaedia Britannica: the Treasury then took the view that this contained all known knowledge and no further books would be required'. The management committee's preference among the candidates who applied for the curator's job was Clifford Musgrave, then director of Brighton Museum and Art Gallery, but he withdrew. The final choice was Philip James, the Art Director of the Arts Council, which disbursed government grants to arts organisations; before the war he had been keeper of the library at the Victoria and Albert Museum. His principal task at the Arts Council had been the creation (in collaboration with Kenneth Clark) of a collection of contemporary art, for display in touring exhibitions. Unfortunately, Dorothy took against him from the first: 'the disadvantage of Mr James is that his own tastes are entirely modern and his knowledge of what will be in his care is negligible *except for the books*,' she wrote to Bracken: 'I frankly would have preferred to entrust this house and its contents to one who was more thrilled by them'. James, who insisted on taking the title of director rather than curator, soon found that his background in arts administration was not much help in dealing with the transformation of a private house into a museum; although he threw himself into the task with energy he lacked the tact and diplomacy necessary to win Dorothy's confidence. It rapidly became clear to him that she was in fact the director in all but name, and when she began countermanding his orders behind his back, the National Trust refused to give him any support.

Although Dorothy was right that James started out with no special knowledge of the works of art in the collection, he made great efforts to master his new responsibility. She was therefore surprised as well as dismayed when he presented her at the beginning of 1959 with a draft text for the guidebook: the problem was not that he was ignorant, but that he had revealed too much. After pointing out justifiably that he had not recorded the contributions made to the collections by Alice and Edmond—he had failed to grasp the point that Waddesdon was a monument to her husband's family—she listed at great length the information that she did not wish to be made public: 'reference is made to a marble vase by Clodion—as this is probably a copy, it would be better to refrain from drawing special attention to it . . . reference is made to furniture in Louis XV "style". It seems unnecessary to point out that these are copies; it should be possible to refer to their upholstery which is beautiful without further comment. As the owners of Waddesdon and Mentmore have always thought these painted panels were by Van Loo, it would be unwise to mention that they are now considered to be 19th century copies as Lord Rosebery may have something to say in the matter. It would be preferable, whenever possible, to avoid to mention the names of private houses from which works of art were brought—such as the Sèvres work table—the fact that it came from Blenheim adds nothing to its interest. It is unnecessary to say that a copy of the monumental clock [in the Morning Room] is at Milton.' James had no option but to obey, but the result was that a veil was pulled over many aspects of the collection and its history which later scholarship has occasionally had to struggle to lift.

To some degree, this was understandable—Dorothy had simply inherited Ferdinand's and Alice's discretion about the source of objects in the collection. Moreover, she was aware that the Trust's acceptance of the house was entirely due to its estimation of the importance of the collection, and this may have made her unusually sensitive to anything that appeared to downgrade any part of it. Without any great innate interest in art or collecting, she relied on friends for advice,

and so subordinated her own understanding of Waddesdon as a house to the preconceptions of a generation of scholars who based their values on those of the museum or auction house, where most of them had received their training. It would take another generation to approach Waddesdon from the point of view of an interest in the history of collecting or 19th-century interior decoration. As the trustees put it in a declaration of the purpose of the trust, which they approved in January 1958, it would seek 'as far as possible to maintain the impression that the house could be lived in so that the works of art can be seen fulfilling the function for which they were designed and made'—it did not add 'for which they were collected'. Although to some degree the National Trust—and in particular James Lees-Milne—had seen that Waddesdon's value lay in its intactness as an ensemble, for most of Dorothy's contemporaries, Waddesdon was seen to be important because it contained major works of art, and anything that tended to suggest those works of art were not invariably of museum quality was to be deplored. The house's pre-eminent value as a 19th-century creation of the highest order was largely discounted.

That attitude was to some degree perpetuated in what was by any estimation an extraordinary achievement, the cataloguing of the collection, for it too implicitly approached the house as a sequence of museum collections. The idea of a series of catalogues for a historic house was unprecedented in England—indeed, no house in the care of the National Trust, and still less any private house, can show anything comparable, although it is now over thirty years since the first volume of Waddesdon's catalogue appeared. The idea seems to have arisen as a result of prompting by Victor, who, as one of the most eminent bibliophiles of his generation, urged the National Trust to undertake a proper catalogue of Waddesdon's books, the one part of the collection that Ferdinand had himself begun to catalogue, as the preliminary to a sequence covering the entire contents of the house. 'In view of the scale and quality of the collection', he wrote in November 1958, 'the catalogues of porcelain, textiles and bindings should become the standard work on these subjects: the catalogue of furniture should become, with the Wallace Collection, one of the two standard works: the catalogue of paintings should become a work of considerable importance.' Although before the war James and Dorothy had been given advice and information about the collection from scholars who were also personal friends, such as Pierre Verlet and Francis Watson, there was great curiosity in the scholarly world about Waddesdon's contents, since almost nothing had been published about them, and requests for photographs, information, and permission to visit began to flood in. This encouraged Dorothy and the other trustees to undertake catalogues if only to keep such enquiries under control. The idea was taken up with great enthusiasm by James, and his proposal for the first five volumes—paintings, drawings and sculpture; French books; armour; porcelain; and furniture—was accepted by the management committee in May 1960. A catalogue committee was set up under the chairmanship of Anthony Blunt, the director of the Courtauld Institute and an old friend of Dorothy. However, by then James, not surprisingly, had resigned, to take up the more congenial task of a book on Henry Moore.

The work on the house prior to its opening was accompanied by a major initiative in the garden. Once again, there was considerable continuity between the new order and the old, despite the fact that the Trust had inherited only a part of the grounds surrounding the house—the division saw 165 acres pass to the Trust, but 540 acres, which included the glasshouses, Dairy and Water Garden, remained part of the estate, which was in Dorothy's hands. Ralph Saunders, who had started work in the garden under Johnson in 1928, and had been foreman of the kitchen garden, was appointed head gardener by the National Trust with a staff of nine (James and Dorothy had employed a gardening staff of 36 at Waddesdon and Eythrope in the 1950s). The approach to the house was replanned, and the main drive, which began at Destailleur's pavilion on the Aylesbury road, was closed; visitors now entered the grounds from the village by what had been an access road. The flower beds and shrubberies at the east end of the house were remodelled, since this area would now be on public display for the first time, following the conversion of the kitchen into a tea room. But the main priorities were the south terrace, grassed over since the 1930s, and the Aviary, which was in a near-ruinous condition. On the terrace, the beds were recut, and annual bedding out was reinstated, with wallflowers and tulips in the spring and pelargoniums and ageratums in the summer, but the effect was only a shadow of what had been achieved in the 19th century, since less than a tenth of the number of plants was used—4,000 instead of the 50,000 recorded in 1900. Nonetheless, it was a bold attempt to reinstate a deeply unfashionable mode of gardening. For the time being, Dorothy kept the glasshouses open, but in October 1962 they were abandoned for good.

The house as it appeared in the late 1950s, not long before it was opened to the public. The Parterre is still grassed over.

THE NATIONAL TRUST

In September 1957, Baron Melides offered the National Trust his collection of 1000 parrots, together with an endowment for their upkeep, with the suggestion that they should be housed at Waddesdon. It was with some embarrassment that the Trust had to reverse its initial acceptance of this gift, following the realisation that the Aviary was in no condition to house the birds. In 1959 estimates were obtained for the Aviary's restoration, initially with the thought that it could be converted into a restaurant, until the Trust's catering manager pointed out its utter unsuitability for the purpose. The restoration was so expensive that it was phased in over several years, and was not completed until 1966. In 1964, the trustees commissioned a new garden for the Aviary from the designer Lanning Roper to replace the long-vanished Victorian bedding-out scheme. The result was a quintessentially 20th-century design: a simple, cool arrangement of lawn edged with low box hedges bordered with white Iceberg roses. The Aviary was initially filled with a rather miscellaneous collection of birds, including pigeons and budgerigars as well as Rothschild's Mynah (named after the 2nd Lord Rothschild, the noted ornithologist who had created the zoological museum at Tring). It was not until 1977 that its running was put on a professional basis, with the appointment of a qualified bird keeper who had come from Colchester Zoo, Ian Hadgkiss. He was asked to create a collection of the sort that had existed in Ferdinand's time—principally softbilled birds, ornamental pheasants, and parrots. These were expensive birds to acquire on the limited budget at his disposal, and so, partly to raise income, he instituted a breeding programme (made possible by the building in the grounds of a new breeding Aviary of 19 flights), which was soon producing 100 parakeets a year. Though its stud book management programme and breeding loans

TOP: *Lanning Roper's scheme for the Aviary. It was replaced by the present scheme, a precise recreation of the arrangement in Ferdinand's time, in 2003.*

ABOVE: *Ian Hadgkiss, Waddesdon's Curator of Birds, feeds a white-cheeked Touraco. Some 38 species are kept in the Aviary including Blue Crowned Laughing Thrush, Rothschild's Mynah, Banded Pitta, Hooded Pitta, Fairy Bluebirds and Brown Breasted Barbets. Many of these range from critically endangered to near threatened in the wild.*

OPPOSITE: *The Conservatory, with late-nineteenth-century terra-cotta figures of a gardener and flower girl by the Gossin Frères, originally in the glass houses. The planting re-creates high Victorian taste.*

from other collections, the Aviary is playing a crucial role in the conservation, preservation and support of endangered and threatened softbill species. Since 1977, 114 species have successfully bred at Waddesdon, including five UK first breeding awards, a record which stands amongst the best in Europe. Ferdinand's original conception of the Aviary as a home for the exotic and unusual could not have been better developed.

Restoration of the Aviary was regarded as a priority by the trustees from the outset because of some doubts about the long-term popularity of Waddesdon, despite Lees-Milne's conviction that it would attract crowds. During the National Trust's protracted negotiations with the Inland Revenue over the question of the size of the endowment, its regional secretary, C.V. Wallace, had stated in July 1958 that the Trust felt 'the character of the Collection was likely to attract a steady flow of specialists, rather than a large number of the general public'. Various means of attracting the maximum number of visitors were considered, including re-establishing the old golf course, and arranging tours of the glasshouses, as well as the temporary exhibitions in the first-floor rooms that Lord Crawford had proposed. Although it was originally hoped that the house would be ready for opening in 1958, it was quickly realised that would have to be postponed for a year, and since the National Trust did not then lay great emphasis on keeping the public informed about its activities, it received many impatient letters from its members asking when the house would be opened. Partly as a result of this widespread curiosity, the first year's opening was a success, with 27,183 recorded visitors. Although the trustees' fears seemed to be confirmed by the fall in the number of visitors to 23,706 in the following year, once the num-

a number which has remained fairly constant ever since, simply because the house cannot accommodate more.

Waddesdon was benefiting from the extraordinary surge of interest in country houses, their collections and gardens that constituted such a marked, and in many ways unexpected, phenomenon, in post-war British life. The availability of government grants for repairs from 1953 onwards encouraged many houses to open their doors for the first time, since funds were provided in return for public access. By the mid 1950s, some 200 houses were open to the public; by the early 1960s this had risen to more than 300. The great houses, which had a long tradition of public opening, set new standards in the facilities they laid on for visitors. Longleat and Woburn Abbey opened their safari parks and Beaulieu its motor museum, helping to establish country houses as major tourist attractions. Thanks to the way many owners had held their nerve, houses which had seemed doomed in 1950 were thriving again only 10 years later. The Cavendishes moved back into Chatsworth in 1958, when its future as a private house was at last secure; the Cokes remained at Holkham, the Howards returned to Castle Howard and the Lascelles decided to keep Harewood. National Trust membership rose from a mere 7,000 in 1945 to 100,000 in 1960 and 200,000 ten years later. Increased car ownership and greater leisure time in the 1960s coincided with a new enthusiasm for art and antiques: as Dorothy put it, 'a mass of sight-seers gyrates discerningly round houses "open to view"' and many had a keener

bers started to rise, in 1962, it was the beginning of an ever-upwards surge, and by 1970 the problem of over-visiting was preoccupying the management committee. Waddesdon was one of the first National Trust houses to control admission by means of tickets that permitted access only at specified times; it was also one of the few houses from which children were completely barred, a restriction not lifted until 1994. By the late 1970s it was attracting some 100,000 visitors a year,

interest in Waddesdon's collections than almost any of the guests she and James had entertained there before the war.

This new enthusiasm was met, at Dorothy's instigation, by the opening of the first floor, beginning with the Bachelors' Wing in 1961, partly so that visitors could be shown some bedrooms and bathrooms— to help convince them that people had once lived in the house—and partly so that additional objects could be put on display. This opening

OPPOSITE ABOVE: *The North Drive lined with visitors' cars bumper to bumper, 1978, a sight that always delighted Dorothy. There is now a car park discreetly hidden from the house.*

OPPOSITE BELOW: *Waddesdon's Keeper of the Collections, Rosamund Griffin, discusses a curtain in the Red Drawing Room with Queen Elizabeth the Queen Mother during a royal visit to Waddesdon in 1994. Lord and Lady Rothschild are at the far right and left. Colonel Crawforth stands next to Miss Griffin.*

LEFT AND BELOW: *The Long Room and the Blue Room, were created on the first floor in 1978. These spaces were remodelled once more during the centenary restoration, completed in 1994.*

Alice and Dorothy's strict regime for the care of Waddesdon's collections is still followed by the National Trust staff. Jane Finch cleans each drop of the chandeliers during the winter season; Patsy Knappett handles this mid-eighteenth-century man's coat and all textiles with the utmost care; and the garden staff cover every outdoor sculpture in November to protect them from winter frosts.

of new parts of the house continued over several years, until by 1980 seventeen rooms had been added to the eleven first shown. Two bedrooms, which still bore the marks of the house's war-time use, were redecorated and furniture was brought out of storage for them. The museum rooms were concentrated in the west wing, part of which had been Ferdinand's private apartment, gutted by R. J. Page to create four new exhibition rooms. Here Dorothy arranged items which had never before been on public display, most notably the textiles, lace, and buttons she had inherited from Adelaïde and part of the collection of drawings and Palestinian antiquities that Edmond had bequeathed to James. The house's commemorative role was emphasised by a display of family relics, ranging from early photographs to Dorothy's wedding dress made by Callot Soeurs and the Ascot Gold Cup won by Bomba. Other rooms were devoted to displays of Sèvres, musical instruments, and costume; the billiard table was moved from the Billiard Room to the staff common room to make way for a display of illuminated manuscripts from Edmond's collection. Although the choice and arrangement of objects was almost entirely Dorothy's, the fitting out of the museum rooms was carried out with advice from the celebrated interior decorator John Fowler, whose extensive work for the National Trust had begun at Claydon in 1956. Fowler was fond of telling the story that when Dorothy first visited his shop in London (to ask for his assistance with the redecoration of Eythrope), he had remarked that he assumed she would have some 'pretty things' to furnish the house—'the best, Mr Fowler, the best'.

The absorbing task of creating the new displays was combined with another, perhaps even more laborious, enterprise, the publication of the catalogues. The first to appear was Ellis Waterhouse's volume on the paintings, in 1967, and it set the high physical standards the series has maintained ever since: a handsomely large format, elegant typography, and abundant illustrations. They were expensive to produce (and at seven guineas each expensive to buy) and would not have appeared at all without a substantial private subsidy from Dorothy. The work of preparing them drew a constant stream of scholars to Waddesdon, giving the house a serious, intellectual spirit of enquiry that had no parallel in English country houses during the 1960s and precious few even now: the closest comparisons were perhaps the livelier departments of the Victoria and Albert Museum or the American houses run along academic lines, such as Winterthur or Williamsburg. Anthony Blunt and Dorothy maintained a close involvement with the catalogues, but most of the work devolved in the first instance on a young assistant appointed in 1960, Geoffrey de Bellaigue. Originally hired to do research for the catalogue of French furniture, he was then asked to write it himself; the two volumes, published in 1974, completely fulfilled Victor's hope that it would be a standard work of reference, and exceeded all expectations in its readability and wit. When De Bellaigue left for the Royal Collection in 1963 (eventually to become its director), his place was taken by Svend Eriksen on a two-year secondment from the museum of decorative arts in Copenhagen, of which he was director. A specialist in 18th-century porcelain, he wrote the catalogue of Waddesdon's Sèvres and also produced the text for a new guidebook, which still forms the basis of the one in use today. He and the catalogue authors were assisted by Maria Brassey, who provided notes concerning the provenance of objects, culled from her own research and her privileged access to such documents as probate inventories, which were not otherwise made available. She also, in Dorothy's words, translated the guidebook text 'from Danish-English into English-English'.

When Eriksen returned to Copenhagen in 1965 he was not replaced, but to a substantial degree his role was absorbed into the post of Keeper of the Collection, to which Rosamund Griffin was appointed. She had begun work at Waddesdon as a guide in 1959, and had then replaced Geoffrey de Bellaigue as a catalogue assistant. In her new role she combined overseeing the catalogues with the conservation of the collection, taking over the responsibility for its maintenance from Miss Morgan, who had by then retired. It was a combination of academic and practical tasks that had no parallel in other country houses owned by the National Trust. Miss Griffin enjoyed Dorothy's total confidence in the running of the house, with the result that what Dorothy called the 'sky-high standards' she had learned from Alice and Mrs Boxall were carried over into a new generation. Miss Griffin's combination of roles meant that she was identified with Waddesdon to an exceptional degree: the seriousness of purpose she observed in Dorothy was combined with an outlook inherited from Waddesdon's existence as a private house. When she arrived, it

Dorothy in the Conservatory. Her concern for and understanding of Waddesdon, still recalled by staff, shines through in her book, The Rothschilds at Waddesdon, *published in 1979.*

ABOVE LEFT: *Dorothy with Mrs Golda Meir, Israel's Prime Minister, in Israel.*

BELOW LEFT: *A model for the Knesset in Jerusalem, financed by a bequest from James de Rothschild and seen through to completion by Dorothy.*

RIGHT: *The Red Lion Steps on the west of the Parterre features a plaque commemorating James and Dorothy de Rothschild's protection of the Cedar Boys.*

OPPOSITE: *Dorothy at Eythrope, about 1980. She continued to visit Waddesdon almost daily, observing the visitors and talking to staff.*

still had the aura of privacy about it: 'people were very quiet', she recalls; 'nobody ever shouted'.

That seamless transition from a private to a public country house was made possible by Dorothy's almost daily involvement in its affairs: she always emphasised to its curators that 'Ferdinand did not create a museum'. She had the complete run of the house, and was treated as its chatelaine by the staff—many of whom had, after all, once worked for her privately: as Miss Griffin recalls, 'she was loved—people weren't frightened of her, but they were in awe of her'. She rewarded their devotion with affection: one guide who had eye trouble was sent to

Dorothy's private optician at her expense, another had flowers provided for a daughter's wedding from the glasshouses at Eythrope. The house was given life by the pleasure she took in it, and many of Waddesdon's staff still remember with affection such touches as the baskets of conkers she and Maria Brassey gathered from the grounds and left in the shop for children to take. Occasionally, she appeared unannounced with private guests when the house was open—the guides once found Kirk Douglas on the front doorstep. She also continued to have a substantial influence on the conservation of the collection, where she emphasised the need to maintain the visual balance of the rooms—at her insistence, cleaned ormolu was always dulled down, for example. Her special interest in the care of historic textiles was evident in the encouragement she gave to the conservator Karen Finch when she was setting up the Textile Conservation Centre at Hampton Court, one of the world's leading private conservation studios. Dorothy's overseeing of the preparations for the annual opening of the house were exhaustive and often exhausting, and no change escaped her notice; she expected meticulous attention to detail and she received it from the house's ex-military administrators, first Brigadier Cowan and then Colonel Crawforth; when the house was open she phoned every evening for a report on the day's events.

Staff occasionally moved from the National Trust to her: in 1970 Brigadier Cowan left Waddesdon to become her agent, a reminder that the house was still set in what remained a well-run private estate. In 1974 she marked the hundredth anniversary of Ferdinand's purchase of Waddesdon with a party in a marquee on the lawn at Eythrope for all her tenants and employees, as well as the National Trust's staff. There were many aspects to Dorothy's life apart from Waddesdon, and on the whole she kept them well separated. Busy with local government responsibilities (she had become a county councillor in 1950, and was an alderman from 1966 to 1974), she also sat on Aylesbury's magistrates' bench for over 30 years, from 1938 to 1969. This public county role was quietly combined with local philanthropic activity, most notably support for Stoke Mandeville hospital. Racing continued to be an enthusiasm, and Dorothy maintained the stud with rather more success than James had managed. Her trainer until 1985 was Bruce Hobbs MC, who had won his first race at the age of fourteen on a hurdler belonging to James; in 1938 he had won the Grand National with Battleship, going down in history as both the tallest jockey (he was over six feet) and the smallest mount ever to win the race.

However, Dorothy's chief concerns outside Waddesdon were for her family and for Israel. Since she was naturally modest, hated fuss, and was occasionally unnerved when she had to organise large social events, few who met her through Waddesdon would have guessed that as she grew older she assumed a matriarchal role for the Rothschilds, in France as well as England. As her great friend Isaiah Berlin put it after her death, she had 'unlimited curiosity for the lives and quirks of the world of her friends and acquaintances, to whose shortcomings she tended to be wholly blind'. To be at the head of the Rothschild family naturally meant a leading role in Jewish affairs, a role focused on her philanthropic interests, many inherited from James, which ranged from the Stepney Jewish clubs to the Jewish Blind Society. But as Isaiah Berlin wrote: 'Her first love remained the State of Israel, in which she became a greatly venerated figure. Any criticism of Israel caused her distress'. As a result of James's will, PICA was wound up, and its possessions transferred to the state. Dorothy was left in charge of a major charitable foundation, Yad Hanadiv, that sponsored educational projects, most notably perhaps the setting up of an 'open university' on the British model, which allows students to take degrees by correspondence courses. She took close interest in the construction of the Knesset building which

James had financed, and towards the end of her life provided the funds for a new Supreme Court Building in Jerusalem (completed after her death). Her long involvement with the Zionist cause was recalled in 1987 at a lunch for the President of Israel at 10 Downing Street, when she told the prime minister, Margaret Thatcher, that it was the first time she had been there since she had visited Asquith during the negotiations that led up to the issuing of the Balfour Declaration, seventy years before. More poignant still was the return to Waddesdon of the 'Cedar Boys', the Jewish orphans who had been sheltered on the estate during the war. In 1983, a chance meeting at a building site in New York between two men who discovered they had both been Cedar Boys prompted a reunion of sixteen of the boys—and girls—at Waddesdon later that year. In 1989, the Cedar Boys paid for a bench in the gardens to commemorate Julian Layton, who had been instrumental in getting them out of Germany, and in 1993 a plaque was unveiled in their presence on the Red Lion steps, on the west side of the south terrace, to commemorate James and Dorothy, 'in gratitude for sanctuary at a time of conflict'.

9

LORD ROTHSCHILD

WHEN DOROTHY DIED IN 1988, at the age of 93, it had long been known that her chosen heir was an English Rothschild—Jacob, the eldest son of Victor, the 3rd Lord Rothschild. A banker (a member of the sixth generation of his family to occupy a leading role in the City of London) and a collector who has had a distinguished public career in the arts, he was almost uncannily well qualified to take on the challenges she bequeathed to him. His softly-spoken, shy demeanour (reminiscent in some ways of descriptions of Ferdinand), conceals an often impatient dynamism that has had a profound impact on Waddesdon. Born in 1936, Jacob Rothschild joined N. M. Rothschild in 1963, served as chairman of the bank's executive committee and had spectacular success managing its associated company Rothschild Investment Trust. After a disagreement with his cousin Evelyn, he left in 1980 to develop his own business interests, which rapidly flourished. His offices were in St James's Place, opposite one of London's few surviving aristocratic town houses of the 18th century, Spencer House, still owned by Lord Spencer but for many years let as offices. When the lease became available in 1985, Jacob Rothschild took the house on as his company's headquarters, and embarked on one of the most ambitious private restoration programmes of a historic building ever undertaken in England. Over the course of the next five years, the magnificent interiors, by John Vardy, 'Athenian' Stuart and Henry Holland, were restored, redecorated and refurnished, to serve once more as the setting for receptions and parties, for which they were designed.

Nathaniel Charles Jacob, Lord Rothschild (b. 1936), who inherited the family interest in Waddesdon Manor upon the death of Dorothy de Rothschild in 1988. Behind him is a painting by Jean-Marc Winkler, commissioned by Lord Rothschild, which shows all the houses built by the family since the eighteenth century.

By then Lord Rothschild—he had inherited his father's title in 1990—was as well known in the committee rooms of the arts as he was in the City. From 1985 to 1991 he was chairman of the trustees of the National Gallery, during the time it was building its long-awaited extension and was embarking upon the restoration of its Victorian galleries, and in 1992 he was appointed chairman of the National Heritage Memorial Fund, the successor to the Land Fund. As a result, he became deeply involved with the fate of country houses and works of art, since the NHMF was the principal public source of funds for the endowment of houses and was frequently called upon to help museums with acquisitions. In 1995, the NHMF took on responsibility for the distribution of money raised for the heritage by the newly established National Lottery, thus placing Lord Rothschild at the centre of debates about the role of the country's historic buildings and collections.

The experience of having overseen the restoration of both a major historic house as well as a close involvement with the funding and running of museums and galleries were all to be drawn upon at Waddesdon. Once she had decided that he was to be her heir, Doro-

thy treated Lord Rothschild like a son: they lunched or dined together at least once a week, and she gradually educated him in the ways of Waddesdon; he was appointed a trustee and a member of the management committee. On her death, he inherited the estate and Eythrope, which became his country home, since his family's seat, Tring Park, with most of its estate, had been sold by his father. Waddesdon demanded his immediate attention, for it was then undergoing the greatest upheaval it had known since the war. In 1984 Dorothy asked the house's newly appointed architect, Peter Inskip of Inskip & Jenkins, to prepare a report on its condition: 'I want to leave the house in a good state when I go', she told him. Not surprisingly, his investigations revealed that 100 years after its construction there was a great deal of outstanding maintenance work to be done, most notably to the roof, where repairs had already been begun. As a result of the report, a five-phase plan for the roof was instituted, of which two had been completed by Dorothy's death. By then it had been decided to undertake a thorough overhaul of the house's services—its wiring, for example, had largely been untouched since the 1920s—as well as its

fire-detection and security systems. As yet, however, there were no thoughts of making any changes to the show rooms, although it was clear that the house would have to be closed to the public while the work was being carried out.

For Lord Rothschild, it seemed a wasted opportunity to undertake repairs and do no more. He proposed instead an imaginative new approach to the future life of the house, which he hoped would relieve the rather formidable impression it made on many visitors. His experience at Spencer House had shown him that it was possible to maintain historic interiors at a high level, while still using them for a variety of purposes other than museum display. It was clear to him that Waddesdon offered the potential for such an approach on its first floor, where the requirements of conservation were different from those of the ground-floor show rooms. The first-floor rooms would probably have to be rethought in any case, for Dorothy's executors had offered in lieu of inheritance tax two major items for display at Waddesdon: an armoire by Bernard van Risenburgh (a cabinet-maker not previously represented in the house) and a Sèvres service ordered by Louis XV in 1766 for Furst von Starhemberg, the Austrian ambassador in France, in gratitude for his help in negotiating the marriage of the future Louis XVI to Marie-Antoinette. These acquisitions prompted the idea of creating an entirely new gallery to show the house's Sèvres and—as a setting for the armoire—reinstating the principal bedroom on the first floor, which formed part of a suite with the Green Boudoir and so would make more sense of that room. Lord Rothschild also proposed placing on loan to the house the set of Bakst panels commissioned by James. A final element that offered exciting new possibilities was the existence of various pieces of 18th-century

OPPOSITE: *Stonework and leadwork being renewed on the south and east fronts during the centenary restoration, 1992.*

BELOW: *The Stahremberg Service, which went on display as part of the centenary restoration.*

boiseries of high quality in storage on the estate. Some may have been fragments for which Ferdinand could find no place at Waddesdon, but most had been removed from his Piccadilly house when it was sold after his death.

All these elements were brought together with impressive skill and flair during the great repair and remodelling project that took place while Waddesdon was closed for over four years, between the end of October 1990 and the spring of 1994—almost as long as it had taken to build the house. The administrator, Colonel Crawforth, and the Keeper of the Collection, Rosamund Griffin, who had recently been joined by a new curator, Selma Schwartz, an expert on porcelain, shared the challenge with outside consultants, some of whom had worked with Lord Rothschild on Spencer House. Alain Gruber gave specialist advice on French decoration, the interior decorator David Mlinaric oversaw with M. Gruber the design and execution of upholstery, curtains and other textiles, and Miss Schwartz took curatorial responsibility for the first-floor rooms, and in particular the displays of Sèvres. The project was managed by Colonel Crawforth in collaboration with Fabia

Bromovsky, who had worked with Lord Rothschild since 1984 on the development of his private and family interests.

Few if any visitors to the show rooms today realise what an enormous upheaval these interiors underwent during the restoration. One major change greatly improved their appearance: their relighting, using the very latest technology. This includes French bulbs imitating candles in an astonishingly realistic way for the chandeliers, and new picture lights to replace the old tungsten fittings, which generated too much heat—it was estimated that the existing lights for the big pictures, most notably the Guardis in the East Gallery, produced as much heat as half a bar of an electric fire. In contrast to the inconspicuous nature of the changes to the downstairs rooms, Waddesdon's first floor has been transformed. In the tradition of the house, French craftsmen were brought over for specialist work on the new interiors. Yves Gilbert, from Le Longevon, near Angers, was responsible for restoring and erecting the *boiseries,* which were painted by Pierre Lesbordes and his wife. The contrast between the French and English craftsmen was noted in the internal newsletter produced for staff during the restoration: 'We have said "au revoir" to the French panelling experts and the parquet floor layers and we welcome M. and Mme. Lesbordes, who are putting the finishing touches to the paintwork. No longer are we able to witness the two teams of French craftsmen at lunch. It was customary practice for them to assemble a dining room table from a piece of panelling and sit around it to a typical French lunch of cheese, bread and red wine, in contrast to the British workmen at the other end of the building who enjoyed their sandwiches in solitary silence reading their newspapers.'

The architect's responsibilities were by no means confined to repairs. Partly for reasons of public safety, Mr Inskip was required to insert a new staircase in the west wing, to link the museum rooms with the west entrance and the wine cellar below. Its handsome plainness is set off by a brass screen designed by Sir Edwin Lutyens, which was brought here by Mr Inskip from another of his repair projects, the headquarters of British Petroleum in London, designed by Lutyens in 1924. At first-floor room level, the staircase opens into rooms containing new displays devoted to family history, including a model of the Supreme Court Building in Jerusalem and an enormous painting by Jean-Marc

OPPOSITE: *The South Bedroom in the Bachelors' Wing. Over the bed is Fragonard's painting,* The Altar of Love; *on the mantel a pair of porphyry vases from Baron Edmond's Paris house flank a handsome clock signed by LePautre, clockmaker to Louis XVI. The chintz on the walls was copied from a fragment found during restoration work.*

Winkler, commissioned by Lord Rothschild, which depicts the houses built by his family since the end of the 18th century. Beyond these rooms are the new Sèvres galleries, arranged according to the plan of Ferdinand's bedroom suite, which formerly occupied this space. The Bakst panels are shown in the circular Tower Room. Until a major theft in 2003, this space also housed the spectacular collection of gold boxes and *objets de vírtu* amassed by Ferdinand, Alice and Edmond. In the principal bedroom apartment, the State Bedroom has had its bed replaced and its panelling completed; visitors are also now shown its companion dressing room (which had been dismantled in the 1970s).

Major work was also carried out in the Bachelors' Wing. The original furnishings, including the billiard table, have been returned to the Billiard Room, and new comfortable upholstered furniture provided for the Smoking Room, since the originals, covered with 17th-century embroidered textiles, were too fragile to go back on display. Appropriate objects, including silver-gilt plate, majolica and rock crystal wares, have been lent by Lord Rothschild to enhance the room's air of a Renaissance collector's cabinet of art and curiosities. The Smoking Room looks over the glazed roof of a lightwell created from the original service courtyard in the 1920s. This neglected area was transformed by the creation of a tiny roof garden, designed by Mr Mlinaric, in which bronze sculptures of birds, originally in the dairy garden, perch amid a formal layout of miniature box hedges. Two bedroom suites have been reconstructed and hung with the red sprigged chintz used throughout this part of the house, and probably elsewhere; it was re-created from a fragment found boarded up in one of the staff offices. Another new element in the Bachelors' Wing is the Blue Sitting Room, designed by Mr Inskip and M. Gruber to display an enchanting set of French 18th-century painted panels, perhaps by Alexis Peyrotte. which were brought here from Dorothy's London house. The room's decoration was inspired by an illustration by Moreau le Jeune for a book in Waddesdon's collection, *Le Monument du Costume français.* Furnished with a day bed made by J.-B. Boulard in 1785 for the French royal family, the room has an air of feminine repose that contrasts slyly with the masculine richness of the claret-coloured Smoking Room and Armoury Corridor.

At the east end of the house, in what had been the administrator's flat, and before that was the private suite that James and Dorothy had taken over from Alice, is a new sequence of rooms: the Red Ante Room, the White Drawing Room and the Blue Dining Room. These are shown to the public in their own right, but they are also designed to be available for parties and other functions, thus bringing new life and activity into the house. The result is a 20th-

century interpretation of 18th-century French interior decoration, carried out with a skill to match the execution of the house's 19th-century interiors. However, there are no delicate fabrics or marquetry needing protection, and visitors can enjoy the novel effect of sunlight streaming into rooms, as it must have done in Ferdinand's time. The White Drawing Room's *boiseries* are made up from two 18th-century sets with additional pieces carved by Yves Gilbert. They were painted by Pierre Lesbordes and his wife using a white rabbit-glue paint made to an 18th-century recipe for *'détrempe au lanc de roi'*, applied so thinly that the grain of the wood remains visible. The room's subtle tones, with only a little gilding on the end walls, is a simple scheme of the type which 18th-century France thought appropriate to a country house, forming a cool, restrained contrast with the glowing richness of the downstairs rooms.

The windows of the White Drawing Room open on the view over the Vale of Aylesbury that first attracted Ferdinand to this site, allowing visitors to look down on the terrace. This has been transformed no less remarkably than the first floor of the house. A restoration of the garden to complement the work being done inside was initiated by Lord Rothschild's second daughter, Beth, working with successive head gardeners, Chris Tolley, Michael Walker and Paul Farnell, initially following a conservation and development plan completed in 1989. In line with Lord Rothschild's desire to raise the standards of the gardens and estate to at least the level maintained before the war, a thorough overhaul of the house's immediate surroundings was begun in the early 1990s. This included such major changes as the creation of a new car park out of sight of the house, so that visitors' cars would no longer line the main approach to the house. Like much of southern England, the landscape had been hit by two exceptionally violent storms, in 1987 and 1991, when several hundred trees were lost. At first regarded as a disaster, the storms in retrospect had a beneficial impact on Waddesdon, for the thinning out which resulted has

OPPOSITE: *The Smoking Room. The display of Renaissance treasures over the chimneypiece is dominated by a fifteenth-century basil pot from Valencia.*

ABOVE: *The eighteenth-century panels depicting delicate birds and summer flowers in the Blue Sitting Room once hung in Mrs James de Rothschild's bedroom at St James's Place, London.*

LORD ROTHSCHILD

OPPOSITE: *The White Drawing Room, home to the silver dinner service made for George III*

ABOVE: *The Blue Dining Room, dominated by Ingo Maurer's chandelier,* Porca Miseria, *a commission for the room in 2004*

RIGHT: *The Red Ante Room, with Reynold's great portrait of* David Garrick between Tragedy and Comedy, *flanked by Romney's* Emma Hart as Circe *and Reynold's* Mrs Lloyd

restored light to gardens that were in danger of becoming gloomily overgrown. However, there was also the problem, that since Ferdinand had created a virtually instant garden, the trees were all of roughly the same age, and, at a century old, the landscape would soon begin to decline without a concerted programme of tree planting. Since 1991 over 5,000 trees have been added to the shelter belts that border the park, and in the gardens more than 50 new specimen trees have been planted. Ferdinand and his gardeners had paid great attention to colour effects in the permanent planting, but by the end of the 20th century the loss of shrubs, particularly along the drives, meant that the garden was looking increasingly monochrome. Here Beth Rothschild and her team encountered a difficulty that is all too common in garden restoration: Victorian gardeners had a wide palette to choose from, and many of the strains they used are no longer commercially available. It proved impossible to find new plants that could match the brilliance of colour in the golden yew for which Victorian Waddesdon was so famous, and so cuttings were propagated from existing specimens. Colour has also been revived by extensive planting of lilac, for which Waddesdon's intransigent clay soil is well suited.

ABOVE: *Beth Rothschild, Lord Rothschild's daughter and a professional gardener. The restoration of the Parterre, the Children's Garden, and the planting of the Millennium Avenue have all been her projects.*

OPPOSITE: *Planting out the carpet bedding on the Parterre, May 1999, the first year that an artist (John Hubbard) was commissioned to create the design.*

The contrast between the effects sought in the 19th century and the resources available to contemporary gardeners was especially acute on the south front's Parterre. Since this is the heart of the garden, both historically and visually, it was decided that nothing would be spared in the effort to recapture as far as possible the impact of Victorian horticulture and design at its most spectacular. In some ways, the task is even more daunting than it was originally, since far more plants are used than in Ferdinand's time, because modern horticultural methods mean that forced plants have to take the place of full-grown annuals, and so a mixture of 110,000 annuals and perennials was required to recapture the effect of the 50,000 annuals used in the late 19th century. Replanting

the Parterre was therefore an enormous undertaking. It was made a little easier by the decision to recut the beds to a version of their 1930s pattern, a simplified version of the Victorian scheme. This was because the complexities of the 19th-century layout, designed to be trimmed by hand, would have meant that mechanical mowers could not have been used. The need for intensive labour was also reduced by installing an automatic irrigation system, which soon proved its worth in a succession of very hot summers in the mid 1990s. The first bedding-out of the Parterre took place in 1993, after two years of trials. As Beth Rothschild recalls: 'When we thought that one plant would show a particularly good red, it frosted in winter. When we thought another plant would be successful, we found it was a favourite food for the badgers.' In 1997 the final element of the Parterre was put into place with the recreation of carpet bedding in the areas to the north and south of the fountain. These flat, intricate arrangements proved enormously labour-intensive: it took 200 man hours to bed out the 57,000 plants used. Technological innovation came to the rescue. Using a system pioneered by a nursery in Cornwall, Kernock Park Plants, the design for the carpet bedding is now worked out on computer, which translates it into a jigsaw of some 900 trays of plants. These trays are then made up in the nursery; and when they arrive at Waddesdon are simply slid into place, meaning that the entire scheme takes only a day to install.

Victorian photographs reveal that the Rothschilds' gardeners also demonstrated their bedding-out skills in some astonishing three-dimensional flower sculptures, most notably perhaps Eythrope's gigantic bird, created from an iron framework filled with earth and moss and planted with althernarheras, lobelias and spergula, to represent 'the colouring seen in some tropical birds', according to the *Journal of Horticulture*. This idea, which seems to have originated with Alfred de Rothschild's gardeners at Halton in the 1880s, was to spread beyond the Rothschilds'

The Parterre from the air, as it appeared in 1999
(the number 167 was part of a daily countdown to the year 2000).

gardens to municipal bedding-out schemes throughout the British Isles. It has now been revived at Waddesdon, initially with a giant bird perched below the west side of the terrace, piquantly positioned to look over the parts of the garden that are in strongest contrast with the labour-intensive artifice of the Victorian bedding out ideal.

In the 1920s, the steep slope below the south-west corner of the terrace had its sea buckthorn and furze replaced with daffodils planted in natural drifts. Named 'Daffodil Valley', it was intended by James and Dorothy to be a memorial to Alice. By the 1990s, the bulbs had been ravaged by a parasitic nematode, and so it was decided to give this area a new appeal by discontinuing its close mowing, and allowing wildflowers to establish themselves. As a result, the slope now provides a display of flowers from springtime onwards, including bluebells and cowslips and numerous orchids, until it is cut for hay in September. This new interest in the ecology of the gardens is evident also in the way that its birds, insects and wildlife are now an attraction in their own right, and are shown to visitors on walks organised by Ian Hadgkiss, the Curator of Birds. The 165 acres of National Trust land around the house are, for example, home to some 100 badgers, inhabiting at least nine setts, so the garden at night can seem as busy as it does by day. When the badgers started to cause a major headache by digging up the lawn on the north terrace, along the main approach to the house, in search of the particularly delicious grubs of a cockchafer beetle that had established itself there, the obvious solution of killing the grubs was not permissible because the beetle proved to be a rare species worthy of protection. So the badgers are now provided with food to take their minds off the grubs and every night dine on a bucket of apples, peanuts and sultanas.

Many of the changes in the way the gardens have been managed over the past century have been adaptations to cope with an ever diminishing workforce. This is not simply a matter of economics: even if the financial resources were available to employ as many gardeners as Ferdinand or Alice had, it is unlikely that many people in the early 21st century would be willing to undertake the routines of a Victorian gardener's job. Waddesdon's standards were indeed punishingly high, but it was the gardeners and labourers who took the punishment and nobody today would ask boys or young men to weed miles of drive or acres of grass by hand. However, a high level of maintenance has been achieved at Waddesdon by the enthusiastic cooperation of a large number of volunteers, many of whom eagerly undertake the jobs that Aubrey Hicks so bitterly complained about when he worked here as a gardener's boy before the First World War. Waddesdon's permanent

OPPOSITE ABOVE: In 2002 the Queen's Golden Jubilee was marked by the creation of a pair of three-dimensional carpet bedding crowns on the North Front

OPPOSITE BELOW: The Great Bird, a re-creation of a late-Victorian application of carpet bedding, originated by the Rothschilds' gardeners.

RIGHT: Gardeners at work: trimming the box hedge in the Winter Garden; clearing drifts of leaves in the Autumn for mulching; and maintaining the beds on the Parterre, which are replanted three times per year.

gardening staff of eleven is supplemented by internships for students from both Britain and overseas, ranging from Poland to Botswana, and there is a regular exchange programme with the botanical gardens in Jerusalem. Waddesdon also offers places for students in the traineeship programme of the Professional Gardeners' Guild, so that at any one time there are usually an additional four or five student professionals at work in the garden. They are supplemented by the volunteers, who include pupils from local schools on work-experience programmes, parties of young recruits from the RAF station at Halton, convalescing patients from Stoke Mandeville Hospital's Head Injury Unit, and regular enthusiasts, many of them retired. Twenty volunteer garden guides offer garden tours three times a week, and there is also a party of some fifteen to twenty Sunday volunteers, who undertake routine maintenance, from dead-heading to raking gravel. So it is occasionally possible for the garden to have some seventy people working in it, easily comparable to the manpower available to Ferdinand.

As the restoration of the gardens progresses under the direction of Paul Farnell, now on the basis of a conservation plan drawn up in 2005, new elements are created or re-established, such as the raised 'tropical' bed of succulents and other exotics on the north terrace, or a new rose garden on the site of a long-vanished one. Most spectacular of all has been the recreation in 2002-03 of the Aviary

Garden. Lanning Roper's 1960s scheme has been replaced by a reconstruction of the beds laid out for Ferdinand, and the sculptures that he chose for the garden, which include an *Apollo* carved around 1699 by Jean Raon and originally intended for the gardens at Versailles, have been returned to their original positions. Their gleaming white marble contrasts magnificently with both the colourful bedding out and the repainting of the restored Aviary in blue and gold, a scheme devised by David Mlinaric to recall French and German rococo garden pavilions. Waddesdon now has a gardens archivist, Sophieke Piebenga, whose research has emphasised that when Ferdinand died the garden was still to some degree a work in progress.

Even such a prominent element as the Frog Fountain Steps, which lead down from the south side of the Parterre to a terrace that once had a fountain, seems never to have been completed in Ferdinand's lifetime. In 2007-08 this area was redesigned as a setting for a new acquisition, three great stone vases from the Italian garden laid out by W.A. Nesfield at Witley Court, Worcestershire—the home of one of the Rothschilds' greatest rivals in the salerooms in the mid nineteenth century, the 1st Earl of Dudley. In 2008, after a two-year consultation, it was decided to undertake the re-creation of one of Ferdinand's most ambitious projects: the double avenue of oaks on the north terrace lining the approach to the entrance front. Most of the full-grown trees that he planted failed to thrive—it seems that the levelling of the hill to create the site for the house had removed too much topsoil—and were subsequently replaced by a mixture of different species. These have now been felled and replaced with oak saplings.

This creative approach to enhancing and developing the gardens has encouraged the introduction of contemporary art into the house's setting. In 2001 a track that formerly led from the glass-houses to the garden was rediscovered and restored as the Baron's Walk, which winds through tranquil glades of trees that part at intervals to reveal exhilarating views over the Vale of Aylesbury. The path, punctuated by newly acquired eighteenth-century sandstone figures of *Venus* and *Adonis*, once in the garden at the nearby Rothschild house of Aston Clinton, leads to a mighty sculpture in travertine, *Terra degli Etruschi*—Earth of the Etruscans—carved by Stephen Cox. This great block of stone, left in its rough state at the top, from which grasses grow, was placed here in 2001 by Lord Rothschild to commemorate those members of his family who owned and cared for Waddesdon. Their names are inscribed on a stone slab set into the ground nearby. A large round stone seat, designed by Cox on the model of Hellenistic drum altars, encourages visitors to pause to enjoy both the view and the contemplative atmosphere. Other acquisitions of contemporary sculpture add an unexpectedly quirky element to the gardens: Angus Fairhurst's 2002 bronze in the Tulip Garden, *A Couple of Differences Between Thinking and Feeling*, depicts a gorilla holding a giant salmon, and in the Aviary Glade, Sarah Lucas's monumental *Perceval* (2006), made of coloured bronze and cast concrete, represents a Shire Horse drawing a cart of gargantuan marrows. A particularly popular element in this new, modern dimension to the garden has been the establishment near the Stables of an adventure trail for children, the Woodland Playground.

Inside the house, new displays and exhibitions are being introduced on a more rapidly changing basis than was possible before the restoration of the 1990s. Particularly eye-catching have been the recreations of historic table settings in the Dining Room, beginning with

OPPOSITE: *The Aviary, as restored in 2002-3.*

RIGHT TOP: *A view looking down Frog Fountain steps to the undulating park beyond.*

RIGHT CENTRE: Terra degli Etruschi, *seen amid its sombre grove of trees with the memorial slab in the foreground.*

RIGHT: *Sarah Lucas's monmental bronze* Perceval *dominates the Aviary Glade. It alludes to a lost agricultural past and pays homage to the working horses once used on every estate.*

293

ABOVE LEFT: *An eighteenth-century dessert re-created in the Dining Room:
the Choiseul Service of 1766 with accompanying Sèvres biscuit groups
with fruit made of sugar, set out around a coloured sand parterre.*

ABOVE: *A sauceboat and tureen dominate this view of Auguste's service
made for George III.*

LEFT: *Ingo Maurer's chandelier,* Porca Miseria, *was commissioned for the
Blue Dining Room, and is made of broken fragments of contemporary porcelain.*

OPPOSITE: *Thomire's gilt-bronze centerpiece, given as an ambassadorial gift
by Louis XVIII reflects candles and flowers in its mirrored base*

an 18th-century dessert setting, using Sèvres dishes from the house's collections combined with *biscuit* figures loaned by Lord Rothschild. The great success of this display, which tapped into the lively current scholarly interest in the history of dining, encouraged a new acquisition for display in the dining room, a magnificent gilt-bronze centerpiece, or *surtout*, made by Pierre-Philippe Thomire in Paris in 1820. Perhaps surprisingly, given his appetite for eighteenth-century porcelain, Ferdinand, like most nineteenth-century Rothschilds, showed little interest in silver of the period. This gap in his outlook has been impressively filled by the acquisition in 2002 of a large part of a silver service commissioned by George III in the 1770s for use in Hanover,

of which he was Elector. Made by the most fashionable of contemporary French silversmiths, Robert-Joseph Auguste, this splendid neo-classical service was enlarged to Auguste's designs by the court goldsmith in Hanover, Franz Peter Bunsen, and further extended for George IV's visit to Hanover in 1821. It was dispersed in the 1920s, when a large part was acquired by the French Rothschilds.

The service is displayed in the White Drawing Room, on the first floor, part of the new suite created in the centenary restoration. Here are shown works of art from Lord Rothschild's private collection, most notably, in the Red Ante Room, two works by Reynolds, a beautiful portrait of Mrs Lloyd and a celebrated depiction of the actor

David Garrick between personifications of Tragedy and Comedy, bought from Agnew by the 1st Lord Rothschild in 1885. In the White Drawing Room, George III's service faces another recent acquisition, a full-length portrait by Antoine-François Callet of Louis XVI, painted in 1782. It originally hung in the French embassy in Piccadilly, in a setting designed to show off the best of French luxury arts, including Gobelin tapestries, Boulle furniture and Sèvres porcelain. That alone would make it an appropriate acquisition for Waddesdon, but what makes it seem particularly at home here, amid fine rococo boiseries, is its magnificent original frame carved by François Buteux. This is just one of several recent acquisitions of paintings that either enlarge on themes already present in the collection, or add elements not previously represented. In the first category, for example, is a pair of paintings by Giovanni Paolo Panini depicting the celebrations staged in 1751 by the French ambassador to Rome to mark the birth

This portrait of Louis XVI accompanied the comte d'Adhémar on his embassy to London, its frame replete with the arms of France and diplomatic imagery.

of a new heir to the French throne, Louis XV's grandson, the short-lived duc de Bourgogne. These magical evocations of courtly entertainments are highly appropriate at Waddesdon, given Ferdinand's interest in depictions of such events. He never showed much feeling for a very different aspect of eighteenth-century French art, genre painting. Its almost total absence from Waddesdon has been addressed by the acquisition of Chardin's *A Boy Building a House of Cards*, painted in 1735. However, it is possible that Waddesdon's most popular acquisition in recent years is a modern work of art: the chandelier in the Blue Dining Room, made in 2003 by Ingo Maurer. Entitled *Porca Miseria*—'Oh my goodness!' is a polite translation—it is is made of fragments of porcelain and cutlery frozen in an explosion over the table.

The new vitality given to the collections by such a lively programme of acquisitions is matched by a scholarly programme without any equivalent in other English country houses. Established by Philippa Glanville, Director of Waddesdon from 1999 to 2004,

the academic programme and other curatorial activities are now overseen by the house's Head of Collections, Pippa Shirley, formerly a curator of metalwork at the Victoria and Albert Museum. The publication of catalogues, overseen by two former Keepers of the Collection - Sir Geoffrey de Bellaigue and Rosamund Griffin - is now drawing towards its close: the catalogue of Ferdinand and Baron Edmond's drawings for architecture, design and ornament appeared in 2007, and was at once acclaimed as a work that would transform scholarly understanding of its subject. When the catalogue of the books and their bindings is published the series will be complete. The research for the catalogues informs not only the presentation of the house, but increasingly, exhibitions and other displays, which address both broad themes, such as the use of porcelain in 18th-century dining, and tightly focused subjects, such as a new acquisition. The drawings and manuscripts are now shown in a spe-

cially created gallery on the top floor, which mounts annually changing displays, some thematic, such as flowers or fashion, some relating to research projects. A new gallery has also been created in the Stables to stage loan exhibitions and to develop Waddesdson's growing engagement with contemporary art. Since 1997, Waddesdon has organised special interest days, prompted by growing public enthusiasm about such subjects as country-house entertaining or housekeeping, as well as furniture, porcelain or paintings. Increasingly, its academic life is conducted on a collaborative basis: for example, it has a partnership with the Eighteenth-Century Study Centre at Warwick University, with which it has undertaken an on-line catalogue of the house's collection of trade cards, and its important part in the international network of Rothschild scholarship is enhanced by its participation in the Rothschild Research Forum website, based at the Rothschild Archive in London. The provision of on-line information about the house and its collections for a global audience—many of whom may never visit

Waddesdon—is a priority for the future. The house's long tradition
of welcoming scholars has resulted in the creation of a well appointed
'academic flat', in which they may stay in the course of research.

They now also have the use of a handsome new library, created
out of former staff offices and designed by David Mlinaric with splendid
mahogany-lined oak bookcases. Seminars and lecture series are held on
a regular basis, making use of a new lecture theatre created in what was
the power house (just to the east of the service wing), which preserves
its gleaming 1920s electrical fittings. Even more ambitiously, there are
plans to convert a group of redundant farm buildings at Windmill Hill
on the Waddesdon estate into a home for the house's archives and a
centre for the Rothschild family's philanthropic interests.

It is in part a tribute to its lively intellectual life that Waddesdon has such a high standing among the world's decorative arts
museums. Judged simply as a collection of French and English 18th-
century art and design, it is often compared with the range of the
Wallace Collection in London or the Frick Collection in New York,
for example. As an appreciation of its essentially 19th-century character has grown, its immense strengths are if anything more apparent

ABOVE: A Concert (*left*) and A Ball (*right*) painted by
Giovanni Paolo Panini in 1751.

RIGHT: *J-S. Chardin's* Boy building a house of cards *echoes 17th-century Netherlandish
painting in the use of light and allegorical overtones of love, fate and the passage of time.*

now than they were when James made his bequest to the National Trust in 1957. Nowhere else is it possible for the public to see a great Rothschild collection in its original setting. Moreover, no other major 19th-cenrury collection of the French decorative arts has preserved its domestic character so intact, complete with its original textiles and decorative finishes. Even those collections that are closest in spirit, such as the Musée Nissim de Camondo or the Musée Jacquemart-André in Paris, are more institutional in character, and none can match Waddesdon's combination of outstanding architecture, collections, garden and landscape. It is the interdependency of that ensemble which the restorations of the 1990s did so much to emphasise.

A fresh appreciation of Waddesdon's essentially nineteenth-century character has led to some important changes to the way that the house is presented. In 2004 the Baron's Room was restored as closely as possible to its appearance in the 1897 photograph of the room in the Red Book. The pictures were rehung, displaced nineteenth-century furniture was returned and the density of display of

ABOVE LEFT: Baron Ferdinand's private sitting room, as restored in 2004.

ABOVE RIGHT: The Library, created out of two former bedrooms and a corridor in the Bachelors' Wing.

LEFT: Indian and Persian textiles and Turkish glass create an atmospheric entrance to the Academic Flat, which provides accommodation for visiting scholars.

OPPOSITE: Floodlighting, which was installed during the 1990s, emphasises Waddesdon's dramatic hill-top setting, recalling one of the châteaux of the Loire.

small *objets d'art* reinstated. The result compellingly evokes not only the way the room looked in Ferdinand's lifetime but also the way that he used it, with intimate arrangements of furniture designed for an intimate social life. The success of this project encouraged a new presentation two years later of the Green Boudoir, which had been shown largely empty ever since the house opened to the public. It has now been furnished according to the description of the room in the inventory taken after Ferdinand's death, with nineteenth-century upholstered furniture and a Venetian glass chandelier. The redisplay of these rooms has emphasised once more the challenges of preserving such an intact Victorian domestic ensemble, especially where the very large collection of delicate textiles is concerned. Waddesdon now has a dedicated textile conservator, whose expertise will be called on in tackling the problem of replacing such major elements of the interiors as the curtains, which will soon be too fragile to be displayed.

No more visible assertion of Waddesdon's vigorous life could have been made than the system of floodlighting created by Pierre Bideaux, who has also been responsible for the architectural lighting for such great châteaux as Azay-le-Rideau and Chenonceau, although he is probably best known for his lighting of the Eiffel Tower. At night, for special events, the house now shines in a setting animated by theatrically placed lighting, so that the statues on the fountains emerge like living figures from the night, as though ready to take part in a Renaissance masque. On certain occasions, Waddesdon is the setting for great receptions, none more significant perhaps than the one hosted by Mar-

garet Thatcher to entertain President Mitterand of France here in 1990 at a summit held to discuss European defence policy. Waddesdon was chosen because of its Anglo-French links; the background to the talks was the radical changes that were ensuing in Europe as a result of the collapse of the Berlin wall and the reunification of Germany—mighty political events that were restoring the network of relations among European countries which Ferdinand and his family had known.

As the two premiers were swept away into the sky in their helicopters, Lord Rothschild was heard to exclaim, 'Now the house is alive again!' His wish that Waddesdon should not simply be preserved but also enhanced and invigorated poses a complex challenge for those charged with its care. Responsibility for the management of Waddesdon lies ultimately with Fabia Bromovsky, its Chief Executive since 1995. She must take a great deal of credit for the immaculate presentation of what is now a major tourist attraction that regularly wins awards for its treatment of visitors. Her task is formidable, as it extends not just to the house, its collections and gardens but to every element of its daily life. When the house is open to the public, from the beginning of April to the end of October every year, the number of staff in the house exceeds that in Ferdinand's day—between 45 and 50 on average act as wardens, guides, attendants in the shop and wine cellar, or cooks and waiters in the restaurants, tending to the needs of visitors with as much concern as the footmen and housemaids of the past. New and highly popular money-making ventures include the magnificently appointed wine cellars and a shop specialising in Rothschild wines (Lord

ABOVE: *Margaret Thatcher and François Mitterand near the Pluto and Proserpina fountain, relaxing during the Anglo-French summit held at Waddesdon, 1990.*

OPPOSITE ABOVE: *An aerial view of Ferdinand's Dairy, constructed for his pedigree cows, now restored and extended in the 1990s by Lord Rothschild to provide a setting for entertaining and other events.*

OPPOSITE BELOW: *Beth Rothschild with Linda and Philip Loder, planting one of the 218 oaks that form the Millennium Avenue.*

Rothschild was given by Dorothy a sixth share of Château Lafite Rothschild, purchased by Baron Edmond's father in 1868). The Five Arrows has been rejuvenated as a successful restaurant and hotel, serving better food and wine than it ever did in the 19th century. The Dairy had continued to function until 1993, although the buildings were by then in a near-derelict state. It has not only been restored but also extended by Julian and Isabel Bannerman, with a new winter garden and boathouses, creating a new setting suitable for conferences or parties. After 50 years of neglect, the rock and water gardens that it overlooks have also been revived. Other commercial ventures include a nursery and plant centre, which is the principal source of plants for the garden.

Waddesdon is a modern demonstration of how traditional estate management can maintain the countryside in a way that sets standards for all. This has had important consequences for visitors to the house, because the improvements to its setting have restored its historic role as the centre of a model estate. Parts of the park turned over to arable farming after the war have been returned to pasture, grazed by sheep and some cattle, and over 185 acres of new woodland have been planted, as well as over 10 miles of new hedgerows. Much of the estate's traditional metal fencing had slowly disappeared when it became too costly to have it repainted annually by the teams of 'greenfinches'. It is now too expensive to be replaced everywhere, but it has been put back where it is visually most significant; elsewhere, virtually invisible electric fencing is used instead.

In the village, the Rothschilds' oxblood and cream estate livery has been revived on the estate's buildings to mark the family's presence, and a concerted programme of buying back property sold in the 1950s and 1960s is in progress; the estate now owns some 120 houses and cottages. Most dramatic of all the changes has been the millennium project initiated by Beth Rothschild and her father, the planting in 1998-99 of a 2,000-yard long avenue of oaks to replace one, probably originally of elm, which was created in the early 18th century to link Winchendon House to Lodge Hill. A long-neglected feature of the landscape—although it may have influenced Ferdinand's orientation of the site of his house—it has been extended by new plantations which give it the form of a Rothschild arrow.

The estate is now larger than it was in Ferdinand and Alice's time, since its 5,642 acres include some 850 rented from neighbouring landowners. Some 3,300 acres are farmed by the Waddesdon Estate, with a mixture of sheep and arable farming; the rest is tenanted. Another major change is that the estate is run commercially: there is no thought of letting it run at the enormous loss tolerated by Ferdinand, when it was little more than a rich man's amusement. The same cannot be said of the house and gardens, which are funded by substantial grants from a family foundation, in addition to James's original endowment. Waddesdon's economic health is regarded as a challenge by Lord Rothschild and Fabia Bromovsky, but the financial conundrum is not easily solved. Revenue from visitor admissions, including an annual rebate from the National Trust in return for the free admission of its members, is bolstered to only a modest degree by the revenue from the shops and restaurants, for all that they have a reputation for quality unmatched by almost any other house open to the public.

Imaginative ways have been found to improve revenue, which as with most historic houses open to the public suffers from the fact that it is necessary to close for part of the year. One particularly successful venture has been the opening of the Bachelors' Wing for a pre-Christmas season, complete with festive decorations, encouraging visits to the shop and restaurants. Even so, the house and gardens can only be maintained at their present high standards with considerable subsidy from Rothschild family trusts. Nobody seriously believes that the house can absorb many more visitors—it is already stretched to the limit on its busiest days—but the grounds are more flexible and the challenge is to attract the public at quieter times of the year, away from peak holiday seasons. Any fears that the high level of public interest in country houses and their collections, which has flourished over the past 40 years, may now be on the decline are countered by Waddesdon's continued popularity: some 350,000 now visit every year, of

whom 120,000 buy tickets for the house. It is astonishing in many ways that Waddesdon has been so successful with the public, since it represents aesthetic values that have been deeply unfashionable for most of the past century. Perhaps it is that very remoteness from 21st-century norms of architecture and decoration that makes it so popular; there is certainly no sense among its visitors that it is enjoyed less than in previous years. It is not much consolation to those responsible for Waddesdon's financial well-being to be reminded that it has never made money; it has always been a subsidised pleasure palace.

No one can doubt that the National Trust's intervention in 1957 was crucial to Waddesdon's survival. The estate's probable fate if there had been no National Trust can be imagined from what has happened subsequently to the Rothschilds' other possessions in Buckinghamshire. In 1974 Tring's exceptionally beautiful park was sliced in two by a new bypass and in 1977 Mentmore was sold by the Earl of Rosebery and most of its contents dispersed at auction. Outside England, little is left for the public to see of the Rothschilds' great traditions of building and collecting: Ferrières, for example, is now owned by the University of Paris and stripped of its contents. But Waddesdon has not simply survived; it has flourished and is maintained at a high level, thanks largely to its creators having prospered as a wealthy and vigorous dynasty for more than two centuries, a record that in England few of the great landowning families can match. It is right that it should be maintained in part as a monument to the Rothschilds' extraordinary history. However, their continued involvement with the house is not simply a historic asset, as it tends to be in other National Trust houses where the donor families maintain a presence: it is crucial to the house's *raison d'être*. A poorly maintained Waddesdon—or even a Waddesdon maintained to the average standards of most historic houses—would arguably not be worth having at all, for it would have become too remote from its original character. At least there has never been any difficulty in matching the financial and personal commitment made by the Rothschilds with the human commitment of time, energy and thought offered by those who care for this formidable inheritance; as John Cornforth wrote in *Country Life* in 1995, 'The place is so completely un-English and in some ways so inhuman; and yet there is also something very English about the way it inspires all who are involved with it and look after it. It seems to get a grip on people and never let go.' The deep affection in which Waddesdon is held was evident in the outrage that greeted a brutal armed burglary in June 2003, when most of the collection of gold boxes was stolen.

That sense of the house being bigger than the people who have lived in it or cared for it suggests something about its complex and contradictory personality. As Mr Cornforth indicated, it has an ambivalent nationality. An English house designed by a French architect for a Paris-born Austrian baron, its furnishings combine English paintings with French decorative arts as a setting for the cosmopolitan social life of a European dynasty. All its owners were fluent in three languages; today, the curatorial staff are drawn from Germany, France and Croatia as well as England. As a result, Waddesdon fits uneasily into the image of the English country house as it has evolved over the past century; an image that claims to embody national identity in its aristocratic and rural guises. The English country house is usually understood to belong to the 18th century, the period which supposedly embodied the canons of taste which most people who struggled to maintain the country's artistic heritage in the 20th century sought to uphold. Waddesdon is a 19th-cenntry house, and for all that it contains major 18th-century works of art, it is not an embodiment of 18th-century values. Ferdinand quite consciously sought to create something that would embody the best of his own eclectic, plutocratic and international world. An appreciation of that identity is still not common, even among historians, who have tended to dismiss Waddesdon as a 'nouveau riche' creation, implying that it has, therefore, no serious bearing on English history and still less on English identity.

Another striking ambivalence about Waddesdon is the way time concertinas here, making a world that is remote for most visitors seem curiously immediate. Some of Waddesdon's staff still have vivid memories of Dorothy de Rothschild, whom Lord Rothschild knew well. Dorothy's husband, James, had known Ferdinand and Alice, and his father, Baron Edmond, was the youngest son of one of the five Rothschild brothers who had founded the family bank after a childhood in the Frankfurt ghetto. These links, forged partly as a result of the long lives of Edmond and Dorothy, make the eight generations that separate Mayer Amschel from Lord Rothschild's children seem oddly brief, and increase the palpable sense at Waddesdon that 'the Baron' and 'Miss Alice' as well as James and 'Mrs James' are still living presences, lingering within the horizon of human memory. That is not always comfortable. Waddesdon is an emotionally ambivalent place, both entrancingly beautiful and uneasily oppressive. For so much of its existence as a private house it was as physically perfect a setting for pleasure as any creation of human hands has ever been. Yet for all the happiness it gave and continues to give, it is haunted by a bat's squeak of sadness, from Ferdinand's lonely depression and Alice's steeliness to the regret that surely lay behind Dorothy's wartime enjoyment at seeing the place filled for the first time with children. All this complicates any attempt to appreciate the house as a social document, which has understandably and rightly been the thrust of recent scholarship on Waddesdon, and has indeed prompted this book.

In the end, Waddesdon cannot be understood except as a work of art, and it shares with the greatest art an aloofness from the everyday which is perhaps its ultimate value. Yet, like all major art, it has proved adaptable to times that are very different from those which produced it. Ferdinand always believed that, as a private house, Waddesdon was an intermediate link in a chain of progress that led from the courts of princes and prelates to the museums of European and American democracy. He would surely be astonished at the dynamic way his prophetic vision has been realised, as hundreds of thousands of visitors pour through Waddesdon's gates every year to admire and enjoy its architecture and art, food and wine, gardens, birds and animals, set in the embrace of a fertile and harmonious landscape. It remains what he set out to create: a place that shows it is possible to aspire to perfection. The inevitable tinge of melancholy associated with such an ambition only makes it all the more compelling.

ENTRANCE
TO WEST WING
AND
WINE CELLARS

AFTERWORD: SUMMER 2009

A DAY IN THE LIFE OF WADDESDON

It is six o'clock in the morning on a Saturday in June 2009. High on a hill in the centre of Buckinghamshire, the turrets and windows of Waddesdon Manor catch the early morning light. The first cars of the day pull up in the staff drive, as the day shift of security guards, led by Paul Worsley, arrives to relieve the night staff. In his cottage on the grounds, the Curator of Birds, Ian Hadgkiss, is already up, and by quarter to seven is checking the young birds in the rearing unit, before setting off on his quad bike to the Dairy, to feed the waterfowl in the Water Garden. By now the gates have been opened and inside the house the members of the security staff have opened the shutters to be ready for the arrival at seven of the cleaners from the village in their minibus. At the same time, the first gardeners begin to examine the Parterre, checking the automatic irrigation system on the newly planted carpet bedding. By half-past seven the housekeepers, led by Hazel Friend and the Steward, Jane Finch, are removing the black covers from the watercolours in the bedrooms and the security guards are setting out the signs around the grounds.

At eight o'clock the kitchens in the house are open, and the head chef, Shaun Blythe, is checking the deliveries. It will be a busy day for the catering staff: as well as the meals to be served in the Manor Restaurant and the Stables, there is a wedding reception to be held in the Dairy this afternoon, and the Manor Restaurant will be opening in the evening for a popular annual event, 'Baron Ferdinand's House Party'. At ten minutes to nine the shop staff, led by Sue Francis, collect the keys from security and begin to set up the shop and check the stock, while Peter Tompkins, who runs the wine shop, is in the cellars, choosing wine for the tasting he has organised for the morning.

The restaurants' front-of-house staff arrives at nine o'clock and begins to lay tables. At ten o'clock the grounds open to the public and the restaurant starts to serve breakfast and morning coffee. Inside the house, a gardener is checking to see that the plants in the Conservatory do not require extra water. The room wardens arrive at ten, as well, ready for a briefing at ten-thirty from Bonnie Bennett, the visitor services manager, about the plans for the day's events. By that time, the cleaners

have finished their tasks, and at ten-thirty they are taken back down to the village of Waddesdon. The associate curator, Ulrich Leben, slips into the Grey Drawing Room with two furniture specialists from the Musée des Arts Decoratifs in Paris, who have asked for a close examination of the Cressent commode. In the Power House, the lecture theatre to the east of the house, Phil Durtnal is organising the first of the audio-visual presentations that are given for visitors to the house—they will continue at regular intervals until three-thirty in the afternoon. Inside the house, guides are preparing for a 'spotlight tour' of the Sèvres in the Red Drawing Room at midday by associate curator Selma Schwartz—these short tours highlight particular aspects of the collection.

At a quarter to eleven, the room wardens are at their posts, ready to greet the visitors for a tour especially for children, which takes place every Saturday morning in the summer. At eleven-fifteen, the public is admitted, on timed tickets, which allow fifty people to enter every quarter of an hour—between 900 and 1000 people tour the house on an average Saturday. The first coach party arrives just after eleven (six such groups have been booked for today). A party gathers outside the restaurant for a tour that will show them the gardens' birds and animals, led by Mr Hadgkiss, and at noon a pre-booked party of thirty Americans visiting English gardens arrives for a special tour with head gardener Paul Farnell.

By one o'clock, lunch in the two restaurants is in full swing, and the number of visitors to the house temporarily tapers off, but just after two, Lord Rothschild arrives with some friends from Eythrope, to view a display on the duc de Choiseul, which marks the recent acquisition for Waddesdon of a portrait of the duke painted in 1786 by Adélheïde Labille-Guiard.

The car park has filled up, and the grounds are busy—on this particular day nearly 2500 people will visit Waddesdon Manor. As the sun climbs higher in the sky, the stewards move around the rooms, adjusting the blinds. Waddesdon's Press Officer, Vicky Darby, walks through with a French journalist who is writing an article on the Manor. The gardeners are making their final check of the irrigation system in the seasonal bedding before they leave for home: it has been a hot day, and some areas have had their water supply increased. Down at the Dairy, preparations are being completed for the wedding reception, which will begin soon after four o'clock. At two-thirty one of the

volunteer garden guides collects from outside the shop a group of 40 visitors who have booked a tour of the garden.

Throughout the afternoon, visitors stream through an exhibition in the Stables on the artist Angus Fairhurst and families make their way to the Woodland Playground. At three-thirty the final visitors are admitted to the house, and as the last ones leave at four o'clock, the rooms are shuttered and the lights turned off. But there is still plenty of activity at Waddesdon Manor: tea is being served in the kitchens, last-minute purchases are being made in the shop, and a crowd has gathered at the Aviary to watch the birds being fed. Waddesdon's head of collections, Pippa Shirley, is in the Smoking Room with a silver specialist from Amsterdam discussing a seventeenth-century silver-gilt cup by Christian Van Vianen. Cars are drawing up at the Dairy for the wedding reception.

At five o'clock the shop closes, and last orders for tea are taken in the restaurants. The visitors' book today records comments made by visitors from the U.S.A., Australia, South Africa, Poland, Japan, Holland, Israel and Hungary. At six o'clock the night security staff are coming on duty. Mr Hadgkiss goes to check the chicks in their incubator; his final task of the day is to put out food for the badgers. At six-thirty the guests for 'Baron Ferdinand's House Party' are gathering for a glass of champagne on the terrace, before setting off on a private tour of the house. As night falls, a member of the security staff leaves the house for one of the regular patrols of the grounds, first stopping to set out the fire hydrants and put up the rabbit gates around the Parterre. At eleven o'clock the House Party guests depart but at the Dairy the lights are still blazing; the reception is not due to end until one o'clock in the morning and the staff will be up until three clearing away. For only a few hours before sunrise, therefore, does silence reign in Waddesdon's grounds, as the badgers feast and the deer roam undisturbed.

ACKNOWLEDGEMENTS
AND BIBLIOGRAPHICAL NOTES

I COULD NOT HAVE WRITTEN THIS BOOK without a very great deal of help from Lord Rothschild and from the staff at Waddesdon Manor. Lord Rothschild read the text in draft, and greatly improved it. Philippa Glanville, the Director and Keeper of the Collections, has not only guided and encouraged me at every stage, she has also read the text several times in draft and made innumerable helpful suggestions. I would also like to thank Waddesdon's chief executive, Fabia Bromovsky, for her support. At every stage of my research. I relied on Colette Warbrick, Waddesdon's archivist, and on Anna Riggs, who has catalogued some of the Eythrope papers. Ruth Smith tracked down historical material for the illustrations with great ingenuity, and took on the difficult task of drafting the captions. Rachel Akpabio, assistant curator, was a particular help with research on Baron Edmond and his collections. Diana de Bellaigue gave me much assistance, as did Mary Balkwill.

I owe a major debt to two of Waddesdon's curators, Selma Schwartz and Ulrich Leben. As well as discussing the house's porcelain collection with me. Selma Schwartz generously passed to me her research notes on the house's visitors during the 19th century, including her own transcripts of material in the Rothschild Archive. Ulrich Leben gave me a most memorable tour of the house's furniture, but I would like to thank him especially for sharing with me his ideas about the house and its owners and for his enthusiasm for this project, which greatly buoyed me up. Both Selma Schwartz and Ulrich Leben read the text in draft and made numerous corrections and suggestions. Rosamund Griffin, the former Keeper of the Collections, kindly allowed me to interview her. I am also very grateful to Pat Batten, the head steward; Tony Morgan, the retired projects manager; and Barbara Roberts, one of the long-standing guide-lecturers, for discussing their work with me. and for telling me their memories of Dorothy de Rothschild.

In the garden, my guides were the head gardener, Michael Walker, and his assistant Paul Farnell, who patiently explained its history and significance for the benefit of a horticulturally ignorant author. Mr

Walker also read the draft text, as did Beth Rothschild, and both strengthened its account of the recent history of the garden and the landscape in which it is set. Andrew Langton, the agent to the Rothschild estate, was an invaluable source of information about the estate, its landscape and the village of Waddesdon. Ian Hadgkiss, the Aviary Keeper, was a highly informative guide. Baroness Liliane de Rothschild read the text in draft and

kindly gave me much advice, together with information about family history. Barbara Scott gave me valuable comments on Alice's collections.

Outside Waddesdon, I received much help from the National Trust, in particular from Simon Jervis, its historic buildings secretary, and Alastair Laing, its advisor on paintings and sculpture. Both read and commented on the text in detail. Mr Laing generously allowed me to make use of his unpublished research on Waddesdon's paintings. Dora Thornton of the British Museum read a draft and most helpfully shared with me her research on the Waddesdon Bequest and other aspects of Baron Ferdinand's collecting. Peter Inskip, the house's architect, read the text and greatly helped my understanding of the centenary restoration. I am grateful to Rebecca Williams for suggesting that I investigate Alice de Rothschild's friendship with Ethel Sands.

Finally, it has been a great pleasure to work with the book's photographer, John Bigelow Taylor, and his wife, Dianne Dubler, whose eyes have revealed more about Waddesdon than words ever can.

The following notes are intended to make clear the principal sources on which I have relied. However, some works have been so fundamental to my research that they need to be acknowledged separately. Mrs James de Rothschild's *The Rothschilds at Waddesdon Manor* (1979) is the principal primary source for the years when James and Dorothy de Rothschild lived at Waddesdon, and it also contains Dorothy's memories of Alice and Edmond. I have also relied very heavily on Waddesdon's catalogues, most notably Bruno Pons's *Architecture and Panelling* (1996) and Geoffrey de Bellaigue's *Furniture, Clocks and Gilt Bronzes* (1974). Waddesdon's guide book is of course indispensable: I used the edition published in 1998, in which the text is by Selma Schwartz, with additions by Ulrich Leben. I am very fortunate that Niall Ferguson's *The World's Banker: The History of the House of Rothschild* (1998) was published before I began my research. A definitive history of the bank, it contains an enormous quantity of information about Ferdinand's family background, based on unrestricted access to the Rothschilds' prewar archives. It has been of immense help to me, not least in sorting out history from myth. I would also like to acknowledge the use I have made of Mark Girouard's short but exceptionally stimulating history of the house, published in 1998 to mark the centenary of Ferdinand's death, and of Brent Elliott's invaluable history of Waddesdon's garden and landscape (1994).

The principal documentary resource for any study of the Rothschilds is the archive at N.M. Rothschild, London. Unless otherwise stated. all quotations from family correspondence are from this source. I am grateful to the archivist there, Melanie Aspey, for her guidance. Waddesdon has recently catalogued its papers, and although very few private documents relating to either Ferdinand or Alice have come to light, the archive there contains a great deal of important material, most notably the typescript of Ferdinand's *Reminiscences,* which covers his life up to his move to London in 1860, with an invaluable chapter on his collecting, 'Bric-a-Brac' (see below). As well as a copy of *The Red Book,* Ferdinand's privately printed account of the building of Waddesdon, the archive also holds his pocket-book accounts (which provide the only detailed information about his spending) and the inventories drawn up after the deaths of Ferdinand, Alice and James. There are also copies and transcripts of material held elsewhere, most notably the Waddesdon visitors' book (which remains in family hands) and extracts from the *Buckinghamshire Herald* covering the 1870s and 1880s. I have made much use in addition of three volumes of press cuttings of obituaries and other articles assembled for Alice after Ferdinand's death.

With Lord Rothschild's permission, I have been able to supplement this material with access to James and Dorothy's private papers at Eythrope. I was also granted access to the National Trust's archival material on Waddesdon for the period 1946-60, and I am most grateful to Simon Jervis and Alastair Laing for arranging this.

Note on the Second Edition (2009)

In the seven years since this book was first published, a great deal has happened at Waddesdon. This second edition has been updated with numerous new illustrations, an extended final chapter and a revised 'Afterword'. I have also updated the Bibliographical Notes and corrected a few errors. I am most grateful to Lord Rothschild, Fabia Bromovsky, and Pippa Shirley, Head of Collections at Waddesdon, for their help in preparing the revision. Edward Parsons, agent of the Waddesdon estate, and Paul Farnell, the head gardener, kindly read and commented on parts of the revised final chapter in draft. I have been helped greatly by the most recent (2008) edition of Waddesdon's guidebook, by Selma Schwartz.

1 FERDINAND ROTHSCHILD AND HIS FAMILY

Outside the material in the house and at the Rothschild Archive, the single most important source for Ferdinand's life at Waddesdon is Edward Hamilton's diary, which is in the British Library. Extracts, focusing on his political life, have been edited by D.W.R. Bahlman in three volumes: *The Diary of Sir Edward Walter Hamilton 1880-1885* (two volumes, Oxford, 1972) and *The Diary of Sir Edward Walter Hamilton 1885-1906* (Hull, 1993). I have also made use of transcripts of additional material relating to Ferdinand and Waddesdon that were made from the original diary by Maria Brassey and are now at Waddesdon.

The best account of the Rothschilds' architectural patronage is Pauline Prevost Marcilhacy's magnificently illustrated *Les Rothschilds:*

bâtisseurs et mécènes (Paris, 1995), which should be supplemented with Jill Allibone's two *Country Life* articles (February 16 and February 23, 1998) on the Rothschild houses in the Vale of Aylesbury. The most important family memoirs covering this period are Lucy Cohen's *Lady de Rothschild and Her Daughter, 1821-1931* (1935) and Constance Battersea's *Reminiscences* (1922). Modern biographical accounts of Ferdinand's English relatives include Richard Davis's *The English Rothschilds* (1983) and George Ireland's *Plutocrats: A Rothschild Inheritance* (2007).

2: BUILDING THE HOUSE

On Devey's work for the Rothschilds, see Jill Allibone, *George Devey Architect 1820- 1886* (1991), where his design for the Schillersdorf dairy is illustrated. Bruno Pons's volume of the Waddesdon catalogue, *Architecture and Panelling* (1996), illustrates drawings in the Destailleur papers in Paris and Berlin and quotes from the unpublished memoir of Destailleur by his son. There is a good analysis of the house's architecture by Anthony Blunt in an article 'Destailleur at Waddesdon', published in a special number of *Apollo* (June 1977) devoted to the house and its collections. These articles were reprinted separately as a book edited by Denys Sutton, *Aspects of the James A. de Rothschild Collection at Waddesdon Manor* (1977). See also the analysis of French styles in country-house architecture in Mark Girouard's *The Victorian Country House* (2nd edition, 1979). I have also made use of an unpublished 1991 lecture on the house's architecture by Peter Inskip.

There is a small group of letters from Ferdinand to Lord Rosebery at Waddesdon, but the main correspondence is in the Rosebery papers at Dalmeny, Lothian. I have used transcripts held at Waddesdon. The main contemporary account of the garden is an article, 'Waddesdon', in *The Gardeners' Chronicle,* June 27, 1885. The house and gardens were also described and illustrated in *Country Life* on December 20, 1892 and August 20, 1898 and December 20, 1902. A selection of *Country Life*'s photographs of the house appears in Michael Hall, *The Victorian Country House from the Archives of Country Life* (2009). On James Pulham, see Sally Festing in *Garden History* 12 (No 2), Autumn 1984. Fred Cripps's story about the birds at Waddesdon is published in his autobiography, *Life's a Gamble* (1957).

For Ferdinand's changes to the village, I have been greatly helped by Geoff Huntingford, 'Waddesdon, Buckinghamshire: Current Conservation Issues in a Village with a Strong Estate Influence', MA thesis in architectural conservation, The Leicester School of Architecture, De Montfort University (August 1999).

3: BUILDING THE COLLECTION

As well as the volumes of the Waddesdon catalogue mentioned above, I have made use of Ellis Waterhouse's on the paintings (1967) and Svend Eriksen's on the porcelain (1968) Equally important are the three volumes of the catalogue of the Waddesdon Bequest by Hugh Tait (1986-1991). For a full account of Anselm and Ferdinand's acquisition of the collection that makes up the Waddesdon Bequest, and its transfer to the

British Museum, see Dora Thornton, 'From Waddesdon to the British Museum: Baron Ferdinand Rothschild and his Cabinet Collection', in *Journal of the History of Collections*, vol. 13, no. 2 (2001). Of Ferdinand's own writings on collecting, the most important is 'Bric-a- Brac', a chapter in his memoirs, published as 'Bric-a-Brac: A Rothschild's Memoir of Collecting', in *Apollo*, July and August 2007. See also his articles 'Century for Century', *The Nineteenth Century* (April 1888) and 'French Eighteenth-Century Art in England', *The Nineteenth Century* (March 1892). A copy of the catalogue of Anselm's collection, *Katalog der Kunstsammlung des Freiherrn Anselm Von Rothschild in Wien,* is at Waddesdon. An essential background to understanding Ferdinand's collecting is provided by Michael Hall's article 'The English Rothschilds as Collectors', in an exhibition catalogue produced by the Jewish Museum in Frankfurt and edited by Georg Heuberger, *The Rothschilds: A European Family* (two volumes, Frankfurt, 1994). On Ferdinand's own collecting of fine art, I have been much helped by an unpublished lecture delivered in 1999 by Alastair Laing, 'The Collecting of English 18th-century pictures by Baron Ferdinand de Rothschild'.

The material preserved at Waddesdon relating to Ferdinand's collecting includes the originals of Ferdinand's correspondence with B.L. Johnstone and the letters from L. Auerbach to Alfred de Rothschild about the sale of the pictures from the Six collection. There is also a group of original invoices from the Wertheimers. I have also made use of Waddesdon's transcripts of material from Agnew's archive. Much useful background information is contained in Gerald Reitlinger's *The Economics of Taste,* most importantly volume 2 (1963), which deals with the history of the collecting of French furniture and porcelain and of Renaissance decorative arts. I was also much helped by two works by Peter Hughes, *The Founders of the Wallace Collection* (1981) and *The Wallace Collection: Catalogue of Furniture* (1996). On the Wertheimers, see Norman L. Kleeblatt (ed.) , *John Singer Sargent: Portraits of the Wertheimer Family* (exhibition catalogue, The Jewish Museum, New York, 1999).

4 : FURNISHING THE HOUSE

Eustace Balfour's letters to his wife are reproduced in the memoirs of his wife, Lady Frances Balfour, *New Obliviscaris* (1930).

On the textiles used to furnish the house, I have been helped by unpublished lectures and notes by Natalie Rothstein at Waddesdon as well as by her article 'European Silks – Historical and Domestic', in *Apollo,* June 1977 (see above). Henry James's remarks on Clarence King appear in Leon Edel, *Henry James: The Treacherous Years (1895-1901)* (1969) See also Thurman Wilkins, *Clarence King: A Biography* (New York , 1958). Ferdinand's books are discussed by A.R.A. Hobson in *The Book Collector* (Summer, 1959) I have also made use of a draft of Giles Barber's introduction to the forthcoming catalogue of the books at Waddesdon.

The sculpture at Waddesdon is the subject of a separate volume of the catalogue of the house's collections, edited by Terence Hodgkinson (1970). On Ferdinand's use of Sander for his orchid collections, see Arthur Swinson, *Frederick Sander: the Orchid King* (1970) .

5 : LIFE AT WADDESDON

A useful source of information about the visitors to Waddesdon is Ferdinand's autograph album, which is still in family hands. It was edited by James Pope-Hennessy as *Baron Ferdinand de Rothschild's Livre d'Or* (Cambridge, the Roxburghe Club, 1952). I have drawn on the following memoirs and diaries by people who knew Ferdinand: John Vincent (ed.), *The Crawford Papers* (Manchester, 1984); Lucy Masterman (ed.), *Mary Gladstone (Mrs Drew):Her Diaries and Letters* (London. 1930); The Marchioness of Londonderry, *Henry Chaplin: A Memoir* (London, 1926); Lillie Langtry, *The Days I Knew* (London, 1925); Frances, Countess of Warwick, *Afterthoughts* (London, 1931); Horace G. Hutchinson (ed.) , *The Private Diaries of the Rt Hon Sir Algernon West GCB* (1922); George Arthur (ed.), *The Letters of Lord and Lady Wolseley 1870-1911*(1922) .

The following biographies contain useful information: Michael G. Lerner, *Maupassant* (1975): Sir Philip Magnus, *Edward VII* (1964); Christopher Sykes, *Four Studies in Loyalty* [on Christopher Sykes] (1946); Anne Taylor, *Laurence Oliphant 1829-1888* (1982). On the Souls, see Jane Abdy and Charlotte Gere, *The Souls* (1984).

On Alfred and Halton, see Andrew Adam, *Beechwood and Bayonets: the Book of Halton* (Whittlebury, 1992). Ferdinand's account of the visit from Queen Victoria is in typescript at Waddesdon. It can be supplemented by an account by Queen Victoria's private secretary, the Hon. Harriet Phipps (the original is in the Royal Archive; I have used a transcript at Waddesdon), and by the Queen's letters to her eldest daughter, the Empress Frederick, published in Agatha Ramm (ed.). *Beloved and Darling Child: Last Letters Between Queen Victoria and her Eldest Daughter 1886-1901* (Stroud, 1990).

Rona's visitors' book is at Waddesdon. The diary of Charles Spencer, 6th Earl Spencer, is in the Spencer papers in the British Library; I have used a transcript of extracts at Waddesdon. On the political background to Waddesdon's house parties, see the discussion of the Rothschilds' politics in Niall Ferguson's *The World's Banker: the History of the House of Rothschild* (see above) and volume two of Richard Shannon's biography of Gladstone, *Gladstone: Heroic Minister 1865-1898* (1999).

My main source for the servants at Waddesdon has been the census return for 1891. For much invaluable comparative material, see Jessica Gerard, *Country House Life: Family and Servants 1815-1914* (1994) .

6 : ALICE

The longest account of Ferdinand's funeral is in *The Jewish Chronicle,* December 23, 1898. Material about Henry Taylor, including his diary and photographs, was presented to Waddesdon in 1994 by Mrs M. Close. The main contemporary account of Alice's life is a memorial pamphlet of 1922 by her cousin Constance Battersea. For her relationship with Charles Dilke, see Roy Jenkins, *Sir Charles Dilke, A Victorian Tragedy* (1958). Constance Battersea's account of her visit to Grasse is published in Lucy Cohen's *Lady de Rothschild and Her Daughters 1821-1931* (see above). On Alice's collecting, see the volume of Waddesdon's catalogue on the arms and armour, by Claude Blair (1974), and an article by Mrs James A. de Rothschild, 'The Feminine Line at Waddesdon', *Apollo,* June 1977. On the gardens at Eythrope, see Lewis Castle, 'Eythrope', *Journal of Horticulture and Cottage Gardener,* June 26, 1890.

Victor Rothschild's letter about Edward VII's visit to Waddesdon was written to John Hayward on February 25, 1959 (original at Waddesdon). On Ethel Sands, see Wendy Baron, *Miss Ethel Sands and Her Circle* (1977). Jacques-Emile Blanche's description of Waddesdon appears in his *Portraits of a Lifetime* (1937)Ottoline Morrell's account of her visit is taken from her manuscript diary. The extract was provided by Adrian. M. Goodman, and is reproduced with his permission. Alice's letters to G.F. Johnson, which cover the period 1901-1918, are at Waddesdon. See also the note on Johnson's career in *The Gardeners' Chronicle,* March 1, 1952 and his obituary in the same magazine, May 8, 1954. Aubrey Hicks's *Memories of Waddesdon 1902-1914* were written in 1972-73 and published by Buckinghamshire County Library in 1990. See also Marcel Gaucher, *Les Jardins de la Fortune* (Paris, 1985), which includes some memories of working for Alice at Grasse and Waddesdon. On Alice's cars, see 'Cars and Country Houses No CVII: Waddesdon Manor' in *The Car,* September 26 , 1906.

7: JAMES AND DOROTHY

On Baron Edmond and his collecting of drawings for architecture and the decorative arts, see Alastair Laing, Martin Meade, J.W. Niemeijer, et al., *Catalogue of Drawings for Architecture, Design and Ornament: The James A. de Rothschild Bequest at Waddesdon Manor,* two volumes (2006). Dorothy de Rothschild's draft notes on Edmond's life, written in 1974, and his own notes for an autobiography, dictated in 1931, are in the Eythrope papers. Edmond and James's involvement with Palestine is the subject of a book by Simon Schema, *Two Rothschilds and the Land of Israel* (1978). Diana Souhami's *Bakst: the Rothschild Panels of the Sleeping Beauty* (1992) is a definitive account of this commission. For Harold Nicolson's visits to Waddesdon, see Nigel Nicolson (ed.), *Vita and Harold: The Letters of Vita Sackville-West and Harold Nicolson* (1992) and James Lees-Milne, *Harold Nicolson, A Biography: Volume II, 1930-1968* (1981). For Virginia Woolf's visits to Waddesdon, see her diaries, edited by Anne Olivier Bell, volume 3 (1925-30), entries for 11 and 13 April, 1930, and her letters, edited by Nigel Nicolson and Joanne Trautmann, *A Change of Perspective: The Letters of Virginia Woolf, Volume III:1923-1928* (1977) , letter of March 16, 1926, to Vita Sackville-West.

The main source for life at Waddesdon in the 1920s and 1930s (including George V's visit) is *The Rothschilds at Waddesdon Manor* (see above), but much

additional valuable information is contained in unpublished lectures given to the house's guides by Dorothy in the late 1950s and early 1960s, which are in typescript at Waddesdon. Dorothy's introduction to Ellis Waterhouse's catalogue of the paintings at Waddesdon is also valuable.

On James's political life and friendship with Churchill, see John Colville, *The Fringes of Power: Downing Street Diaries 1939-1955, volume I: September 1939-September 1941* (1985) and Robert Rhodes James (ed.), *Chips: The Diaries of Sir Henry Channon* (1967) .

8: THE NATIONAL TRUST

My main source is the National Trust's archive, supplemented with background information from John Cornforth, *The Country Houses of England 1948-1998* (1998) and Peter Mandler, *The Fall and Rise of the Stately Home* (1997); see also Jennifer Jenkins and Patrick James, *From Acorn to Oak Tree: The Growth of the National Trust: 1895-1994* (1994). James Lees-Milne's diary account of his first visit to Waddesdon is published in his *Caves of Ice* (1983). A good contemporary account of the impression made by Waddesdon when it opened to the public is Mark Girouard's article 'Waddesdon Manor, Buckinghamshire: A Treasure House of 18th-century Art' in *Country Life,* August 20, 1959. Isaiah Berlin's obituary of Dorothy was published in *The Independent,* December 12, 1988.

9 : LORD ROTHSCHILD

The principal published source for the centenary restoration is a series of articles in *Country Life*: by John Cornforth on the new first-floor rooms (June 8, 1995), and on the lighting of the works of art (March 27, 1997); by Jeremy Musson on the flood lighting (July 6, 1995); by John Martin Robinson on the conversion of the Dairy (May 1, 1997); and by Michael Hall on the Bachelors' Wing (June 4, 1998) .

I have also benefited from unpublished lectures on the house and its restoration delivered by Lord Rothschild to the Metropolitan Museum of Art, New York (1999) and the Huntington Museum (2000). Much of my account of the garden restoration is based on an unpublished lecture by Beth Rothschild, 'The History and the Restoration of the Garden at Waddesdon Manor' (1998). On the additions to the collection, see Michael Hall, 'An Acquisitive Gene: Lord Rothschild's Collecting for Waddesdon', *Apollo,* July and August 2007. The paintings by Panini, Callet and Chardin are discussed by Juliet Carey in 'New Paintings at Waddesdon Manor: Recent Acquisitions for the Rothschild Collection', *Apollo,* September 2008.

MAYER AMSCHEL ROTHSCHILD
1743–1812

Frankfurt · Vienna · London · Naples · Paris

AMSCHEL
1773–1855

SALOMON
1774–1855

NATHAN MAYER
1777–1836

CARL MAYER
1788–1855

JAMES
1792–1868
m.
BETTY
(Vienna)

ANSELM
1803–1874
m.
CHARLOTTE
(London)

BETTY
1805–1886
m.
JAMES
(Paris)

ALICE
Waddesdon
1847–1922

FERDINAND
Waddesdon
1839–1898
m.
EVELINA
(London)

CHARLOTTE
1807–1859
m.
ANSELM
(Vienna)

LIONEL
Tring
1808–1879
m.
CHARLOTTE
(Naples)

ANTHONY
Aston Clinton
1810–1876

MAYER
Mentmore
1818–1874

CONSTANCE
1843–1931
m.
LORD
BATTERSEA

HANNAH
1851–1990
m.
LORD
ROSEBURY

EVELINA
1839–1866
m.
FERDINAND

NATHANIEL
1ST LORD ROTH-
SCHILD
1840–1915

ALFRED
1842–1918
Halton

LEOPOLD
1845–1917
Ascott

WALTER
2ND LORD ROTH-
SCHILD
1868–1937

**NATHANIEL
CHARLES**
1877–1923
m.
ROSZIKA VON
WERTHEIMSTEIN
1870–1940

EVELYN
1886–1917

ANTHONY
1887–1961

EVELYN
b. 1931

MIRIAM
b. 1908

VICTOR
3RD LORD ROTH-
SCHILD
1910–1990
m.
(1) BARBARA
HUTCHINSON
1911–1989
(2) TERESA MAYOR
b. 1915

JACOB
4TH LORD ROTH-
SCHILD
b. 1936
m.
SERENA DUNN
b. 1935

HANNAH
b. 1962

BETH
b. 1964

EMILY
b. 1967

NATHANIEL
b. 1971

CHARLOTTE
1819–1859
m.
LIONEL
(London)

ADOLPHE
1823–1884
m.
JULIE
(Vienna)

WILLY
1828–1901
m.
MATHILDE
(Vienna)

EDMOND
1845–1934
m.
Adelaide
(Naples)

ADELAIDE
1853–1935
m.
EDMOND
(Paris)

JAMES ARMAND
Waddesdon
1878–1957
m.
DOROTHY PINTO
1895–1988

THE FAMILY TREE OF THE ROTHSCHILDS
connected with Waddesdon Manor
with the names of the family's houses in Buckinghamshire

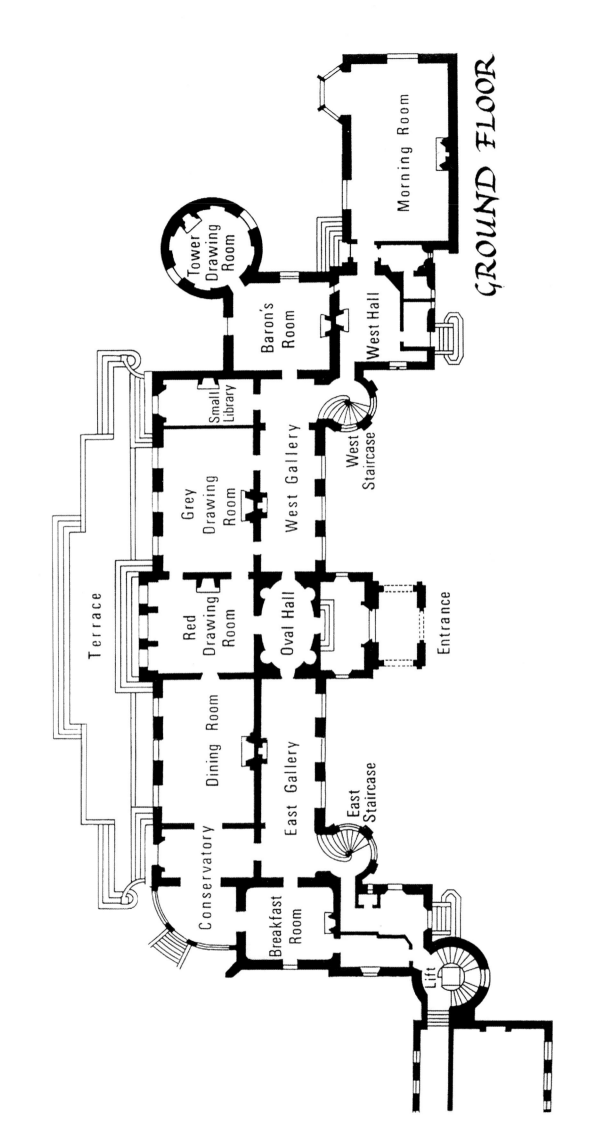

GROUND FLOOR

Morning Room

Tower Drawing Room

Baron's Room

West Hall

Small Library

Grey Drawing Room

West Gallery

West Staircase

Terrace

Red Drawing Room

Oval Hall

Entrance

Dining Room

Conservatory

East Gallery

Breakfast Room

East Staircase

Lift

PHOTOGRAPHY CREDITS

FOR PERMISSION TO USE IMAGES we are grateful to the Alice Trust and the Rothschild Family Trust.

All other images are credited to Waddesdon Manor, The Rothschild Collection (The National Trust) with the exception of those listed below. We are grateful to photographers John Bigelow-Taylor, Dianne Dubler, Mike Fear, Hugh Palmer, Stan Eost and Peter McDonald.

Academie d'Architecture, Paris, 46 ,62, 63, 64, 65, 154, 155

Bildarchiv Osterreichische Nationalbibliothek, Vienna, 26

The British Museum, 94, 95, 96, 97

Helga Brown, 246

Centre historique des Archives Nationales, Paris, 48, 49, 50

Christie's, 138

Country Life Picture Library, 172, 267

Courtauld Institute of Art, 113

The Earl of Rosebery, 37

RAF Halton, 124, 165

English Heritage, National Monuments Record, 128

Tim Imrie-Tait / Country Life Picture Library, 285

Kunstbibliothek, Berlin, 51, 57, 137

National Portrait Gallery, London, 78, 79

The Rothschild Archive, London, 25, 34, 150, 186, 187

The Royal Archives, 2001 © Her Majesty Queen Elizabeth II, 177

Royal Horticultural Society, Lindley Library, 204

Sir Geoffrey Shakerley, 181

Dan Stevens, 270

Times Newspapers Ltd, 298

INDEX